THE KOREAN
DIASPORA
IN THE WORLD
ECONOMY

THE KOREAN DIASPORA IN THE WORLD ECONOMY

Edited by
C. Fred Bergsten
and Inbom Choi

Institute for International Economics
Washington, DC
January 2003

C. Fred Bergsten has been director of the Institute for International Economics since its creation in 1981. He was also chairman of the Competitiveness Policy Council, which was created by Congress, throughout its existence from 1991 to 1995 and chairman of the APEC Eminent Persons Group throughout its existence from 1993 to 1995. He was assistant secretary for international affairs of the US Treasury (1977-81), assistant for international economic affairs to the National Security Council (1969-71), and a senior fellow at the Brookings Institution (1972-76), the Carnegie Endowment for International Peace (1981), and the Council on Foreign Relations (1967-68). He is the author, coauthor, or editor of numerous books on a wide range of international economic issues, including *No More Bashing: Building a New Japan-United States Economic Relationship* (2001), *Whither APEC? The Progress to Date and Agenda for the Future* (1997), *Global Economic Leadership and the Group of Seven* (1996), *The Dilemmas of the Dollar* (second edition, 1996), *Reconcilable Differences? United States-Japan Economic Conflict* (1993), and *Pacific Dynamism and the International Economic System* (1993).

Inbom Choi, former Institute visiting fellow, is chief economist at the Federation of Korean Industries. He was assistant secretary to the president for economic affairs and director of international economic policy in the Office of the President of Korea (1995-96). He has been a research fellow at the Korea Institute for International Economic Policy since 1990. He has also been a consultant to the World Bank and a visiting professor at Georgetown University. In 1998 and 1999, he was selected by the Asia-Europe Meeting (ASEM) as one of the Next Generation Leaders of Asia. He is coauthor of *Free Trade between Korea and the United States?* with Jeffrey J. Schott (2001). He is the author of *Competitiveness of Korean Products in the U.S. Market* (1993, in Korean), *Trade Barriers in Government Procurement Practices of Developed Countries* (1992, in Korean), and *Effects of FDI on Productivity in the Manufacturing Industries of Korea and Taiwan* (1991, in Korean), among others.

INSTITUTE FOR INTERNATIONAL ECONOMICS
1750 Massachusetts Avenue, NW
Washington, DC 20036-1903
(202) 328-9000   FAX: (202) 659-3225
http://www.iie.com

C. Fred Bergsten, *Director*
Brigitte Coulton, *Director of Publications and Web Development*
Brett Kitchen, *Director of Marketing and Foreign Rights*

Typesetting by General Typographers, Inc.
Printing by Kirby Lithographic Company, Inc.

Printed in the United States of America
05 04 03   5 4 3 2 1

Library of Congress Cataloging-in-Publication Data

Korean diaspora in the world economy / coedited by C. Fred Bergsten and Inbom Choi.
    p. cm.
  ISBN 0-88132-358-6
  1. Korea (South)—Economic conditions—1960 2. Koreans—Foreign countries—Economic conditions.
  3. Korea (South)—Emigration and immigration—Economic aspects.
  4. International business enterprises—Korea (South) I. Bergsten, C. Fred, 1941- II. Ch'oe, In-bom, 1957-

HC467.95 .K674 2003
330'.089'957—dc21   2002192248

Contents

Preface   vii

Acknowledgments   xi

1   Prelude
    The Korean Diaspora and Globalization:
    Past Contributions and Future Opportunities   1
    Special address by C. Fred Bergsten

2   Korean Diaspora in the Making:
    Its Current Status and Impact on the Korean Economy   9
    Inbom Choi

    Comments on Chapter 2   28
    Taeho Bark

3   Chinese Business Networks and Their Implications for
    South Korea   31
    Young Rok Cheong

    Comments on Chapter 3   56
    Kihwan Kim

4 The Impact of Korean Immigration on the US Economy   **61**
Marcus Noland

Comments on Chapter 4   73
Soogil Young

5 The Status and Role of Ethnic Koreans in the Japanese Economy   **77**
Toshiyuki Tamura

Comments on Chapter 5   98
Jang Hee Yoo

6 The Economic Status and Role of Ethnic Koreans in China   **101**
Si Joong Kim

Comments on Chapter 6   128
Byong Hyon Kwon

7 The Global Economic Outlook and Business and Investment Opportunities for Overseas Koreans   **131**
C. Fred Bergsten, Marcus Noland, and Il SaKong

About the Contributors   **145**

Index   **149**

Preface

About 6 million Koreans, close to 10 percent of the current population of the Korean peninsula, now live and work outside the peninsula around the world. This important but little noticed "Korean diaspora" began in the early 20th century. In particular, Korean migration into the United States began in 1903 with the migration of Korean laborers to the sugar plantations of Hawaii. To celebrate the 100th anniversary of Korean immigration into the United States, and to analyze the Korean diaspora's past and potential future economic impact, the Overseas Koreans Foundation (OKF) and the Institute for International Economics held a major conference in Seoul in October 2002 and are now releasing this volume in January 2003.

The conference in Seoul was part of the 1st World Korean Business Convention for overseas Koreans, sponsored by the OKF, to bring together business leaders of the Korean diaspora from all parts of the world. Since the largest number of overseas Koreans reside in the United States (about 2 million), it was appropriate for an American research institution, the Institute for International Economics, to cosponsor the economic component of that event. This volume is the result of that collaboration.

The volume attempts to do three things. First, it places the Korean diaspora in the context of both Korean history and the diasporas from other parts of the world. Second, and primarily, it analyzes the impact of overseas Koreans on both the host economies to which they have migrated (mainly the United States, Japan, and China) and the home economy of Korea itself. Third, and much more speculatively, it considers some possible future paths of the diaspora in light of the possible future evolution both of the world economy (and especially its further globalization) and of Korea itself, including its southern and northern components.

The Overseas Koreans Foundation, a nonprofit organization established in October 1997, embraces those affairs affecting as many as 6 million ethnic Koreans living overseas. It also encourages networking among the Korean diaspora in the areas of culture and education exchanges throughout the world as well as research focused on the overseas Koreans' agenda. One of its main objectives is to promote business networking among Korean entrepreneurs and to give them ongoing opportunities for their business interaction online as well as offline. As its first step, the 1st World Korean Business Convention was organized. The OKF is convinced that this IIE-OKF international seminar will provide a conceptual background and road map for successful networking in the years to come.

The OKF expects this conference and the resulting volume to help expand understanding of the Korean diaspora and the contributions it has made to both Korea itself and to the other countries that have been involved. The Foundation hopes that the effort will lead to continuing networking among leaders of the diaspora and to even greater contributions from it in the future. To that end, the Foundation has created the World Korean Business Network that will initiate a series of future activities to promote those objectives.

The Institute for International Economics has devoted extensive attention to Korea throughout its history since 1981. Its major publications on Korea itself include *Free Trade between Korea and the United States?* (2001) by Inbom Choi and Jeffrey J. Schott, *Avoiding the Apocalypse: The Future of the Two Koreas* (2000) by Marcus Noland, *Measuring the Costs of Visible Protection in Korea* (1996) by Namdoo Kim, and *Korea in the World Economy* (1993) by Il SaKong. In addition, the Institute has released a number of studies on East Asia more broadly, which include substantial sections on Korea. The studies include, most recently, *East Asian Financial Cooperation* (2002) by C. Randall Henning and *New Regional Trading Arrangements in the Asia Pacific* (2001) by Robert Scollay and John P. Gilbert. In addition, a group of public and private leaders from the two countries meet annually to address current issues between them and to build personal relationships that will help to further strengthen their relationships.

The Institute for International Economics is a private nonprofit institution for the study and discussion of international economic policy. Its purpose is to analyze important issues in that area and to develop and communicate practical new approaches for dealing with them. The Institute is completely nonpartisan.

The Institute is funded largely by philanthropic foundations. Major institutional grants are now being received from the William M. Keck, Jr. Foundation and the Starr Foundation. A number of other foundations and private corporations contribute to the highly diversified financial resources of the Institute. About 31 percent of the Institute's resources in our latest fiscal year were provided by contributors outside the United States, including about 18 percent from Japan. The Overseas Koreans Foundation supported this volume.

The Board of Directors bears overall responsibility for the Institute and gives general guidance and approval to its research program, including the identification of topics that are likely to become important over the medium run (one to three years), and which should be addressed by the Institute. The Director, working closely with the staff and outside Advisory Committee, is responsible for the development of particular projects and makes the final decision to publish an individual study.

The Institute hopes that its studies and other activities will contribute to building a stronger foundation for international economic policy around the world. We invite readers of these publications to let us know how they think we can best accomplish this objective.

C. FRED BERGSTEN
Director
Institute for International Economics
January 2003

BYONG HYON KWON
Chairman and President
Overseas Koreans Foundation
January 2003

Acknowledgments

We would like to thank Ambassador Byong Hyon Kwon, Chairman and President of the Overseas Koreans Foundation, who initiated and strongly supported this project. Our appreciation also goes to the hard-working staff of the Overseas Koreans Foundation, in particular David Lee, Byeong Sun Song, and Jong-Mi Lee, who provided not only administrative support for the whole project but also logistical support for the October conference in Seoul.

We would also like to thank all the participants in the conference, including those who attended and especially those who participated in the discussions. Our utmost thanks are, of course, due to the authors and discussants whose papers and comments appear in this volume.

Finally, many thanks to Brigitte Coulton, Marla Banov, and Madona Devasahayam for their efficient and hard work, especially given a short work schedule, in preparing the manuscript for publication.

C. Fred Bergsten
Inbom Choi

Prelude

The Korean Diaspora and Globalization: Past Contributions and Future Opportunities

Special address by C. FRED BERGSTEN

When Byong Hyon Kwon, South Korea's former ambassador to China and Australia, asked me to help him prepare the conference on which this book is based and to add an economic dimension to it, I responded immediately for three reasons.

First is my deep affection for Ambassador Kwon. In his remarks to the conference, he was very kind in giving me some credit for the development of the Asia-Pacific Economic Cooperation forum (APEC) but in fact he was the one who made APEC a possibility. When South Korea was chairing APEC in 1991, he negotiated something that had never been done before in history. It was the involvement of all "three Chinas," as they then were—the mainland, independent Hong Kong, and Taiwan—in an international institution where all could participate together. This made APEC a real possibility. Ambassador Kwon deserves the credit for whatever APEC has turned into, and I was thrilled to be able to work on it with him.

The second reason for my desire to participate in the conference and contribute to the book was that I personally, and our Institute for International Economics, have devoted enormous attention to South Korea over the years. In fact, in my very first job back in 1964, I was part of a super-secret task force at the US Department of State that worked with the Korean authorities at the time in developing the original

C. Fred Bergsten is the director of the Institute for International Economics.

development strategy that propelled Korea into becoming one of the greatest success stories in economic history. My assignment was to determine the proper exchange rate for the *won* and I therefore prepared a laborious calculation comparing Korea with all the other countries in the region. I came up with an exchange rate that was then adopted as part of the Korean development strategy.

At that time, South Korean exports of manufactured goods totaled about $10 million. Today, of course, they are far in excess of $100 billion. I always felt that what we accomplished then, working closely with our Korean friends, was a huge success. I have always been proud of it, and have always been happy to work very closely with friends in Korea on Korea's superb economic development ever since.

The third—and perhaps the most important—reason that I was thrilled to have a chance to participate in *this* event was that I personally reside in the middle of the Korean diaspora. I live just outside Washington in a town in Virginia called Annandale in the midst of Fairfax County. Those of you who know the region know that Annandale is in fact at the heart of the Korean diaspora. In the town of Annandale, there are more than 300 Korean businesses and 37 Korean restaurants. Every church has its Korean component. There is a Seoul Plaza shopping center a mile or so from my house. Korean businesses account for half of all the business revenue that is collected in Annandale.

So, living in the midst of the Korean diaspora, I was delighted to have a chance to analyze it and participate in this historic conference. The conference has tried to bring together many prominent participants in, and observers of, the overseas Korean community to enable us to think together about its future and how it can contribute even more to both South Korea and all the countries in which the overseas Korean population plays such an active and constructive role.

What we tried to do is to organize a conference on the economic aspects of the Korean diaspora, to try to understand it better, to see what its effects have been, and to come up with ideas for how it could even more effectively and more positively contribute both to South Korea and to the world economy as a whole. In doing so, we of course wanted to look at the Korean diaspora in the broader context of globalization.

As historians look back at the past 50 years, and I suspect at the 21st century as well, it will probably be viewed as the golden age of globalization, when countries and people around the world were increasingly integrating their activities and having economic exchanges with each other at a level never seen before in human history. We know that globalization brings huge benefits to all the countries that participate in it. Indeed, it remains true that no country in history has ever succeeded in building a developed and high-income economy without participating in the global economy. Globalization is imperative for economic success.

South Korea is the most dramatic example of that experience. As I mentioned, it went from being a poor, underdeveloped economy, fewer than 40 years ago, to one of the most successful and prosperous economies in the world today. As analysts, economists, and historians look at the evolution of globalization, South Korea is the poster child. It is held up as the example above all of how participation in the global economy can propel a country from poverty to being one of the most successful in the world.

The most dramatic contrast is with North Korea, one of the few countries that has excluded itself from globalization and therefore has remained one of the poorest and least developed societies on the face of the globe. There can be no clearer understanding of the benefits of globalization, and the costs from failing to participate in it, than an analysis of events on this peninsula. It is therefore particularly appropriate to look at how this country and its people have participated so actively in the process during this period.

At the Institute for International Economics, we have done a series of studies looking not just at globalization's macroeconomic effects but also at its impact on individual industries, workers, and communities, and at how it brings them tremendous benefits. We have looked at the United States, which has also globalized rapidly during the past 50 years, and found that workers in globalized industries earn 10 to 15 percent more than workers in industries that are the same in all other respects but have not taken an active role in the world economy. We have looked at how communities benefit enormously from having their workers and companies participate in the world economy.

Moreover, one of the largest elements in globalization, in addition to international trade and international investment, is the flow of individuals—the migration of people from one set of countries to another, the same phenomenon that we discussed and analyzed in this conference in its focus on overseas Koreans and the Korean diaspora. Indeed, there was an earlier historical wave of globalization, in the 19th century, which in fact was led by the flow of people. The huge migration of Europeans—in particular to the United States, Canada, Australia, and South America—was a defining element in that first wave of globalization. Yet we know that—as we now celebrate the 100th anniversary of Korean migration to the rest of the world—Koreans did not participate very much in that first wave of immigration and globalization in the 19th century.

However, the chapters in this book show that Koreans have now been making up for that late start very extensively during the past 50 to 100 years. The flow of Koreans seems small in comparison with the flows of Chinese or Indians or other large diasporas about which we know much more. But the results are in fact different when we analyze the flow of Koreans more closely.

If one looks at the number of Koreans who are involved in this diaspora—about 6 or 7 million, depending on how it is defined—it turns out to be a much larger share of the Korean population than the flow of over-seas Chinese, overseas Indians, or indeed overseas communities from most other countries. The percentage of Koreans who have moved abroad and into the world economy is a much larger share than that of any other large Asian country.

The papers presented at the conference, which now form the chapters of this book, look at the impact of overseas Koreans on both overseas economies and on South Korea. Chapter 4 analyzes the impact of Koreans in the United States on the economy of the United States, and the results are rather stunning. The Korean population in the United States is a small share of the US economy, but it has a disproportionately favorable impact. The Koreans in the United States have a saving rate double that of the average American, something we need badly because our national savings are far too low. Koreans in the United States graduate from college at a rate double that of the average American, providing a highly skilled and highly educated addition to our labor force. The second generation of Koreans has an average income 70 percent above that of the average American, indicating both their attainment and the contribution they make to the US economy. In chapter 4, my colleague Marcus Noland—who is a well-known expert on South Korea, the Korean economy, North Korea, and the outlook for Korean unification—reached the stunning conclusion that if somehow we were able to double the number of Koreans who were participating in the US economy, we would increase the growth rate of per capita income by 0.1 to 0.2 percent.

But the chapters in this book also demonstrate that the benefit from the flow of Koreans to the rest of the world is considerable for South Korea it-self. It is a win-win proposition. Another of my colleagues at the Institute, Inbom Choi, concludes in chapter 2 that Koreans in the United States have generated an increase in trade between the United States and South Korea of about 15 to 20 percent, a further important increment to the ex-change between our two countries. This obviously adds to economic wel-fare, social benefits, and personal satisfaction in both countries.

So it is very clear that the Korean diaspora has had a large—indeed, disproportionately large—impact, one that has been extremely favorable on both South Korea and the countries to which the overseas Koreans have gone. But that is all in the past. And so, as we celebrate the 100th an-niversary of the Korean diaspora, it is good to look forward and see what the future might have in store and what might happen during the next 100 years as Korea's involvement in the world economy expands even further.

As we look to the future, a key point is that globalization, widespread as it now is, is almost certainly still in its early stages. We know that be-cause studies have been done of how much impact borders still have on national economies. They have looked at the impact that national divi-sions still have on economic development to try to find out what effects further globalization would have on various countries.

One way to do that is to look at the relationship between the United States and Canada. One might think that the national border between the United States and Canada could not be very important. The two countries basically speak the same language, virtually all Canadians live within 150 miles of the border, and the two countries have had a free trade agreement for more than 20 years. Hence one might think that the border would have very little impact. In fact, however, studies of the relationship that compare trade between US and Canadian cities or US and Canadian states with trade within those countries, across pairs of states or pairs of cities, holding everything else constant except for the border, show that trade within Canada or trade within the United States is still 15 to 20 times as great as trade between the United States and Canada, indicating that the border still has a tremendous impact.

Similar studies have been done for Europe, looking at trade between France and Germany, which have had a common market for 50 years. It turns out that trade within these two countries is still many times as great as trade between them, despite the fact that they are next to each other and that they now have a single economy and even a single currency. The point is that globalization still has a long way to go before the impact of national boundaries has been reduced to the point where international exchange functions largely as national exchange. Therefore, the benefits of the movement of people, and of trade and investment between countries, are still in their infancy, and large future benefits are yet to come.

As I look at both South and North Korea in that future world of increasing globalization—and perhaps look forward a number of decades, not just years—it strikes me that three possible fundamental developments might further enhance the role of Korea in the globalization process and indeed the world economy as a whole. The first, of course, is the inevitable unification of the peninsula. Marcus Noland has studied unification in great depth, and what one sees is that the economic joining of North and South Korea will create a much larger country and, after the inevitable adjustment phase, a much more successful one.

We know that the cost of unifying the Korean peninsula will be very large. Noland estimates that it will cost something like $600 billion over a 10-year period to integrate the two Koreas, once that process becomes politically possible. But once it occurs, the highly skilled, capital-intensive economy of South Korea will be joined to the underdeveloped, labor-intensive economy of North Korea, bringing together labor and capital in new combinations that will provide the opportunity for substantial further expansion—not just the improvement of North Korea to the South Korean level but also a further impetus to economic growth in South Korea and the peninsula as a whole. And therefore, in the 21st century and this age of increasing globalization, the inevitable unification of the peninsula will further boost the economy of Korea and the role it can play in the world economy.

The second factor will be the increasing convergence between South Korea and the other leading economies in the world, particularly Japan. As we all know, the Japanese economy has been stagnant for the past decade—the "lost decade," as it is frequently called in Japan. It is encouraging that recent personnel changes in Japan may lead it out of that stagnation, help it undertake needed reforms, and start its economy growing again. But even with these improvements in Japan, it is quite clear that the Korean economy, with its annual growth potential of 5 to perhaps 7 percent, is going to continue expanding much more rapidly than Japan. This situation means that at some point in the 21st century—maybe even within about 20 years if Japan fails to improve its performance, but surely at some point in the next few decades—per capita income in Korea is likely to equal or surpass that in Japan.

In one sense, these equalizing per capita incomes will simply be part of the global convergence process whereby successful developing countries move up the income scale, catch up with the former leaders, and often pass them. But in this part of Asia, given its history, it will be particularly significant for Korea to approach the Japanese standard of living, and possibly even reach it, within the foreseeable future.

Yet that is only the start of that particular story, given the population and demographic changes that are also taking place. The unification of the Korean peninsula will create a country whose current population would be about 70 million. Japan's population is now about 110 million but it is starting to decline, and many Japanese demographic projections suggest that in the course of the 21st century it will actually be cut in half to something like 60 million, lower than the population of a unified Korea today. Meanwhile, Korea's population will continue to increase at least modestly. So, sometime in the 21st century, Korea is likely to have a larger population than Japan.

Now put together these two developments: a Korea that has a larger population than Japan, and a Korea whose per capita income is approaching that of Japan, or perhaps even reaching it. The inexorable result of the two would of course be that Korea's economy would become larger than Japan's. I say this not to criticize Japan or in any way to denigrate its own economic development two or three decades ago, which was in fact the most remarkable economic success story in history to that time.

But times change. Countries that once were world leaders, like the United Kingdom in the 19th century, drop to a more intermediate position. Countries like Argentina, which in 1930 had the world's third highest per capita income, drop to much less favorable positions. Countries rise and countries fall. I simply make the comparison between Korea and Japan because of their proximity and the region's history, and because it dramatizes the role that Korea will be able to play more and more in both the region and the world.

Finally, I point to the third major development that I think will also heavily influence Korea's role in the globalization process in the coming decades: the effort to put in place new institutional arrangements of cooperation among East Asian countries, including free trade and financial agreements among the countries that belong to the Association of Southeast Asian Nations (ASEAN) and those of Northeast Asia—the so-called 10 plus 3. On the financial side, these countries have already concluded the Chiang Mai Initiative, under which the major East Asian countries have agreed to financial cooperation totaling about $35 billion.

With regard to trade, South Korea and Japan are talking about a free trade agreement. Korea, Japan, and China are studying the possibility of a Northeast Asian free trade agreement. More broadly, the 10 ASEAN countries are actively discussing free trade agreements with the countries of Northeast Asia and even negotiating with some of them.

The form that this movement has taken at the moment, however, strikes me as worrisome for Korea. Therefore, Korea should be sure that it plays an active role in this process to benefit fully from it and avoid being adversely affected.

The form that the Asian regional economic process now seems to be taking comprises two sets of bilateral negotiations: one between the ASEAN countries and China, and the other between the ASEAN countries and Japan. Indeed, China and the ASEAN countries have reached agreement to form a free trade arrangement within 10 years, and they are already talking about implementing its first stages in the near future. Negotiations between Japan and the ASEAN countries are behind the Chinese process, but they are also trying to work out free trade provisions among them.

My fear is that if these ASEAN-China and ASEAN-Japan agreements proceed, Korea could be left out. There would be free trade between China and the Southeast Asians, and between Japan and the Southeast Asians, but not between Korea and that important part of the world, nor between Korea and its economic partners on either side, China and Japan.

Therefore it seems to me that, from a South Korean standpoint, it is critically important to return to the original concept of an East Asia-wide free trade agreement, combining the 10 Southeast Asian countries with the three Northeast Asian countries—China, Japan, and South Korea—in a single unit. This would avoid discrimination within the region, which could otherwise adversely affect Korea.

Regional arrangements of this type clearly have become some of globalization's driving forces during the past decade. They will almost certainly be its major driving forces in the decades ahead. As Korea assumes the larger economic role described above, it would be tragic for Korea, and very unfortunate for the region and the world, if Korea were not centrally involved in the process. I therefore hope that Korea will take up that role and make the full contribution of which it is capable.

All of these developments provide a major opportunity not only for the South Korean economy but also for overseas Koreans. The chapters of this book portray the very positive impact that overseas Koreans already have been having on both the world economy and the countries where they live. The book's chapters also conclude, however, that both overseas Koreans and South Korea itself could do even more to encourage that outcome. The book suggests a number of ways for that to happen. We believe that the book and the conference that led to it are a very promising, encouraging, and creative start for that process and are delighted to have been offered the opportunity by Ambassador Kwon to participate so actively in it.

2

Korean Diaspora in the Making: Its Current Status and Impact on the Korean Economy

INBOM CHOI

Does the Korean Diaspora Exist?

Today, the notion of a diaspora is often used casually in a way of describing a dispersion of people of a common national origin. However, is it correct to say that there is a Korean diaspora just because there are many Koreans living outside the Korean peninsula? The concept and definition of a diaspora have changed over the years and are still being studied and debated by many scholars and experts. It is helpful to examine the concept and definition of a diaspora before discussing the Korean diaspora and its impact on the Korean and world economies.

What Is a Diaspora?

"Diaspora" is not an everyday English word, and many people may not understand its exact meaning. Of course, those who have studied religion, sociology, demography, history, political science, or economics would probably know its meaning. Historically, there are three concepts of a diaspora: original, classical, and contemporary.

Inbom Choi is the chief economist at the Federation of Korean Industries. He was a visiting fellow at the Institute for International Economics when he wrote this paper.

The word "diaspora" originates from the Greek verb *speiro*, meaning "to sow," and the preposition *dia*, meaning "over." The ancient Greeks used this word to mean migration and colonization.[1] For the Greeks, diaspora essentially had a positive connotation. Expansion through military conquest, colonization, and migration were the predominant features of the Greek diaspora. This original concept of a diaspora, signifying expansion and settler colonization, can loosely be applied to the late European (especially British, Portuguese, and Spanish) expansionist settlements of the mercantile and colonial periods.

Eventually, however, the meaning of a diaspora changed to become quite negative, to describe a forced dispersion of people out of their homeland to their countries of exile. And for some groups, such as Africans, Armenians, Jews, and Palestinians, the expression acquired an even more negative and brutal meaning. For them, the word "diaspora" signified a collective trauma and banishment to live in exile against their will. The most famous such trauma, of course, is that of Jews. In fact, so closely did the word "diaspora" become associated with the fate of Jews and the biblical use that usually when it is written with a capital "D," the Diaspora means, as the *Oxford English Dictionary* states, "the settling of scattered colonies of Jews outside of Palestine after the Babylonian exile, or Jews living outside Palestine or modern Israel." This is a very narrow definition of a diaspora. A little broader meaning is the dispersion of Christians isolated from their own communion and scattered across the Roman Empire before it adopted Christianity as the state religion.[2] These definitions associated with Jews and early Christians form the classical concept of a diaspora.

The contemporary concept of a diaspora is a way of understanding migration, cultural differences, identity politics, and so on. Thus, this broader definition of "diaspora" refers to a dispersion of people of a common national origin or of common beliefs living in exile. An even broader definition would simply refer to people of one country dispersed into other countries. These contemporary definitions of a diaspora especially refer to one particular phenomenon: cross-border migration.

Over the years, many social scientists have tried to provide a more specific definition of this broad concept of a diaspora. In fact, for decades, social scientists studying the issue of the diaspora have tried to tighten its definition, which today often is used as a synonym for "overseas," "ethnic," "exile," "minority," "refugee," "expatriate," "migrant," and so on. Depending on how restrictively the term "diaspora" is defined, these experts offer vary-

---

1. The Greeks colonized Asia Minor and the Mediterranean in the Archaic period (800-600 BC).

2. Originally, the Hebrew word *galut* (Deuteronomy 28:25) was employed to refer to the forced exile of the Jews in Babylon (586 BC). The word "diaspora" was later used in the sense of the forced dispersion of Jews and Christians.

ing characteristics or features of a diaspora.[3] In general, however, they seem to be focusing on five key criteria for the existence of a diaspora:

- dispersal of a large number of individuals from an original homeland to two or more foreign regions;

- an involuntary and compelling element in the motivation for people to leave their home country due to severe political, economic, or other constraints;

- a group's conscious and active efforts to maintain its collective identity, cultural beliefs and practices, language, or religion;

- people's sense of empathy and solidarity with members of the same ethnic group in other countries of settlement, leading to efforts to institutionalize transnational networks of exchange and communication; and

- people's collective commitment to preserve and maintain a variety of explicit and implicit ties with their original home country, provided it is still in existence.

Depending on how strictly one applies these criteria to identify a diaspora, there can be a wide range of diasporas. For example, if one argues that all five criteria should be met for a community to be identified as a diaspora, then we would have a rather narrow definition of a diaspora. Conversely, if one argues that only a couple of these criteria would be enough to identify a diaspora, then we have a rather broad concept of a diaspora.

Different Types of Diasporas

By comparing various diasporas in terms of their motivation to move out of their homeland to other countries, we can categorize different types of diasporas. Following the method used by Cohen, various diasporas can be grouped into five categories: victim or refugee, imperial or colonial, labor or service, and trade or commerce.[4]

---

3. For example, Connor (1986) defines "diaspora" very loosely as any segment of a people living outside its homeland. Conversely, Safran (1991) offers a very limited definition of diaspora, which applies to very specific cases and would prevent, for instance, the Greek, Chinese, or Lebanese transnational communities from being considered diasporas. See Dorais (2001).

4. Cohen (1997) also considers one more type of diaspora: a cultural or hybrid diaspora. He gives an example of the Caribbean people abroad. Caribbean people are not native to the area and are from a mixture of African slaves, indentured workers from India, and European settlers. Today, those Caribbean people living outside the region form a loose diaspora centered on their common culture.

As can be seen in table 2.1, a particular diaspora can be categorized into more than one type because the history of a diaspora often shows different motivations for people to leave their home country at various times. Thus, in a way, it is almost impossible to come up with a categorization of perfect matches between a particular ethnic group and a specific type of diaspora. In fact, it is quite the contrary. For example, Jews were not only a victim diaspora, but also one that was periodically successful in trade and commerce. Likewise, the Chinese were indentured laborers—therefore classified as a labor diaspora—as well as a successful trading diaspora. This type of categorization of diasporas may not be the best, and in fact many sociologists might use other methods. But in this way, we can at least compare major motivations for diasporas.

The victim or refugee diaspora is of course the result of a terrible experience of forced migration. The most important element here is the catastrophic origin of the diaspora. The best known case is, as noted above, that of Jews. However, there are other cases of victim groups with profiles not much different from that of Jews. The horrific African slave trade and the brutal treatment of Armenians by Turks[5] resulted in victims and refugees who formed diasporas of their own. Sometimes, even the Irish diaspora propelled by the potato famine in Ireland in the mid-19th century is identified as a victim diaspora.[6] A more recent case is the Palestinian diaspora. When the United Kingdom withdrew from Palestine in May 1948, the Israeli army occupied the vacuum and the ethnically based state of Israel was proclaimed. It has been estimated that two-thirds of the Arab population of Palestine left their homes and became refugees. Ironically and tragically, the Palestinian diaspora had been created by the homecoming of the Jewish diaspora.

The expansion of the powerful nations in Europe led to the development of their own imperial diasporas in their colonies abroad. British, Dutch, French, German, Portuguese, and Spanish colonists moved outward to most parts of the world. The British were particularly successful in establishing overseas settlements. However, for these settlers in their colonies, the term "diaspora" is not used normally by many sociologists because they emigrated several generations ago and do not continue to

---

5. Although the origins of the Armenian diaspora were in commerce and trade, the Armenians can be characterized as a victim diaspora because the Turks, following the massacres of the late 19th century, forcibly deported two-thirds of Armenians (estimated to be 1.75 million people) to Syria and Palestine.

6. The huge transatlantic migration of the Irish during the period 1845-52, following the famine, is considered a trauma. Studies have shown that hidden behind a seemingly laissez-faire government policy toward the Irish famine was a deliberate British government policy of population control, modernization of agriculture, and land reform, which ended up propelling the massive and continuous transatlantic migration of the Irish in the 19th century. See Cohen (1997) and Kinealy (1995).

Table 2.1   Different types of diasporas

Type	Examples
Victim or refugee	Jews, Africans, Armenians, Palestinians, Irish
Imperial or colonial	Ancient Greek, British, Spanish, Portuguese, Dutch, French
Labor or service	Indentured Indians, Chinese, Japanese
Trade or commerce	Venetians, Lebanese, Chinese

Source: Cohen (1997).

retain their identity as a collective group or keep ties with their original home countries, which are key features of a diaspora. For example, the term "diaspora" is not normally used when describing the presence of descendants of British people in Australia, Canada, Kenya, New Zealand, South Africa, the United States, and Zimbabwe. Nor is the term applied to the many German colonies established in Central and Eastern Europe and in several Latin American countries.[7]

The labor or service diaspora is the result of migration for the purpose of finding work—mainly involving unskilled labor. Examples of this type of diaspora include Indian workers in the plantation colonies during the period of British colonialism, North African construction workers in France, Chinese railroad workers in the United States, and Japanese workers in sugarcane plantations in Hawaii. These diasporas were, of course, the results of the 19th-century system of indentured labor abroad and therefore were somewhat related to the victim diaspora due to the coercive element of recruitment. However, these are not generally considered as victim diasporas because, in all three Asian cases, the people who were indentured formed a very small fraction of the total migrant population, the migrants had the legal right to return, and the recruitment process and work conditions were legally regulated, however badly.[8]

Stories of trade diasporas have been around for many years—for example, Homer's *Iliad* and *Odyssey* and Shakespeare's "The Merchant of Venice." The best known trade diasporas are those of Venetians, Lebanese, and Chinese. Merchants from one community would live as aliens in a town in another country; learn the language, the customs, and the commercial practices of their hosts; and then start the exchange of goods. Some kept moving back and forth between home and host countries, but many others stayed and settled in their host country.

The result of these activities was an interrelated net of commercial communities forming a trade network and diaspora. In the case of

7. Exceptions would be the Germans in Argentina and Chile, because they retain their identity. This phenomenon is sometimes called "minorities of superiority," which refers to the wish of these minorities to perpetuate their identity, which they see as culturally superior.

8. See Cohen (1997).

Chinese, at least as many traders as indentured laborers had begun to spill from the Chinese mainland into the rest of Southeast Asia. Moreover, the merchants' long-term influence was far greater than that of indentured laborers. It would be therefore more appropriate to describe the Chinese diaspora primarily as one of trade rather than labor, if one has to choose only a single category.

Globalization is bringing the parts of the world much closer together than ever before, creating more international migration and transnational corporations, and creating global cities with multiethnic, multicultural, multilingual populations. Globalization has enhanced the practical, economic, and affective roles of very adaptive diasporas. As diasporas become more integrated into the globalized world, their power and importance will be enhanced.

Diasporas Come and Go

Like other historical formations, diasporas form and disappear over time. As was mentioned above, many imperial or colonial diasporas are disappearing because of their weakened collective identity and ties with the original homeland. Some diasporas expand while some others shrink—not only because their dispersion continues or ceases, but also because they keep or lose their collective identity. For example, the Chinese diaspora continues to expand as more Chinese people migrate to other countries looking for jobs and business opportunities. But at the same time, the Chinese diaspora communities continue to maintain their collective ethnic identity—for example, by their continued commitment to teach the Chinese language to their second and third generations.

Conversely, the Japanese diaspora has in fact stopped growing and in a way has begun to disappear. Like Chinese contemporaries, many Japanese left their country in large numbers, initially to Hawaii for jobs on sugar plantations, and after the US annexation of Hawaii mainly to the west coasts of the United States and Canada. However, since the end of World War II, Japanese emigration has effectively ceased. Most Japanese who had settled in East Asia returned to Japan. Although there is still a large Japanese community in Latin America and on the west coasts of the United States and Canada, they have begun to lose their collective identity and cohesiveness, which is a key element of a diaspora. For example, many second- and third-generation Japanese-Americans do not speak Japanese.

Some diaspora communities have a strong enough political will to create nation-states. The best known case is Israel, but others include Cape Verde, Haiti, Liberia, and Singapore. Various other small states, which are often islands, are essentially made up of diaspora communities: Guyana, Mauritius, Suriname, and Trinidad.

The Making of the Korean Diaspora

Koreans are strongly rooted in their homeland. Thus, few people from Korea had left the country before Japanese colonization in 1910. During the period 1910-45, a sizable number of Korean workers left their homeland and settled in Manchuria, on Sakhalin, and in Japan. Korean emigrants during this period can generally be characterized as indentured labor migrants, and thus they could be called a labor diaspora. But many of them were forced to leave their home country under the colonial rule. They could therefore, with some justification, also be described as a victim diaspora because of the coercive element in their emigration or recruitment.

During this period, many Koreans, most of whom were North Koreans, also migrated to China and settled there as a result of their unhappiness with the Japanese colonization of their homeland. After World War II ended in 1945, many of them stayed in China after the Japanese left the Korean peninsula. The postwar Soviet occupation on Sakhalin prevented any possible return movement by the Korean minority there, and others remained in Siberia, on the border with Manchuria. Many Koreans who were living in Japan at the end of World War II also stayed and settled there in pursuit of better economic opportunities.

The character of Korean migration has changed from the 1960s, when the Korean economy began to develop and the government adopted an active emigration policy as part of domestic population control. As a result of this policy, many Koreans left their homeland to find better economic opportunities in other more industrialized countries. Most of these Koreans moved to the United States. After 1975, and increasingly in the 1980s and 1990s, more than half a million South Koreans immigrated to the United States, especially to Los Angeles, according to the US census.

As of 2001, according to South Korean government statistics, there are more than 5.7 million Koreans living outside the Korean peninsula. Does this mean that there is a Korean diaspora? As was discussed above, diasporas have several key characteristics. Most of these features are present in the case of Korean migration.

Chaliand and Rageau (1995) included the Korean diaspora in their atlas of world diasporas, but they raised two questions about the Korean migration being identified as a diaspora: One is the magnitude of migration, and the other is the limited destination. They argued that—though there had been quite an early migration to Japan of about 400,000 Koreans in 1930 and the emigration continued and accelerated after the 1960s—the total number of overseas Koreans lacks the massive proportions of a typical diaspora, such as the Irish case, in which more than half of the population emigrated from their homeland. However, if one can call the Japanese emigration a diaspora, the Korean diaspora certainly qualifies, because the number of Japanese living abroad is not very large. Moreover, the numbers of overseas Chinese and Indians are not that large relative to the huge populations still living in their home countries.[9]

The other question Chaliand and Rageau raised was that the overseas Koreans are essentially concentrated in three countries—the United States, China, and Japan—though small colonies exist on Sakhalin and in eastern Siberia. The question is whether this is a true dispersion or not. It is true that more than 80 percent of overseas Koreans are concentrated in these three countries. But the Irish also moved to only a couple of countries linguistically similar to their home country—the United States and Canada. Nevertheless, overseas Koreans are scattered all over the world. There are 15 countries with more than 10,000 Koreans and 5 countries with more than 100,000.

Moreover, Korean diaspora communities are very active in forming ethnic Korean community associations. These associations act as a centripetal force, pulling Koreans together, and they make conscious efforts to maintain the Koreans' collective ethnic identity, which again is one of the key elements of a diaspora. In fact, there are more than 2,000 of these ethnic Korean community associations all over the world. One can certainly claim that the Korean diaspora exists.

The Current Status of the Korean Diaspora

How many Koreans are living outside the Korean peninsula? It is certainly not easy to answer this question—even though, as stated above, the South Korean government estimated in 2001 that there are 5.7 million Koreans living abroad—because it is not easy to collect accurate data on population, particularly of minority populations in foreign countries. Nevertheless, the Korean Ministry of Foreign Affairs and Trade provides official estimates of overseas Koreans.[10]

The Ever-Growing Diaspora

As of 2001, again, it is estimated that there are about 5.7 million Koreans living in 151 countries outside the Korean peninsula. This population has grown 17 percent during the past 10 years. The number of overseas Koreans has always shown a positive annual growth rate, meaning that

---

9. It is estimated that there are 50 million overseas Chinese and 20 million overseas Indians, which are roughly 3.9 percent and 2.0 percent of their homeland populations, respectively. In Korea's case, overseas Koreans take up 8.2 percent of the total population in the Korean peninsula, which means the sum of the South Korean and North Korean populations.

10. See the Web site of the Korean Ministry of Foreign Affairs and Trade, http://www.mofat.go.kr.

the Korean diaspora is ever expanding. In particular, the 10-year period 1973-82 showed the highest growth rate of overseas Koreans; the number more than doubled, from about 700,000 in 1972 to 1.7 million in 1982, not counting the ethnic Koreans in China and the countries belonging to the Commonwealth of Independent States (CIS).[11]

During this period, almost 100,000 Koreans were added to the existing overseas Korean population every year. The year 1991 was particularly important for the Korean diaspora; for the first time, a complete picture of the Korean diaspora was revealed by identifying the numbers of ethnic Koreans in China and the CIS countries—which was about 2.4 million at the time, about 1.9 million in China and about 0.5 million in the CIS countries. Thus, the total number of overseas Koreans was estimated at about 4.8 million in 1991 (table 2.2). Through 2001, as the number grew to 5.7 million, an average of about 82,000 were added each year. It is clear that the Korean diaspora is still growing.

Dispersion of Overseas Koreans

The 5.7 million overseas Koreans are scattered across 151 countries. There are 24 countries with more than 2,000 ethnic Koreans, and 15 countries with more than 10,000. But overseas Koreans are concentrated in 5 countries or commonwealths, each with more than 100,000 ethnic Koreans; as is shown in table 2.3, these are the United States, China, Japan, the CIS, and Canada, which together account for 5.3 million, or 93 percent, of all overseas Koreans.

The United States has a larger number of ethnic Koreans than any other country in the world. There are more than 2 million ethnic Koreans in the United States, which is 38 percent of all overseas Koreans.[12] In the United States, ethnic Korean communities are concentrated in two areas: about 30 percent in the Los Angeles area and about one-quarter in the New York area. In the Los Angeles area alone, there are more than 200 various associations of ethnic Koreans. Seven US metropolitan areas have more than 100,000 ethnic Koreans; in order of Korean population, they are Los Angeles, New York, Chicago, San Francisco, Seattle, Houston, and Washington. In Hawaii, where the first Korean immigrants to the United

---

11. This number does not include ethnic Koreans in China. Because the South Korean government did not have diplomatic relations with China and the Soviet Union until the late 1980s, it could not provide the estimate of ethnic Koreans in China and the CIS countries until 1991.

12. This estimate by the Korean government is very different from the estimate of the 2000 US census, which puts the number at about 1 million. Because many people, particularly minorities, often do not respond to the census, its data on ethnic groups are likely to be underestimated.

Table 2.2   Expansion of the Korean diaspora, 1991-2001

Year	Number of overseas Koreans
1991	4,832,414
1995	5,228,573
1999	5,644,229
2001	5,653,809

Source: Korean Ministry of Foreign Affairs and Trade Web site, http://www.mofat.go.kr.

Table 2.3   The Korean diaspora by country and region of residence, 2001

Country, group, or region	Number	Percentage share
Major country or group		
United States	2,123,167	38
China	1,887,558	33
Japan	640,244	11
CIS	521,694	9
Canada	140,896	2
Region		
Asia	2,670,723	47
North America	2,264,063	40
Europe (including CIS)	595,073	11
Latin America	111,462	2
Middle East	7,200	—
Africa	5,280	—
Total	5,653,809	100

CIS = Commonwealth of Independent States

Source: Korean Ministry of Foreign Affairs and Trade Web site, http://www.mofat.go.kr.

States landed in 1903 as sugar plantation workers, now only about 30,000 ethnic Koreans reside. In Canada, most ethnic Koreans live in the Toronto and Vancouver areas.

Closer to home, there are 1.9 million ethnic Koreans in China, followed by 0.6 million ethnic Koreans in Japan and 0.5 million in the CIS countries. In Japan, the largest ethnic Korean community is located in the Osaka area. More than 200,000, or about 34 percent of all ethnic Koreans in Japan, live in the Osaka area. Among the CIS countries, Uzbekistan has the largest number of ethnic Koreans (about 230,000), followed by Russia (about 157,000). Almost half of the ethnic Koreans living in Latin America are in São Paolo, and about a quarter are in Argentina.

The latest hot spot for Korean emigrants is New Zealand. Throughout the 1990s, many Koreans left South Korea for New Zealand. The number of ethnic Koreans in New Zealand was only about 3,000 in 1992, but it grew very fast to about 18,000 in 2001. It is interesting that the motivation for this new wave of Korean migration to New Zealand is to escape from the poor living environment of Korean society, particularly for the sake of their children's education. The highly competitive South Korean educational system is driving these people from their homeland. They would rather raise their children in easy-going, environmentally cleaner, less expensive New Zealand, with its English-speaking educational system. Unfortunately, many heads of the households cannot find the high-paying jobs they are used to in South Korea, and therefore return to Korea to work, leaving their separated families behind.

The Diaspora's Impact on the Korean Economy

A diaspora could have an impact on the home country's economy in three basic ways. First, it could affect the trade and investment flows of the home country's economy, as can easily be seen with many trade or commerce diasporas. Second, it could affect the balance of payments of the home country through fund transfers between overseas settlers and their remaining families and relatives in the home country. Third, it could affect the home country's human resources and labor market.

Trade and Investment

Trade and investment have a long history of interrelationship with diasporas. Some of the best known diasporas are considered to be trade or commerce diasporas—the Chinese and Indian diasporas. In fact, there have been many academic studies analyzing the positive impact of diasporas on trade and investment flows between the home and host countries. These studies try to focus on informal trade barriers, especially weak enforcement of international contracts and inadequate information about international trading opportunities.[13]

As these studies have shown, business and social networks created by diasporas operate across national borders and thus can help overcome these types of informal trade barriers. For example, Saxenian (1999) shows that a transnational community of Indian engineers has facilitated the outsourcing of software development from California's Silicon Valley to such cities as Bangalore and Hyderabad. In other words, diasporas play the roles of alleviating problems of contract enforcement and providing information about business opportunities in international trade and investment activities.

As one can imagine, it is difficult to enforce contracts in international trade. There is always the risk of facing the failure of the other party's

---

13. For a complete survey of these studies, see Rauch (2001).

commitment to the contract. By doing international business through the network of a diaspora, one can reduce this risk significantly. For example, within the Armenian community in the 17th and 18th centuries, contracts could be made on a handshake and still avoid the opportunistic behavior of agents involved because of the trust created by the Armenian diaspora's moral community.[14]

In the case of the Chinese diaspora, the network has created a system of implicit penalties as a community, which are far greater than the short-term benefits one might gain through opportunism. If a business owner violates an agreement, he or she is blacklisted within the network, which is far worse than being legally sued because the entire network refrains from doing business with the blacklisted owner.[15] The threat of collective punishment of deviant agents by all merchants in the network deters opportunism and creates trust in international transactions, which in turn promotes the expansion of trade and investment.

Diaspora networks can also be used to transmit information about current opportunities for profitable international trade or investment. Transnational networks can facilitate business agent matching through the provision of market information, by informing suppliers about consumers' tastes in a particular country. As a result, suppliers will know what to supply and how to adapt their products to consumer preferences in a given country. One good example is the case of South Korean wig exports to the United States. According to a study,[16] Korean wig manufacturers had to depend entirely on Korean immigrant wig importers for market information about US wig fashions. Wig producers in Korea could obtain information on new styles and market trends from these immigrant wig importers, even though they were not able to develop new styles of their own.

At the same time, transnational diaspora networks can help investors to find joint-venture partners, producers to find appropriate distributors, and manufacturers to find good parts suppliers. The case of the Chinese transnational network is well documented in a study of the bamboo network.[17] Thus, through a network effect, diasporas can have a positive impact on bilateral trade. In addition, diasporas can also create trade through a taste effect, which means that immigrants' taste for goods from their countries of origin can directly create new trade flows to their country of residence. The most common example of this newly created trade through a taste effect is an increase in imported food. Most immigrants have a ten-

---

14. See Curtin (1984).

15. See Weidenbaum and Hughes (1996).

16. See Chin, Yoon, and Smith (1996) for a case study of the wig business in Los Angeles during the 10-year period starting in 1968.

17. See Weidenbaum and Hughes (1996).

dency to continue to stay with their ethnic dietary patterns and habits, and therefore they need to consume traditional foods and buy the necessary ingredients, which are normally imported from their home country.

The positive impact of a country's ethnic groups or immigrants on its bilateral trade has been studied empirically in the past, using gravity models which analyze the determinants of bilateral trade flows. For example, an empirical study of US bilateral trade during the period 1970-86 confirms the positive impact of immigrants on US trade.[18] A similar study, also done on Canadian bilateral trade, found the same evidence of Canada having more bilateral trade with countries from which it has more immigrants.[19]

To assess the impact of the Korean diaspora on South Korea's trade, a gravity model is also used to estimate the impact of the number of overseas Koreans on the country's bilateral trade.[20] The estimation uses Korea's bilateral trade with its 171 trading partner countries and the number of ethnic Koreans in those countries for 1999 and 2001.[21] The estimation result shows that the estimated coefficient on the number of overseas Koreans is positive (+0.18) and highly significant (99 percent confidence level) in the total trade volume equation, confirming the findings of earlier studies.[22]

This finding means that South Korea trades more with a country where more ethnic Koreans reside than with a country with a smaller number of ethnic Koreans. When the export equation is estimated separately, the estimated coefficient of the number of overseas Koreans is again positive (+0.16) and highly significant (99 percent confidence level), which means that Korea exports more to a country where more ethnic Koreans reside than to a country with fewer ethnic Koreans. When the import equation is estimated separately, the estimated coefficient of the number of overseas Koreans is again positive (+0.14) and highly significant (99 percent confidence level), which means that Korea imports more from a country where more ethnic Koreans reside than from a country with fewer ethnic Koreans. The fact that the export elasticity is larger than the import elas-

18. See Gould (1994).

19. See Head and Ries (1998).

20. I would like to thank Ben Goodrich for excellent research assistance for this analysis. The gravity model used here is based on one developed by Jeffrey Frankel (1997). The data are mostly drawn from the IMF's *World Economic Outlook* database and its *Direction of Trade Statistics* data.

21. The years 1999 and 2001 are the only ones for which the data on the number of overseas Koreans are most completely available. Although the dataset contains 171 trading partners, the actual number of observations for the estimation was 334 because some observations for certain variables are missing data values.

22. A random-effects generalized-least-squares regression estimation method was used.

ticity can be reasonably interpreted as meaning that export elasticity combines a taste effect and a network effect, whereas import elasticity only reflects a network effect.[23]

This result could also mean that more overseas ethnic Koreans find prospective business opportunities by importing and selling Korean products in their country of residence than by exporting products of their country of residence to South Korea, perhaps because Korean products are competitive. Thus from this analysis, it can be argued that the overseas diaspora of ethnic Koreans create Korea's trade with those countries where they reside and in fact create more exports than imports. This result could also be loosely interpreted as meaning that a 100 percent increase in the number of overseas Koreans would appear to increase Korea's exports by 16 percent and its imports by 14 percent, with a very small standard error.[24]

Foreign direct investment (FDI) by overseas ethnic Koreans has not been large, especially in comparison with that of the Chinese diaspora. Traditionally, however, FDI has not been an important part of Korean economic development.[25] Nevertheless, there was some FDI from overseas Koreans in the earlier stage of South Korea's economic development. Most of this FDI was from the ethnic Koreans in Japan. One well-known example was the case of the Lotte Group. Lotte chairman Kyuk-ho Shin apparently had accumulated wealth in Japan as an ethnic Korean and decided to invest in his homeland of Korea. Yet the dominant modality of FDI in Korea has been through minority stakes in joint ventures, mostly because of the regulations and restrictions on FDI. However, this pattern has been changing since the recent economic crisis in Korea; the ensuing liberalization of foreign investment rules has led to more FDI inflows to Korea in recent years.

The recent trend in FDI inflows in South Korea is its significant increase into services sectors like information technology and finance. In particular, information technology and other related high-technology industries have attracted FDI from overseas ethnic Koreans. For example, Chairman Son Masayoshi of Japan's Softbank has invested a significant amount in computer software and related industries in the past several years. Some other ethnic Koreans in Silicon Valley have also invested a significant amount in the software industry. Thus, there is a trend of

---

23. See Rauch (2001) for details of this type of interpretation on this result. Gould (1994) and Head and Ries (1998) show basically similar results for the United States and Canada, respectively.

24. Standard errors for the export and import coefficients are 0.043 and 0.078, respectively. This interpretation is a somewhat loose one because the dataset used in this analysis does not have enough time dimensions. It is difficult to argue that these elasticities are long-run elasticities.

25. See Choi and Schott (2001) for more discussion on FDI in South Korea.

increasing interest in investment by overseas Koreans. This FDI is insignificant, however, when compared with that of the Chinese diaspora in China.

China has drawn upon an enormous ethnic Chinese pool of nearly 50 million people, mostly based in Asia. The economic success of the Chinese in Hong Kong, Singapore, Taiwan, and elsewhere created investment opportunities in mainland China. China offered favorable treatment to overseas compatriots as it gradually opened its economy to FDI during the first reform period of the 1980s. The ethnic network facilitated a massive shift of production, through FDI in export processing as well as in trading activities, into lower-cost China.[26] The bulk of FDI into China came from Hong Kong and Taiwan. FDI from ethnic Chinese also provided valuable management skills and access to well-established global business networks. Conversely, until recently, the Indian diaspora's FDI has been limited because the Indian diaspora has had a bigger presence in the professional services sector as opposed to manufacturing and the Indian government has had a restrictive policy against FDI, just as did South Korea.

Fund Transfers

One of the key elements of a diaspora is the fact that overseas ethnic groups maintain, through various means, strong ties with their original homeland. One way of maintaining ties with families, relatives, and friends at home is to send them money. In fact, this phenomenon of overseas ethnic groups transferring funds to their homeland is very common among most diasporas, particularly where the home-country economy is in a poor state. Naturally, people living and working in the higher-wage countries would transfer funds to the lower-wage countries.

A simple indicator of this cross-border fund transfers is the "current transfers" item in a country's balance of payments account. Current transfers comprise general government transfers and other private-sector transfers, including workers' remittances. But for most countries, the amount of government transfers is a very small portion of total current transfers. Thus, many countries with large overseas diaspora communities usually show large inflows of current transfers.

As is shown in table 2.4, India receives huge inflows of funds through current transfers. In 2000, India had $13.5 billion of current transfers from abroad, which was 2.9 percent of GDP. China also receives a large quantity of current transfers, though their share of its GDP is small be-

---

26. For a story of the Chinese and Indian diasporas' investment in their home countries, see Joydeep Mukherji, "View from the Silk Road: Comparing Reform in China and India," *Standard & Poor's Credit Week*, February 6, 2002.

Table 2.4 Trend in current transfers for South Korea, India, and China, 1997-2001 (millions of US dollars)

Country and year	Current transfers Inflow	Current transfers Outflow	Inflows as a ratio of GDP (percent)
South Korea			
2001	6,548	6,911	1.55
2000	6,500	5,820	1.41
1999	6,421	4,506	1.58
1998	6,737	3,384	2.13
1997	5,288	4,621	1.11
India			
2001	n.a.	n.a.	n.a.
2000	13,504	51	2.94
1999	11,958	35	2.74
1998	10,402	67	2.51
1997	13,975	62	3.48
China			
2001	n.a.	n.a.	n.a.
2000	6,861	550	0.64
1999	5,368	424	0.54
1998	4,661	382	0.49
1997	5,477	333	0.61

n.a. = not available

Source: IMF, International Financial Statistics.

cause of its huge GDP. But more important, China and India both have outflows of current transfers that are very small compared with the size of inflows of current transfers, and thereby have a large surplus in current transfers.

However, in the case of South Korea, not only are its inflows of current transfers relatively small (less than 2 percent of GDP) but also its outflows of current transfers are large, partly because of its higher income level. Korea's outflows of current transfers are increasing by more than $1 billion every year. Korea even had a deficit of current transfers in 2001. Part of the reason for this large outflow of funds in the form of current transfers is that there are many foreign workers in Korea, who send back a large portion of their earnings to their families in home countries. Yet, a large portion of the outflow in current transfers accounts for those funds transferred to Korean families abroad. Some of those funds are sent to Korean students abroad, who are not really part of the Korean diaspora.

Still, a large quantity of funds is transferred to ethnic Koreans living abroad. Perhaps the recent South Korean trend of emigrating to industrial countries (e.g., New Zealand, as mentioned above) could explain some of this outflow, because many heads of families come back to Korea for higher-paying jobs and send money for living expenses to their families abroad. This is a unique phenomenon.

The Labor Market

As a diaspora develops and expands, it affects labor markets both in the home country and abroad. First, because people are leaving the country, there is a loss of human resources from the domestic economy and a gain for their host countries. One problem that a country should be concerned about, when it faces sizable emigration, is brain drain. This is quite a common and serious problem for many developing countries because many skilled, high-quality workers tend to leave the country in pursuit of higher-paying jobs and a better living environment abroad. South Korea had some experience with this problem in the 1950s and 1960s after the Korean War, when many highly educated people left Korea to study in the United States and settled there instead of returning home. But starting in the late 1970s, Korea was able to attract back many of these US-educated scholars and scientists.

At first, the South Korean government provided many financial incentives for them to return. Then, recognizing that research and development activities can contribute significantly to the economy's growth, the government took steps to create institutions for research and development and allocated the necessary funds. As a result, during the late 1960s, key institutions such as the Korea Institute of Science and Technology were created and flourished. Later on, the science town of Daeduk was created to host many research institutes. By offering heavy incentives to these institutes, Korea was able to recruit many ethnic Korean scientists living in industrial countries, especially from the United States. Thus, these ethnic Korean scientists, who moved back to Korea either permanently or temporarily for several years, contributed significantly to the development of Korea's science and technology capacity. Starting in the 1990s, there has been a trend among many overseas ethnic Koreans to wish to return to Korea as the country has developed significantly and become quite an attractive place to live.

In this sense, overseas ethnic Koreans have contributed to the development of the South Korean economy by transferring their knowledge and skills—which they obtained and strengthened in the more advanced countries of their residence—to their homeland. Recently, overseas ethnic Koreans' expertise in service industries (e.g., financial services) has begun to be transferred to Korea. Although one often hears about these transfers, it is of course very difficult to quantify such contributions by the Korean diaspora.

Meanwhile, the rapid economic development has brought high wages and income to South Korea. As a result, by the mid-1990s, Korea began to experience some shortages of labor, particularly in sectors with what are known as "3-D" (dirty, difficult, and dangerous) jobs. Just like most other industrial countries, Korea began to import cheap labor from abroad, mostly from Southeast and South Asia. But these imported workers' job opportunities were limited to those 3-D jobs because they could not speak the Korean language. As wages in Korea rose very high in the first half of the 1990s, the service industries began to seek cheaper labor from the pool of ethnic Koreans in China, whose biggest advantage was the fact that they could communicate in Korean. This meant that they could work in service industries like the restaurant business.

This labor market matching—demand for cheaper labor in South Korea matched by excess supply of ethnic Korean labor in China—brought a massive influx of ethnic Koreans from China into the Korean labor market. Now, one can easily run into these ethnic Koreans from China in many restaurants, working as waitresses, busboys, and short-order cooks. In this sense, overseas ethnic Koreans are contributing to the Korean economy by providing the home-country labor market with cheaper workers who are equipped with the necessary (language in this case) skills. This is also a very uncommon phenomenon among diasporas. Not one of the many examples of global diasporas listed in table 1.1 can be identified as having this characteristic—an overseas ethnic community that provides cheaper labor to its homeland.

Summary and Conclusion

The Korean diaspora is alive, expanding, and still in the making. It has more than a century of history. The diaspora's 5.7 million ethnic Koreans are scattered all over the world in 151 countries. Some have left South Korea involuntarily, and others voluntarily. But all of them actively try to maintain their collective identity and culture as Koreans. Overseas ethnic Korean communities seem to have an ethic of empathy and solidarity. But most of all, they try to maintain their ties with their homeland, Korea. These characteristics of overseas ethnic Koreans, again, are the key elements of a diaspora.

The Korean diaspora is concentrated in five countries or commonwealths, with more than 100,000 ethnic Koreans in each, which together account for 5.3 million or 93 percent of all overseas ethnic Koreans. The United States and China have the largest numbers of these Koreans, with respectively 2.1 million and 1.9 million, or 38 and 33 percent, of them.

Diaspora networks contribute to the creation of trade through the taste effect and the network effect. The above analysis shows that the Korean diaspora does have a positive impact on trade by creating more exports than imports. It is estimated that a doubling of the number of overseas Koreans appears to increase South Korea's exports by 16 percent and Korea's imports by 14 percent. Foreign direct investment by the Korean diaspora has not been very significant for the development of the Korean economy, unlike in the case of the Chinese diaspora.

South Korea's pattern of current transfers in its balance of payments account is indicative of an interesting and unique aspect of the fund transfers by the Korean diaspora. In contrast to the other diasporas, such as those of the Chinese and Indians, the Korean diaspora seems to be taking money out of the homeland rather than sending it to Korea.

The Korean diaspora did not really cause a brain drain but instead contributed to the development of South Korea by transferring back home the knowledge and skills they obtained in more advanced countries. And most interesting, ethnic Koreans from China are providing a low-wage labor resource for the homeland.

It is important to study the many aspects of the Korean diaspora because it concerns not only overseas ethnic Koreans but Koreans at home as well. One area where more research needs to be done is in building a statistical database for many variables related to the Korean diaspora, particularly trade and investment data. It is recommended that an organization like the Overseas Koreans Foundation should pay more attention to building this database in the future.

References

Chaliand, Gerard, and Jean-Pierre Rageau. 1995. *The Penguin Atlas of Diasporas*. New York: Viking Penguin.

Chin, Ku-Sup, In-Jin Yoon, and David A. Smith. 1996. Immigrant Small Business and International Economic Linkage: A Case of the Korean Wig Business in Los Angeles, 1968-77. *International Migration Review* 30: 485-510.

Choi, Inbom, and Jeffrey Schott. 2001. *Free Trade Between Korea and the United States?* POLICY ANALYSES IN INTERNATIONAL ECONOMICS 62. Washington: Institute for International Economics.

Cohen, Robin. 1997. *Global Diasporas: An Introduction*. Seattle: University of Washington Press.

Connor, Walker. 1986. The Impact of Homelands upon Diasporas. In *Modern Diasporas in International Politics*, ed. Gabi Sheffer. New York: St. Martin's Press.

Curtin, Philip D. 1984. *Cross-Cultural Trade in World History*. Cambridge: Cambridge University Press.

Dorais, Louis-Jacques. 2001. Defining the Overseas Vietnamese. *Diaspora* 10: 3-28.

Frankel, Jeffrey A. 1997. *Regional Trading Blocs in the World Economic System*. Washington: Institute for International Economics.

Gould, David. 1994. Immigrant Links to the Home Country: Empirical Implications for U.S. Bilateral Trade Flows. *Review of Economics and Statistics* 76: 302-16.

Head, Keith, and John Ries. 1998. Immigration and Trade Creation: Econometric Evidence from Canada. *Canadian Journal of Economics* 31, no. 1: 47-62.

Kinealy, C. 1995. *The Great Calamity: the Irish Famine, 1845-52*. London: Gill & Macmillan.

Rauch, James E. 2001. Business and Social Networks in International Trade. *Journal of Economic Literature* 39: 1177-1203.

Safran, William. 1991. Diasporas in Modern Society: Myths of Homeland and Return. *Diaspora* 1: 83-99.

Saxenian, Anna Lee. 1999. *Silicon Valley's New Immigrant Entrepreneurs*. San Francisco: Public Policy Institute of California.

Weidenbaum, Murray, and Samuel Hughes. 1996. *The Bamboo Network*. New York: Free Press.

Comments on Chapter 2

TAEHO BARK

I have learned much from Inbom Choi's chapter. I had never encountered the word "diaspora" until I read his chapter, despite the fact that I lived in the United States for more than 10 years. Thus, reading the chapter was a particularly good opportunity for me to learn about the Korean diaspora.

The motivation for and main characteristics of the Korean diaspora seem to vary according to the time period. For example, there seems to be a clear difference between the periods before and after the 1960s. In the future, I expect the Korean diaspora to follow the trend of the more recent period, especially in seeking better opportunities. However, in this case, the migration will be temporary rather than permanent. It will be an interesting exercise to look at the changes according to the time period and major destinations. Political, commercial, and social motivations may well explain the migrations.

In chapter 2's section on the Korean diaspora's impact on South Korea's economy (p. 19), it was pointed out that the ethnic Koreans' investment in Korea has not been significant. This finding seems to be related to the Korean foreign direct investment policy, which has not welcomed investment from abroad so as to protect domestic firms from foreign competition. In the future, however, I think ethnic Koreans' role in Korea's economic development will increase. For example, ethnic Koreans from Asia can make huge contributions to the low-skilled workforce in Korea, whereas ethnic Koreans from the United States can strengthen the Korean economy in the services sectors and high-technology businesses.

One thing the chapter did not mention is the fact that ethnic Koreans can play an important role in mediating trade and investment disputes between South Korea and the United States. I am not saying that ethnic Koreans should become lobbyists. Rather, it is important to emphasize that they can diversify their business interests between the two countries,

Taeho Bark is Seoul National University's dean of international affairs and dean of its School of International and Area Studies. He also serves as the commissioner of the Korea Trade Commission.

which might be helpful in eventually mitigating possible conflicts in the future.

In the coming years, more ethnic Koreans from all over the world will likely return to or visit South Korea for various reasons. In this context, it will be very important to investigate other countries' experiences, particularly with regard to the efforts home-country governments have made to facilitate the interaction between ethnic nationals living abroad and the homeland.

As for government policy, it needs to be emphasized that Korean nationals living abroad might not want any special favors from their home country. Instead, they might want to be treated equally with their fellow Koreans living in South Korea. In particular, the home-country government should not intervene on behalf of ethnic Koreans in other countries. If the home-country government would like to help Koreans abroad, it can best do so by promoting programs initiated by the private sector, such as cultural and educational events.

Because I work at Seoul National University, it is useful to share some of my own experiences. Recently, the number of ethnic Koreans visiting South Korean universities has been increasing. They may come to Korea either to learn the Korean language and culture for a semester or two or to seek a formal degree. However, at my university, most of the lectures, especially for the undergraduate courses, are conducted in Korean. This really discourages those ethnic Koreans who do not speak Korean. We need to make more efforts to invite these young Koreans born and living abroad to visit South Korea in a more accessible linguistic context so that they can come to know and understand more about their origins.

In response to this need, Seoul National University is about to launch a new program, Learning Contemporary Korea: Gateway to East Asia, in the spring semester of 2003. This program will offer a package consisting of three components: learning the Korean language and culture, taking a couple of courses to be conducted in English, and working at an outside organization as an intern. I hope that this program will create a good momentum for introducing contemporary South Korea to both ethnic Korean students and to students from other countries around the world.

3

Chinese Business Networks and Their Implications for South Korea

YOUNG ROK CHEONG

In the past 20 years, no country seems to have beaten China in its grand comeback in both global political and economic arenas. China has become a key player in formulating the world order since gaining membership in the United Nations in 1972. China has also recorded an average annual real growth rate of more than 10 percent—shocking the world. In human history, no other country has shown such tremendous economic growth while having such a huge population. And with regard to the source of China's rapid economic growth, the contribution of overseas Chinese[1] has often been mentioned by many China watchers.[2]

First of all, overseas Chinese not only provided the People's Republic of China with capital at the initial stages of its Economic Reform and Open Door policies in 1978 and thereafter, but they also gave it a developmental model to be copied. Even more important, overseas Chinese global business networks were a key element in rescuing China from the economic bottleneck it suffered when confronted with sanctions from Western countries after the Tiananmen Square incident. Yet it is too early to judge whether there is a strong relationship between these overseas Chinese networks and China's rapid economic development.

Young Rok Cheong is professor of economics at Seoul National University.

1. Defining "overseas Chinese" is somewhat complex. In this chapter, the term "overseas Chinese" means the Chinese living abroad, regardless of their citizenship.

2. Barry Naughton has been among them.

In the fall of 2001, many overseas Chinese celebrities from around the world arrived one after the other at the Nanjing airport, where they received a warm welcome from local government officials. Among them were well-known Hong Kong business tycoon Henry Fok and Nobel Prize winner Yang Zhenning of the United States.[3] They were joining Chinese political leaders Jiang Zemin,[4] Zhu Rongji, and Chen Qichen to celebrate the Sixth World Chinese Entrepreneurs' Convention—a very important moment of clarifying that this somewhat informal and self-sufficient overseas Chinese organization is strongly supported by the Chinese central government.

This convention manifested a change in Chinese policy toward overseas Chinese. The government has sought overtly to actively utilize their resources directly in its state building. This is attributable to the new circumstances under which China has pursued its rapid economic development. The convention will surely facilitate Chinese economic development in the 21st century, although it is still too early to say if the convention was launched in strong coordination with the Chinese central government to alleviate the agony of the Asian financial crisis.

South Korea has also successfully achieved economic development since World War II with an export development strategy that has relied on foreign demand. After going through the Asian financial crisis, however, it is making many efforts to follow the global trends of extensive market opening and establishment of worldwide business networks. Naturally, a close look at the role of overseas Chinese in modernizing China may also offer important lessons for Korea. Korea also has almost 6 million overseas Koreans,[5] who could have played a more important role in both promoting its economic development and even in resolving the national conflict between South and North Korea. Unfortunately, Koreans have tended to despise overseas Koreans, thus keeping almost 10 percent of the total global ethnic Korean population from playing a positive role in their nation's development. Steps would need to be taken to broaden the country's economic base so that overseas Koreans could participate in its development.

It is often said that the 21st century is a "network" age.[6] As the world has become more and more interdependent, threats of massive wars seem to have diminished, whereas economic and business networks have

---

3. Fok runs his business in Hong Kong and holds the vice chairmanship of the CPCC, whereas Yang became a symbolic leadership figure of science and technology in China by winning the Nobel Prize in 1957 and is also a key proponent of reviving Chinese science and technology.

4. He delivered his welcoming remarks via Jing Shuping, then host of the conference and chairman of the Bank of the Minsheng.

5. Overseas Koreans are dispersed mostly in the United States, Japan, China, and Russia and the other members of the Commonwealth of Independent States.

6. Peter F. Drucker is among them.

become more important in the global market. The economies of scale that dominated in the previous period seem to have given way to network economies. As such, research on business networks themselves might provide an outline of the future. Especially with regard to business networks of overseas Chinese, several questions come to mind: whether these networks have been successful or not, how they have been evolved thus far, to what extent the government has helped, and finally whether the Chinese model could be applied to South Korea.

In this regard, this chapter basically tries to clarify a couple of the points above. The second section reviews business networks of overseas Chinese and then considers their implications for the Korean case. Several limitations and challenges ahead are then examined in subsequent sections. Because the chapter is not purely academic, it relies on a review of diverse published materials and interviews with experts on this matter.

The Evolution of Overseas Chinese Business Networks

Current Status

During the past 30 years, the size and distribution of the overseas Chinese population has changed. Largely, they are divided into two groups. The first group consists of immigrants who were not well educated. They are from Guangdong's[7] Jiangmen area, Zhujiang's delta area, Fujian's Fuzhou area, and Zhejiang's southern area. The second group is made up of highly educated immigrants, including scholars and students from mainland China studying in the United States, Canada, Australia, and Europe. Due to the rapid growth of the population and new migrations of overseas Chinese since the 1970s, their number increased from 10 million to 15 million in the early of 1950s to 30 million to 35 million in the 1980s and 1990s.

Since the mid-1970s, about 4 million overseas Chinese from mainland China, Hong Kong, and Taiwan have moved to foreign countries. They have been expected to adapt to local cultures all over the world. Overall, these new overseas Chinese immigrants are well educated in comparison with the earlier ones. According to the data of the Chinese Education Committee, a majority of scholars and students studying abroad between 1983 and 1995 selected the United States as their country of residence. And most of them have wanted to go into business after finishing their education.

As of 1998, the total number of Chinese people in the world including mainland China was 1.38 billion, which accounted for 22.4 percent of the global population. As for overseas Chinese, approximately 35.71 million

7. In this chapter, the pinyin system is used to transliterate Chinese names.

live in Southeast Asia, which accounts for 80 percent of their total population. In addition, 13.2 percent live in the Americas, 5.5 percent in Europe, and 1.4 percent in Australia and New Zealand. There are 98 countries with an overseas Chinese population of more than 1,000; of these people, more than 10,000 live in each of the 52 countries and more than 100,000 in each of the 25 countries.[8] The 11 countries with the largest overseas Chinese populations and shares of their total populations are listed in table 3.1.

As the table shows, Indonesia (7.31 million) topped the list for overseas Chinese population, followed by Thailand (6.36 million), Malaysia (5.52 million), Myanmar (3.0 million), and the United States (2.73 million). According to the share of total population, Singapore (78 percent) topped the list, followed by Malaysia (26.3 percent), Brunei (14.7 percent), Thailand (10.2 percent), and Suriname (9.2 percent).

It is estimated that the history of overseas Chinese dates back to the period of the South Sung Dynasty. The Chinese migrated for many reasons; we will briefly touch on five. First, many fled the country when internal conflicts erupted or dynasties changed. An especially large number fled in the wake of the Yuan Dynasty's triumph over the Sung Dynasty. At the end of the Ming Dynasty, another large number escaped abroad when the Manchu people conquered the Han people in Beijing. Others left when the Taiping rebellion[9] broke out and the Communists took over mainland China in 1949.

Second, some Chinese moved abroad to avoid paying high taxes or being exploited by landowners. Between 1661 and 1812, the rate of population growth in Fujian jumped five times, whereas its land area increased only 32 percent. In Guangdong, the rate of population growth rose 20 times while its land increased merely 20 percent. As a result, the lack of land and worsening working conditions forced many Chinese to move to Taiwan and other Southeast Asian countries, collectively known as Nanyang.[10]

Third, many Chinese moved abroad when China was invaded by the Western colonial powers aimed at territorial expansion. After the Opium War, the Chinese national economic system collapsed under the pressure of colonial leadership. A huge number of farmers, laborers, and factory workers were indentured to foreign countries or had to move abroad.[11]

Fourth, many Chinese moved overseas due to changes in the immigrant policies of their new countries of residence. For example, the United States allowed a large number of Chinese laborers to enter at the time a nation-

---

8. There are 13 Asian countries, 5 European countries, 5 American countries, and Australia and New Zealand.

9. It was in the 1880s.

10. Nanyang was taken as an overseas Chinese residence because it was the first area they settled in massively.

11. They are called indentured laborers, or *coolies.*

Table 3.1 The 11 economies with the largest overseas Chinese populations and percentages of total population

Rank	Overseas Chinese population (millions)		Percentage of overseas Chinese in total population	
1	Indonesia	7.310	Singapore	77.9
2	Thailand	6.358	Malaysia	26.3
3	Malaysia	5.520	Brunei	14.7
4	Myanmar	3.000	Thailand	10.2
5	United States	2.730	Suriname	9.2
6	Singapore	2.680	French Polynesia	8.8
7	The Philippines	1.030	Myanmar	6.4
8	Vietnam	1.000	Panama	4.4
9	Russia	1.000	Indonesia	3.6
10	Canada	0.920	Laos	3.1
11	Peru	0.500	Canada	3.1

Note: Hong Kong and Taiwan are excluded.

Source: Committee on Overseas Chinese in Taiwan.

wide railroad system was built to develop the country's Pacific frontier. When the United States passed the Chinese Exclusion Act of 1882, which prohibited the entry of Chinese laborers into the country, Chinese migration diminished. However, the restrictions were lifted in part in the 1960s, and many Chinese came to the United States in the 1970s and 1980s. About that time, Australia, Canada, Indonesia, the Philippines, and Singapore also liberalized their immigration policies toward the Chinese.

Fifth, pragmatic Chinese characteristics contributed to the growth of overseas Chinese; the Chinese are more likely to consider their personal happiness important than their love for the country. Therefore, they tend to move to foreign countries to look for a better life.[12]

Recently, many Chinese intellectuals have moved overseas as they have been lured by the strategy of other countries to hire the best and brightest foreign nationals. Overall political and economic elements, together with individual choices, have worked as push and pull factors to increase the growth of overseas Chinese.

Many researchers have observed the emergence of a Chinese economic bloc in recent years (table 3.2). However, it is not easy to estimate the accurate size of overseas Chinese capital due to the rapidity of capital mobility and Chinese secrecy characteristics. In the 21st century, an economic bloc is likely to prosper in China, Hong Kong, and Taiwan. As table 3.2 shows, the bloc had only half the GDP of the United States in terms of the purchasing power parity in 1990. However, it is expected to exceed the US level in 2002.

It is also very interesting to measure the magnitude of overseas Chinese capital at the global level. During the past 30 years, their commu-

---

12. This is called the self-selection model.

Table 3.2 Estimated GDP of the Chinese economic bloc relative to selected large economies (trillions of US dollars)

Economic bloc or economy	GDP in exchange rate conversion terms		GDP in purchasing power parity terms		Per capita income at purchasing power parity
	1991	2002	1990	2002	
Chinese economic bloc	0.6	2.5	2.5	9.8	7,300
United States	5.5	9.9	5.4	9.7	36,000
Japan	3.4	7.0	2.1	4.9	37,900
Germany	1.7	3.4	1.3	3.1	39,100

Note: The Chinese economic bloc includes China, Hong Kong, and Taiwan.

Sources: Lu Peichun (1995), Overseas Chinese networks.

nities have achieved rapid economic growth. Although their trade network in East Asia and Southeast Asia has existed for 600 years, huge sums of overseas Chinese capital were accumulated between the 1960s and the 1980s, when Hong Kong, Singapore, Taiwan, and South Korea grew to become the "four dragons" of Asia. Between the 1970s and the 1980s, Indonesia, Malaysia, and Thailand, the major bases for overseas Chinese, developed rapidly. As a result, they became the largest beneficiaries of what was known as the East Asian economic miracle. According to the World Bank, the value of their companies rose from $400 billion in 1991 to $600 billion in 1996.

As of 2000, it also was estimated that there is about $300 billion in floating overseas Chinese capital.[13] It was estimated that there are about 150 overseas Chinese businesspeople with more than $500 million in property. In particular, it was estimated that they account for 6 percent of the Southeast Asian population and 86 percent of its property. They dominate at least 70 percent of the national economy of each country in South Asia. *Asia Week* published interesting data on the total stocks held by their 500 largest businesspeople showing that the amount was $566.8 billion in 1999, $616.3 billion in 2000, and $456.8 billion in 2001.

Characteristics

The overseas Chinese are famous for their collective character. Whenever they migrate, they soon form a community known as a "Chinatown." They are used to forging networks based on blood ties, friendships, and professional accomplishments. The so-called *guanxi* (network of connections) exerts great influence over their society. They organize a wide range

---

13. This estimate is taken from a news article on the September 2001 international convention of overseas Chinese in Nanjing.

of networks to consolidate their influence for survival or better settlements. Because they generally do not take firm root in foreign societies, they rarely invest in manufacturing, which requires a longer time frame for investment returns. Instead, they concentrate their investment in real estate, hotels, and finance, from which the flow of capital is relatively quick and smooth. They are also active in underground economic activities.

It was not until the end of the 19th and early 20th centuries that the overseas Chinese began to accumulate capital. They largely ran small businesses in commerce and served as agents representing the interests of local people or foreign capital. As a result, they had an image of being small and medium-sized businesspeople.

Overseas Chinese capital began to function in modern forms after new independent states were born in the wake of World War II. However, an economic disparity between overseas and local people was an obstacle to their accumulation of overseas capital in some countries, such as Indonesia and Malaysia.[14] The rapid growth of the global economy has provided opportunities for overseas Chinese to accumulate capital since 1960. Their capital has moved from the traditional sectors of small business to various modern industrial sectors.

In the early 19th century, the overseas Chinese in Southeast Asia started to establish networks based on blood ties, friendships, and professional accomplishments to protect their profits. By the 1940s, these networks were getting stronger and unified in each country. In the 1970s, the networks were incorporated into one network encompassing the Southeast Asian region. After the 1980s, overseas Chinese from Hong Kong, Taiwan, and other Southeast Asian economies moved to the United States and Europe, which enabled them to establish a global network linking the United States, Europe, and Southeast Asia.

In the 1990s, they formulated an international strategy to form a global network of overseas Chinese. The strategy focused on establishing an Asia-Pacific economic region to link their capital in Asia to the high-technology industry of North America. According to the strategy, they would concentrate on high-value-added products instead of financing labor-intensive manufacturing products.

Overseas Chinese networks are characterized by a solid bond of blood ties, friendship, and professional accomplishments—as seen in secret societies (*bang*) and various alumni meetings. They forge a strong bond within the networks. However, they are often hostile toward other networks. In Southeast Asia, different lines of overseas Chinese from Fujian, Guangdong, and Kejia compete against each other for shares of economic interests. In Australia, Canada, and the United States, new overseas Chinese are likely to compete against old ones from Fujian and Guangdong.

---

14. South Korea is also notorious for dispelling overseas Chinese.

Originally, secret societies were established as a sort of social insurance to protect their life and property against ruthless emperors and the ruling class during the Yuan and Ming Dynasties. Under the Qing Dynasty, these *bang* became subject to the government's oppression. As a result, they went underground and remained secretive. Overseas Chinese also organized secret societies by region and business. They organized all kinds of secret societies and *hui* (associations) to maintain order within the group. Various meetings exist, such as clan, hometown, and public ones, for those who are in the same business. They tend to develop a strong relationship among group members. However, they are likely to exclude other ethnic groups and nonmembers.

Hometown background may be the strongest factor to affect the organization of networks. Language is another important element of the hometown background. There are hundreds of dialects in China. The Chinese cannot communicate with one another if they are located 100 *li* away.[15] Therefore, dialects can be a good way to distinguish the Chinese. They can tell food, clothes, social status, and other general sociocultural characteristics by dialects. Even if they use the same writing system, they can hardly communicate with those who speak different dialects. As a consequence, they are likely to organize networks with those who speak the same dialect. For example, those who are affiliated with the Fujian Secret Society cannot join the Guangdong Secret Society because they do not speak Cantonese. However, those who can speak Cantonese can become members of the Guangdong society even if they are not from Guangdong.

The overseas Chinese from Guangdong, including Chaozhou, Hainan, and Kejia, account for more than 70 percent of the total overseas Chinese population, with about 30 percent of the population being from Fujian. However, conglomerates and big capitalists from Fujian dominate those from Guangdong. In Taiwan, 70 percent have a Fujian background, with the rest being aboriginals, Kejia, and mainlanders.

The overseas Chinese have made use of their networks for their development. They have established Chinatowns all over the world. This suggests that they have strong networks to protect their interests. Unlike in the United States, Europe, and Japan, in Southeast Asia they have tended not to be separate from local people to avoid friction with them. However, they have maintained invisible networks of mutual assistance.

Their international conference is their largest open and established international organization. They hold the conference every 2 years. At least 1,000 overseas Chinese participate in it—even if they speak different dialects or are from different clan groups. The conference is conducted in Mandarin and English, and simultaneous interpretation is provided for those not speaking either.

---

15. The Chinese unit 10 *li* is equivalent to 2 kilometers. Hence, 100 *li* equals 20 kilometers.

In the 1990s, changes in the international situation and the organizations of overseas Chinese resulted in the creation of new networks. For example, the alumni from the same schools and those who studied in the United States organized their own networks. This phenomenon implies that in addition to traditional networks such as the Guangdong and Fujian Secret Societies, various alumni groups also will become networks.

Taiwanese Government Policy

The Nationalist Chinese policy toward overseas Chinese dates back to the end of the Qing Dynasty, when the Qing government adopted measures to protect overseas Chinese lives and rights. The policy was based on the principle of *jus sanguinis* and the loyalty of the Chinese on the basis of blood ties and ethnicity. After the *Guomingdang* government moved to Taiwan in 1949, the policy was not stalled, but it constantly changed in response to the governments of the People's Republic of China (PRC), the United States, and other major countries.

The Nationalist government assumed the role of savior and protector of the overseas Chinese who were then dispersed in more than 100 countries under the slogan of "All People One Heart." The Guomingdang announced a series of programs for them: to protect their rights and privileges, to promote close cooperation among their networks to counter the Chinese Communists and the Soviet Union, to support educational projects for them so that they could have access to the Chinese cultural tradition, to provide incentives for them to invest in Taiwan and work for the government, to train their younger generation as party leaders, to support the activities of underground anticommunist organizations in mainland China, to enhance the status of those who work with the Nationalist government, and to pursue ideal and practical objectives with the countries that do not have diplomatic relations with Taiwan.

The Nationalist government's plan for the Cold War fell apart in the early 1970s. In 1971, the United States revised its containment policy against China, which had been supported by US political, economic, and military assistance to Taiwan. All of a sudden, the Nationalist government lost this US protection. The United States changed its position by deciding not to prevent China from entering the United Nations and to pursue reconciliation with China, which led to President Richard Nixon's visit to China in 1972. As a result, many Western countries and Japan recognized China instead of Taiwan. Consequently, the Taiwanese strategy of the 1950s was abandoned and revised.

To strengthen its control over the overseas Chinese in the United States, the Nationalist government of Taiwan took a few important measures in the early 1980s. First, it invested millions of US dollars in a few Chinese-language newspapers in the United States that were facing bankruptcy.

Second, it increased its support for Chinese-language schools in the United States. Third, all the Huiguan and Gongsuo launched campaigns to have them pledge their loyalty to the Taiwanese government in San Francisco. Fourth, the Nationalist government and the Guomingdang were increasingly oppressive, including kidnapping those who favored the PRC.

However, the political situation changed again in the 1980s. The policy and measures of the Nationalist government proved to be ineffective and negative—isolating the Nationalist government from the global networks of overseas Chinese—and were abolished in the 1990s. The Nationalist government stopped relying on overseas Chinese efforts, and it began to lobby the United States and other countries directly.

PRC Government Policy

The PRC government changed its attitudes toward overseas Chinese with the evolution of their status. It first established government agencies to favor them for national unification and economic development. It has offices dealing with their matters in the State Council, the Standing Committee of the National Peoples' Congress, and the Political Consultation Conference. In the Communist Party, the Department of the Unification Front is responsible for them. Such civilian bodies as the National Returned Overseas Chinese Association run branches nationwide and promote their rights and benefits.

Most of all, however, the major duties of each PRC organization relating to overseas Chinese affairs are to lure their investment, to invite their famous members to visit mainland China, and to protect their rights, property, and relatives in China. If they have difficulty making investments or staying in the country, they can get help solving their problems by going directly to the General Office of Overseas Chinese Affairs under the State Council.

In the 1950s, the objective of the Chinese government's policy[16] toward overseas Chinese was to promote economic and political interests. Economically, the policy allowed them to send money and goods to their relatives, to explore sales markets for Chinese goods around the world, and to make investments. Politically, they served as activists on the unification frontline, supporting Chinese revolutionary diplomacy. The Chinese government handled them based on the basic principle of dual nationality. The PRC would respect the decision on one's own nationality

---

16. Article 98 of the PRC's 1954 Constitution declared that the PRC government will protect the legitimate rights and benefits of overseas Chinese. The Overseas Chinese Affairs Commission was set up to handle matters of overseas Chinese. Overseas Chinese were allowed to take part in state affairs by stating their participation in the National Peoples' Congress.

and not force holders of Chinese nationality or applicants for Chinese nationality to adopt the foreign nationality.[17]

The Chinese government evaluated the high achievements of overseas Chinese in business and assured their importance. Its four basic policy guidelines toward them were announced in May 1989: first, not to recognize their dual nationality but to encourage them to obtain the nationality of the host country; second, to demand that the host government guarantee their rights and benefits; third, for them to learn to respect the laws of the host country and coexist with the people of the host country in harmony; and fourth, to promote their unity by cultivating their patriotism and love for China. The policies also focused on attracting capital, technology, and intellectual expertise for both domestic economic development and overseas market development.

The Chinese policy toward overseas Chinese is summed up in the 1991 PRC Protection Law on Returned Overseas Chinese and Overseas Chinese Relatives. This law consists of 22 articles. In particular, article 3 describes the basic guideline: "On the rights and duties of returned overseas Chinese and [overseas Chinese] relatives, no organization should discriminate against them . . . the state will treat them adequately." In particular, this specific measure was determined by the State Council, which implies the importance of the domestic policy toward them.

The key elements of the guidelines on the Chinese authorities' policy for overseas Chinese are to support their survival and development in the host country, and to use them as bridges of friendship and cooperation between China and foreign countries. In particular, the guidelines focus on the need to contact influential overseas Chinese through relatives and hometown business associations to invite many of them to participate in modernizing China. The Chinese government's gradual approach has succeeded in attracting a huge quantity of investment and much support from them.[18] It has made efforts to remind them of the fact that China is the mother country of all Chinese people.

Competition Between the PRC and Taiwan

As was noted above, networks of overseas Chinese businesspeople have become very important for both mainland China and Taiwan because of

---

17. The nationality of those below 18 years of age will be the same as that of their parents, and after they reach 18 years of age they will determine their nationality.

18. Overseas Chinese as well were aware of the changing situation in China. They showed a favorable response to China. Lu Sunlin, director of the Taiwan Chamber of Commerce in Ho Chi Minh City, says, "Chinese officials contacted pro-Taiwan overseas Chinese with no demands." They merely say, "we want to be your friends," "we are brothers." He notes that "their approaches are remarkably effective in the process of changes in China." (*Far Eastern Economic Review*, June 21, 2001.)

their growing influence and economic development. During the Cold War, pro-Taiwan global networks of overseas Chinese businesspeople were powerful, whereas PRC networks of these businesspeople have been increasingly influential since the PRC's Economic Reform and Open Door policies were implemented in 1978.

The effort to encourage the formation of networks among the overseas Chinese was initiated by the Taiwanese government. The Global Economic and Trade Meeting was held first in 1963 in Tokyo. The meeting was intended to promote the exchange of information among overseas Chinese on economies, trade, investment, diplomatic policies, and the economic development of Taiwan. The meeting has since been held every 2 to 3 years in major cities of the world. The 21st meeting was held in 1998 in Taiwan, at which 970 overseas Chinese businesspeople from 55 countries participated. The 22nd meeting was held in April 2000 in Brazil. The Taiwanese government established a network of these global businesspeople under the Overseas Chinese Affairs Commission. Since 1972, this commission's network has educated 4,320 businesspeople on management, international trade, and factory management. In October 1999, 333 of them opened the first general meeting.

In May 1999, a joint international investment committee for overseas Chinese businesspeople was also held in Taipei. About 200 overseas Chinese and 80 Chinese businesses participated in the meeting on overcoming the Asian financial crisis and challenges for the 21st century. Under the guidance of the Overseas Chinese Affairs Commission of Taiwan, the meeting aimed at securing pro-Taiwan networks of overseas Chinese businesspeople and exchanging information on their investments. The Taiwanese government also managed to promote their global financial conference for friendship and exchanging information. Recently, the meeting was held in 2000 under the sponsorship of the US California Bank. There are also various other overseas Chinese business networks in each country, such as general Chinese business associations and Taiwanese merchants' associations.

The World Chinese Entrepreneurs' Convention (WCEC) is another good example of overseas Chinese organizing an international network. They established a national economic consultative body in response to the regionalism of the European Union and the North American Free Trade Agreement, and the globalism led by the World Trade Organization (WTO) in the 1990s. In 1991, then Singapore Prime Minister Lee Kuan-Yew proposed a global network of overseas Chinese to promote linkages between China and Southeast Asia. In his view, cooperation among them will become more and more important in the global age of the 21st century.

Accordingly, Lee supported a division of labor among economies: China as a production base, Hong Kong and Singapore as financial centers, and North America and Europe as final consumption markets. In particular, overseas Chinese international networks were important as domestic and international markets for Singapore. The overseas Chinese global meeting reflected the inevitability and concerns of the Chinese system increasing the volume of trade, investment, and tourism in the age of globalization.

As was seen in the Tiananmen Square incident, social turmoil following the reform of the Chinese system threatened the Chinese Communist Party. Chinese reform needs help from overseas Chinese in taking paths of steady economic growth that will stabilize the country's social and political system. China can look at the successful cases of overseas Chinese under different systems in the transitional period. For instance, China has paid attention to Singapore for its successful reform measures. First, Singapore has achieved its social development during a period of 32 years, under the rule of the single government party. Second, Singapore is geographically and politically appropriate as a benchmark of national development for China. This is why the Singaporean Chinese Business Association has initiated an international overseas Chinese business network to promote economic cooperation and mutual understanding among industrial and commercial fields.

Moreover, the first WCEC meeting was held in Singapore in August 1991. It has been decided to hold a meeting every other year in major cities of the world; the second and third meetings were in Hong Kong and Bangkok, respectively. About 800 people from 30 countries attended the first meeting in Singapore. The Hong Kong meeting in November 1993 had 1,000 attendees discussing current global economic development and the role of overseas Chinese in the changing economy. The third WCEC meeting was held in Bangkok in 1995.

About 1,300 people from 20 countries attended the fourth WCEC meeting in Vancouver in August 1997. Participants discussed the influence of electronic communication and information technology (IT) in global market communication, and how to strengthen cooperation in the IT industries among overseas Chinese businesspeople.

China dispatched a large number of delegates to the fifth WCEC meeting in Melbourne to strengthen its linkages to the global network of overseas Chinese and thereby became a key country in the Chinese economic bloc. About 400 representatives from government and business sectors attended the meeting in 1999. Conversely, Taiwan sent a small number of delegates due to the earthquake and the protest over the participation of a larger number of Chinese from the mainland.

The sixth WCEC meeting was held in Nanjing in September 2001. About 3,300 participants came from 77 countries. The Beijing government spent $1.1 billion, and the meeting resolved that China will lead the global economic bloc of overseas Chinese. On the basis of the meeting, the network of overseas Chinese businesspeople in Australia, Canada, China, Hong Kong, Singapore, and the United States is becoming more and more visible.

Currently, the PRC government has allocated more than 200,000 people and a large amount of money to deal with overseas Chinese. Conversely,

Taiwan's Overseas Chinese Affairs Commission has only 360 people with an annual budget of $56 million. The Taiwanese government appeals to their moral values by revealing the human rights violations of the mainland Chinese. Recently, it tried to help overseas Chinese from Taiwan participate in local politics to show them that its political system is superior to that of the PRC. However, Taiwan's strategy is unlikely to be effective because of insufficient material and human resources as China takes active steps to attract the overseas Chinese.

The Role of the Council of 100

The Council of 100 consists of successful overseas Chinese in the various fields of finance, management, high technology, politics, economic trade, and entertainment and is organized as a nongovernmental organization to enhance the status of overseas Chinese in American society.[19] Although it is not clear when it was established, it was supposed to have been after the Tiananmen Square incident in 1989, corresponding to the time the global meeting of overseas Chinese (WCEC) was launched. March Fong Eu, a leading member in the council and then the California secretary of state, attended the first WCEC meeting in Singapore in 1991, which shows the relationship between the Council of 100 and the WCEC. The theme of the 1993 general meeting was the Greater Chinese Economic Zone.

Among the council's major activities are to encourage China-United States reconciliation. On the basis of the significance of United States-China relations in opening China to the world for its development, the council offered scholarships to universities in mainland China to promote understanding of the United States. The scholarships intended to recognize basic differences between the two countries and to pursue mutual benefits. The council has promoted cultural exchanges and thus made great contributions to improving United States-China relations.

Internet Network of Overseas Chinese Businesspeople

At the second WCEC meeting in 1993, Lee Kuan-Yew, the former prime minister of Singapore, proposed exchanging information on the economy, trade, and investment among overseas Chinese businesspeople world-

---

19. The council's current leadership is as follows. The Advisory Group is led by Yo-Yo Ma (a musician), I.M. Pei (a world-renowned architect), the late Chang-Lin Tien (the former chancellor of the University of California, Berkeley) and Shirley Young (an overseas Chinese leader). The Representative Group is led by Henry S. Tang, chairman; Charlie Sie, vice chairman; Alice Young, treasurer; Dennis Wu, general secretary; and Nelson Dong. Its headquarters are in New York.

wide. Under the Chinese Business Association of Singapore, an Internet leadership service was started on December 8, 1995. In 1999, the Singapore Chinese Business Association and the *United Morning Post* jointly invested in the global network of overseas Chinese businesspeople to set up an Internet service, http://wcbn.asial.com.sg, which is available in English and Chinese. It collects information on overseas Chinese businesses in 20 countries, and plans to have information on more than 100,000 businesses.

Another effort is made by the Taiwanese government. Taiwan's Overseas Chinese Affairs Commission set up the Global Chinese Business Network (GCBN), http://www.gcbn.net, in 1998, which is linked to the Taiwanese government's Basic Construction Plan for National Information and Communication to provide information to overseas Chinese. Besides WCBN of Singapore and GCBN of Taiwan, Internet sites for global overseas Chinese businesspeople have been created by Chinatowns, Overseas Chinese Business Associations, and clan meetings.[20]

The Overseas Chinese Contribution to China's Development

Thus far, this chapter has intensively reviewed the evolution of overseas Chinese business networks. Yet these networks still need to prove their effectiveness in the practical arena. In this regard, it is helpful to elaborate on evidence of the networks' effectiveness using the example of the PRC's Economic Reform and Open Door policies.

First of all, it is necessary to emphasize that there was also explicit preferential treatment[21] by the PRC of overseas Chinese from Hong Kong, Macao, and Taiwan. It is noteworthy that the General Office of Overseas Chinese Affairs was set up in the 1980s to help overseas Chinese under

---

20. Chinese Overseas Promotion Association, http://www.coea.org; Worldwide Chinese Association, http://www.worldwidechineseasso.org; Overseas Chinese Youth Association, http://www.ocya.org; Huaren, http://www.huaren.org; CWO, http://www.cwo.org; China-Town.net, http://www.china-town.net; San Francisco Chinatown, http://www.sfchinatown.com; Singapore Federation of Chinese Clan Associations, http://sfcca.org.sg/; and JS Info, http://www.huaqiao.jsinfo.net.

21. Immigration Control Law on the Citizens of the PRC 1986; Law of the Chinese Labor Department (1983.9); Law to Exempt the Income Tax on Foreign Money to Be Sent for Family Members in China by Overseas Chinese Relatives (1980.10, State Council); Housing and Residential Areas for the Overseas Chinese who Returned to China for Good (1984.12.24, General Office of the State Council); Temporary Measures to Purchase or Build Houses Based on the Money Sent by the Overseas Chinese (1980.3.5, General Office for Overseas Chinese Affairs under the State Council); Regulations on the Employment of Overseas Chinese who Returned to China and Their Children (1983.3.21, General Office for Overseas Chinese Affairs Under the State Council; Law on Education for Overseas Chinese who Returned to China and Their Children (1983.3.21, General Office for Overseas Chinese Affairs Under the State Council).

the State Council. In 1980, China established the first Special Economic Zones (SEZs) in Shantou, Shenzhen, Xiamen, and Zhuhai, which are located in the vicinity of Hong Kong, Macao, and Taiwan. The SEZs are the hometowns of many overseas Chinese living in Hong Kong, Taiwan, and Macao and have provided them with various privileges, including taxation and facilities.[22]

Preferential treatment can be more important if it is implicit than if it is explicit. Projects receiving preference are often given to global overseas Chinese businesspeople. This sort of preferential treatment is closely linked to the traditional *guanxi*, which is very important in business. For example, Beijing's real estate development project business in the central district[23] has been dominated by Li Kashing, an overseas Chinese world celebrity from Hong Kong. Recently, Jiang Mianheng, son of Jiang Zemin, has been working in the semiconductor business, together with Wang Yongxiang, son of the owner of Formosa Plastic.[24]

Second, the influx of overseas Chinese capital to China has played a key role in developing the Chinese economy. As a developing country, China stands to attract the largest amount of foreign direct investment (FDI); see table 3.3. As of the end of 2001, the total FDI flow to China was $393.5 billion in accumulation on an actual basis. The FDI in 2001 increased by 15.2 percent, amounting to $46.9 billion, which reflects the positive expectations of foreign investors after the entry of China into the WTO. It also reflects Southeast Asia's recovery from recession and the Taiwanese government's easing of restrictions on investment in China. Recently, new investments have been made in semiconductors and petrochemicals.

FDI has accounted for a significant portion of the Chinese economy in the areas of industrial production, trade, tax income, and employment. The investments have made important contributions to improving high technology, management techniques, and skilled technical labor. The entry of China into the WTO will improve the transparency of regulations and policies, the business environment, and the openness of new business such as information services as an important base for further expanding FDI.[25]

China has risen as a global manufacturing nation thanks to the investments of overseas Chinese. The countries where overseas Chinese reside account for the major portion of FDI in China. In the mid-1990s, they ac-

---

22. When overseas Chinese invested in the SEZs, income tax was exempted for two years and reduced to half for three years afterwards.

23. Wangfujing, located in the center of Beijing City, and as such being a most bustling street, is one of the representative areas of those developments.

24. Wang Yong Qing, the owner of Formosa Plastic, is one of the leading Nationalist Party entrepreneurs.

25. The Chinese Academy of Social Science expects actual foreign direct investment to increase to $100 billion in 2005—twice as much as the current amount.

Table 3.3 Distribution by economy of foreign direct investment flows to China, 1995-2000 (billions of US dollars)

Economy	1995	1996	1997	1998	1999	2000
Hong Kong and Macao	20.50	21.26	21.03	18.93	16.67	15.85
United States	3.08	3.44	3.24	3.90	4.22	4.38
British Virgin Islands	0.30	0.54	1.72	4.03	2.66	3.84
Japan	3.11	3.68	4.33	3.40	2.97	2.92
Taiwan	3.16	3.47	3.29	2.92	2.60	2.30
Singapore	1.85	2.24	2.61	3.40	2.64	2.17
Korea	1.04	1.36	2.14	1.80	1.27	1.49
United Kingdom	0.91	1.30	1.86	1.17	1.04	1.16
Germany	0.39	0.52	0.99	0.74	1.37	1.04
Others	3.17	3.91	4.06	5.17	4.87	5.56
Total	37.52	41.73	45.26	45.46	40.32	40.71

Source: *Chinese Foreign Trade Yearbook 2001.*

counted for 70 to 75 percent; at present, the rate of FDI has sunk below 60 percent. However, their share is still being maintained at about two-thirds of the total investment. As of the end of 2000, 53 percent of the total FDI was from overseas Chinese capital. There are 136,400 investment companies based in Hong Kong, Malaysia, Macao, or Singapore operating in China (67.1 percent of the total). A major portion of overseas Chinese capital has come from Hong Kong. Between 1979 and 1994, 78 percent ($93 billion) of FDI was accounted for by Hong Kong capital. Between 1997 and 2000, 78 percent ($65 billion) out of $83.5 billion was accounted for by Hong Kong capital. This was because of the geographical proximity of Hong Kong, its relations with China, and the status of Hong Kong in Southeast Asia and Chinese societies. As Hong Kong's manufacturing businesses moved to the Zhujiang Delta areas of China, overseas Chinese businesspeople's investments were made in such tertiary industries as finance and trade.

Between 1991 and 2000, Taiwanese investment in China reached about $17.1 billion, according to the estimation of the Taiwanese authority. According to the Chinese authority, it was estimated at $25 billion. The actual investment amount is estimated at $70 billion to $100 billion. Given the loss of investment in Southeast Asia caused by the Asian financial crisis, it is expected that Taiwanese investment in China will increase unless there is political tension mostly related to issues of "taidu" (independence of China).

Third, it is impossible to separate trade from investment. The size of Chinese imports from and exports to countries dominated by overseas Chinese shows the strong relationship between them and China. According to Chinese data,[26] Hong Kong recorded $56 billion (exports,

---

26. Based on the Web site of the Ministry of Foreign Trade and Economic Cooperation, http://www.moftec.gov.cn.

$46.6 billion; imports, $9.4 billion); Taiwan, $32.3 billion (exports, $5 billion; imports, $27.3 billion); Singapore, $10.9 billion (exports, $5.8 billion; imports, $5.1 billion); Malaysia, $9.4 billion (exports, $3.2 billion; imports, $6.2 billion); Thailand, $7 billion (exports, $2.3 billion; imports, $4.7 billion); Indonesia, $6.7 billion (exports, $2.8 billion; imports, $3.9 billion); the Philippines, $3.6 billion (exports, $1.6 billion; imports, $2 billion); and Macao, $0.9 billion (exports, $0.8 billion; imports, $0.1 billion) in 2001. Europe recorded $97.6 billion (exports, $49.2 billion; imports, $48.4 billion); Japan, $87.7 billion (exports, $44.9 billion; imports, $42.8 billion); the United States, $80.5 billion (exports, $54.3 billion; imports, $26.2 billion); and South Korea, $35.9 billion (exports, $12.5 billion; imports, $23.4 billion) in 2001.

Overseas Chinese served as an important channel for promoting the sales of Chinese products in the international market. The Southeast Asian region close to Hong Kong and Taiwan was favorable for their investment, considering the importance of blood ties and linguistic and cultural identity. With this investment, the productivity of the Chinese provinces has increased drastically. This is shown by the fact that nongovernmental investments led by joint-venture companies (including township enterprises and overseas Chinese companies) account for half of current Chinese trade.

An increase in the new immigration by overseas Chinese, their big investments of Taiwan, their economic strength in Southeast Asia, and an increase in the number of their elites in advanced nations, all helped change their social, economic, and political structure in relation to China.

The Chinese provincial governments also have invited overseas Chinese of the same town or family to invest, as follows. First, a global trade network was formed to promote economic benefits. Second, information exchange with the hometown was facilitated under the government's sponsorship. Third, major figures from the hometown were included in the leadership, which then could take advantage of their personal networks. The provincial government also could exercise influence over them. Fourth, the organizational style was less forceful than traditional organizations; overseas Chinese were offered business opportunities in their global business meetings, which were held to promote business activities. Through the networks of overseas Chinese businesspeople, Chinese potentialities could be developed.

The capital investments by overseas Chinese were first concentrated in Fujian and Guangdong, where most of them had originated, and later extended to other areas. Between 1979 to 1987, $2.04 billion—39.1 percent of the total $5.22 billion overseas capital invested in the mainland—was invested in the four SEZs. Up through 1993, more than 50 percent of overseas capital flowed to Guangdong and Fujian. From the early 1990s on, overseas capital was not concentrated in Guangdong and Fujian but dis-

works of global overseas Korean businesspeople through a cooperative body with businesspeople in Korea. Like OKTA, it has its secretariat office in Seoul.

The International Network of Korean Entrepreneurs was established in October 2001 to strengthen the national competitiveness and globalization of the Korean venture capital industry through mutual exchanges and cooperation among global Korean venture businesspeople. It plans to set up branches in 50 countries by 2004, including in the United States (New York, San Francisco, Washington), Australia, China (Beijing, Shanghai, Dalian), Brazil, Indonesia, Canada (Toronto), Japan (Tokyo), and the United Kingdom.

There are also a number of organizations for overseas Korean businesspeople in various countries. The Overseas Korean American Businessmen's Association[30] was created in Silicon Valley in 1997. It has about 1,000 members, including Korean-American businesspeople, scientists, business executives, venture capitalists, and professors. They try to organize networks of Korean businesspeople. The Korean American Commerce and Industry Federation[31] was established in New York in 1981. It is designed to promote the rights and privileges of Korean-American businesspeople and to foster cooperation among Korean-American economic organizations.

The Korean Chamber of Commerce in Japan was organized in 1962. Its local branches in all the provinces of Japan are intended to protect the rights and privileges of Korean-Japanese and to provide information on commerce and industry. The director is Hong Chaesik. The Korean Japanese Credit Association[32] was set up in 1956 aimed at promoting cooperation among Korean-Japanese. It provides Korean-Japanese with loans and has an investment trust to assist in capital formation.

The Korean Chinese Business Association[33] was created in 1993 to help South Korean companies advance in the Chinese market, whose environment is quite new due to a different economic system and long antagonistic relationship, following the normalization of Korean-Chinese diplomatic relations. Korean companies in Beijing are organized under the sponsorship of the Korean Chamber of Commerce and Industry. There are 28 branches nationwide, which provide information on the Chinese market and promote friendship among members.

The Korean National Economic Community Meeting was started with the participation of the members of OKTA and WFOKC, led by the Overseas Koreans Foundation and KOTRA, to overcome the Korean for-

---

30. Currently, Brandon Kim of Altos Ventures is the president of the association.

31. The president is Lim Changbin, who has a textile business in Atlanta.

32. The chairman is Lee Jongdae, who is the chairman of the Commercial Bank in Yokohama.

33. The president is Park Yunsik, who is general manager of LG Corporation in Beijing.

eign exchange crisis in 1998. Its first meeting was held in Seoul in October 1998, followed by a second one in Chicago in October 1999, a third one in Seoul in October 2000, and a fourth one in Los Angeles in November 2001. Meetings are held in South Korea and the United States every other year. In sum, these meetings promote the exports of domestic companies to overseas markets through overseas Korean buyers and the investment of overseas Korean capital.

Applying the Overseas Chinese Networking Model to Koreans

The overseas Chinese community consists of 36 million people (excluding Hong Kong and Taiwan), who make up 2.6 percent of the total Chinese population. The overseas Korean community has 6 million people, 9.8 percent of the total Korean population—living primarily in the United States, China, Japan, and Russia. There are at least four critical differences between overseas Koreans and Chinese. First, there is no country not on the Korean peninsula having Koreans as the dominant political leadership. Conversely, with regard to Chinese, along with mainland China, three separate economies are ruled by Chinese leadership: Hong Kong, Singapore, and Taiwan. If they are well connected, they can promote their common interests through their networks based on homogenous composition of Han people. This suggests that if such a South Korean effort directed toward overseas Koreans is not carefully handled, it could inhibit the sovereignty of host countries of overseas Koreans.

Second, there is a lack of leading Korean businesspeople with global prestige. Overseas Chinese business leaders, however, have a widespread presence across the world due to their long history of immigration and their much larger population. In Korea, voluntary and spontaneous migration has a relatively short history. As a result, there are relatively few overseas Korean business celebrities, which may work against forming global overseas Korean networks.

Third, there have been significant differences between government policies toward overseas Chinese and Koreans. During Mao Ze-dong's period, China adopted an isolationist policy, which created distrust between overseas Chinese and their home country. However, the policy was modified to focus on economic aspects during the Deng Xiaoping era, resulting in a policy of attracting overseas Chinese to promote mutual cooperation between them and China. Conversely, South Korea considered overseas Koreans as having abandoned their home country, which somewhat resembles Mao's policy. In particular, some politicians even exploited the overseas Korean community politically.

Fourth, there have been differences in perceptions of overseas Chinese and overseas Koreans toward their home countries. Overseas Chinese believed that they would be well treated and would make money on their investments in China. Overseas Koreans, however, received more skeptical responses to their investments from their home country, which resulted in their loss of interest in investing. Yet even though South Korea treated them coldly, overseas Koreans participated in donating funds to help Korea in the Olympics and the IMF crisis. There is an increase in the number of Korean businesspeople who have been successful in IT and biotechnology industries in the United States and Japan. Most of them still have pessimistic attitudes toward investing in Korea, given the way businesses there are managed, and toward returning to Korea under the current overseas Korean policy.

China's policy toward overseas Chinese has been accommodative and active under the current central government's leadership. The government passed laws and arranged offices for them. They are led by the unique Chinese personal network, *guanxi*, which links individuals, hometown associations, business associations in the same industry, and associations of people with the same family name. In particular, it is worth noting again that under the leadership of Singapore prime minister Lee Kuan-Yew and Chinese political leader Deng Xiaoping, a global overseas Chinese business meeting (WCEC) was held in 1991 (see above).

Yet China's policy toward overseas Chinese is an important benchmark for South Korea's policy toward overseas Koreans. The policy under review is to seek the possibility of connecting the overseas Korean community with overseas Chinese businesspeople. If China's policy continues to be successful and Korea's policy continues to fail, Korea's national competitiveness will lose its edge. However, the systematic improvement of Korea's policy to utilize overseas Koreans' potential talents may have a great positive impact on Korean economic development.

Given the points mentioned above, the potential assets of overseas Koreans are best evaluated as precious human and material resources. Judging from the contribution of overseas Chinese to China, it is also expected that overseas Koreans can benefit South Korean economic development—as an investment source, for trade expansion, as a talented personnel pipeline, and in constructing a new and advanced economic system. Therefore, there should be changes in Korea's policy toward overseas Koreans in the direction of organizing networks of overseas Koreans to coexist with their home country. The government should adopt a policy of restoring trust in overseas Koreans. It should take a pragmatic approach to mutual interests in economic relations instead of taking a political approach to overseas Koreans.

In particular, overseas Koreans should organize networks to contribute to a new economy led by information technology and biotechnology. The government should grant incentives for their contributions to Korea. For example, the government could arrange measures to give preferential treatment to overseas Koreans that would not violate international norms.

There should be efforts to remove obstacles to the participation of overseas Koreans in the domestic economy.

Therefore, a global overseas Korean businesspeople's convention should be formed and positively established, despite South Korea's limits in developing ways to overcome its difficulties in the 21st century. There should be a caveat in the Korean case, however. If the government became too deeply involved in overseas Korean matters, it might inhibit the sovereignty of host countries. Therefore, a prudent measure is needed. It is worth a cautionary note that it has been 10 years since the sixth WCEC meeting was held in Nanjing, China.

Because the 21st century is an age of networks, overseas Koreans must network worldwide in their economic and business activities. To function effectively, the proposed global overseas Korean businesspeople's convention should observe a few basic principles. It should be nonpolitical[34] and consist of networking professional groups, followed by global networks operating organizations in the United States, Japan, China, and Russia, in addition to South America and Southeast Asia. Its thrust should be to organize networks in local communities to promote the convenience of overseas Koreans utilizing their existing organizations. The leaders of these constituent organizations should include scientists, engineers, bankers, lawyers, businesspeople, and other professional groups, as seen in the Chinese case. In this regard, the selection of core group leaders (voluntarily led by the United States) as modeled after the Chinese Council of 100, is promising.

The South Korean government, however, has to help create business opportunities to attract more overseas Koreans with intellectual expertise—implementing programs to invite their scientists, and starting programs so that their children can learn about Korea on their vacations (like Taiwan's programs to invite young people). The government also needs to organize a system to provide information on business opportunities and domestic situations via various channels, including the establishment of an overseas Koreans' office in cyberspace to unify the concerns of overseas Koreans that are handled in various departments. And Korean domestic organizations must dispatch Korean delegates to a global meeting of overseas Korean businesspeople.

Another option is creating exclusive industrial zones for overseas Koreans that resemble China's Special Economic Zones. In addition, there should be Korean national scholarships for overseas Koreans, modeled after those of the Chiang Ching-kuo Foundation for International Scholarly Exchange. Scholarships for overseas Koreans will help them to play a leading role in overseas Koreans' business networks.

The revision of special laws for overseas Koreans is also required, similar to that undertaken for Chinese or Japanese laws. The establishment of

---

34. A strict division between the politics and economics is required.

a council of economic advisers for overseas Koreans is necessary, as is the construction of a business center for them. In this regard, a study of the Chinese policy toward overseas Chinese would offer a valuable lesson for South Korea's policy toward overseas Koreans. The study would be important to Korea, whose 6 million people overseas can play a leading role in promoting national reunification, spurring economic development, and preserving cultural values.

References

Clegg, S., and S.G. Redding, eds. 1990. *Capitalism in Contrasting Cultures*. Berlin: Walter de Gruyter.

Dan, Chun. 1999. Haiwai Huaren Jingji Yanjiu (A Study of Overseas Chinese Economy) (in Chinese). Maizian Publishing Company. Shenzhen, China.

Drucker, Peter F. 1999. *Management Challenges for the 21st Century*. Butterworth-Heineman. Oxford.

EAAU (East Asia Analytical Unit). 1995. Overseas Chinese Business Networks in Asia. Department of Foreign Affairs and Trade, Australia.

Greenhalgh, S. 1991. Families and Networks in Taiwan's Economic Development. In *Business Networks and Economic Development in East and Southeast Asia*, ed. G. Hamilton. Hong Kong: University of Hong Kong Press.

Kunio, K. 1988. *The Rise of Ersatz Capitalism in Southeast Asia*. Singapore: Oxford University Press,.

Lever-Tracy, C., D. Ip, and N. Tracy. 1996. *The Chinese Diaspora and Mainland China: A New Economic Synergy*. Houndmills, UK: Macmillan.

Lu, Peichun. 1995. Overseas Chinese Business Networks in Asia. Department of Foreign Affairs and Trade, Australia.

Naisbitt, John. 1936. *Megatrends: The New Directions Transforming Our Lives*. Warner Books.

Naughton, Barry. 1997. "The Emergence of the China Circle." *The China Circle*, ed. Barry Naughton, 1-37. Washington: Brookings Institution.

Ohmae, Kenishi. 1995. *The End of the Nation State*. Free Press. New York.

Pan, Lynn, ed. 1998. *The Encyclopedia of the Chinese Overseas*. Archipelago Press. Landmark Books. Singapore.

Redding, S.G. 1990. *The Spirit of Chinese Capitalism*. Berlin: Walter de Gruyter.

Redding, S.G. 1991. Weak Organisations and Strong Linkages: Managerial Ideology and Chinese Family Business Networks. In *Business Networks and Economic Development in East and Southeast Asia*, ed. G. Hamilton. Hong Kong: University of Hong Kong Press.

Shapiro, Carl, and Hal R. Varian. 1998. *Information Rules: A Strategic Guide to the Network Economy*. Harvard Business School Press. Boston.

Sit, V.F.S., and S.L. Wong. 1989. *Small and Medium Industries in an Export-Oriented Economy: The Case of Hong Kong*. Hong Kong: University of Hong Kong Press.

South China Morning Post, various issues.

The Australian, "Asian Billionaires in 2000: The 100 Wealthiest Families," January 27, 2000.

The Australian, "The Top 100 Companies in 10 Asian Markets," April 19, 1999.

Winkler, E., and S. Greenhalgh, eds. 1990. *Contending Approaches to the Political Economy of Taiwan*. Armonk, NY: M. E. Sharpe.

Yazhou Zhoukan (The Chinese 500 is contained in the issue published in the first week in November each year).

Zhao, Hongying. 2001. "New Immigrants from China and their Characteristics" (in Chinese). *Yearbook of the World Chinese Entrepreneurs 2000/2001*, 135-37. Beijing, China.

Comments on Chapter 3

KIHWAN KIM

In chapter 3, Young Rok Cheong has done an outstanding job in three areas. First of all, he presents an excellent account of how overseas Chinese communities have evolved over time. Second, he gives a detailed account of the efforts made by not just the Chinese government in Beijing, but also the governments of Singapore and Taiwan, to enlist the support of overseas Chinese for development in their respective jurisdictions. Third, he has done a good analysis of the ways in which overseas Chinese have contributed to the economic development of China through investment and trade.

Cheong's main findings in these areas may be summarized as follows. The history of Chinese emigration goes back quite far. In fact, it can be traced back as far as the Sung Dynasty in the eleventh and twelfth centuries. As a result, the overseas Chinese population today is very large, numbering no less than 36 million or 2.6 percent of the total Chinese population. At least 52 countries have an overseas Chinese population of more than 10,000. However, a large majority of overseas Chinese--about 80 percent of the total--is found in Southeast Asia. Overseas Chinese communities today account for many prominent leaders in business as well as other fields.

To accelerate their own economic development over the years, the governments of China, Singapore, and Taiwan have pursued deliberate policies to organize overseas Chinese. These policies have taken several forms, including government-sponsored conferences to which prominent overseas Chinese are invited, explicit recognition of outstanding professional performance, special tax incentives for overseas Chinese investment, and scholarships for promising young overseas Chinese. It is also interesting to note that, until recently, the Chinese and Taiwanese governments in particular competed with each other to win loyalty and support from overseas Chinese for their political causes.

Kihwan Kim is chairman of the Seoul Financial Forum and the Korean National Committee for the Pacific Economic Cooperation Council. He also serves as an international adviser to Goldman Sachs.

Overseas Chinese have made tremendous contributions to the economic development of China. As of the end of 2000, according to Cheong, overseas Chinese were responsible for 53 percent of the total foreign direct investment outstanding in China. The lion's share of that investment, however, came from Hong Kong. Overseas Chinese have also served as important conduits for two-way trade between China and the countries where they reside. In short, with respect to the information on these three areas, Cheong's chapter is encyclopedic.

Yet when it comes to evaluating the implications of overseas Chinese communities for South Korea, the chapter leaves much to be desired. This is due in large measure to its failure to look more closely into overseas Korean communities as well as to appreciate some fundamental differences between South Korea and China politically and culturally. To be sure, Cheong notes that the population of overseas Koreans today is about 6 million, or 9.2 percent of the total population on the Korean peninsula. But he fails to tell us how overseas Koreans are geographically distributed. Nor does he tell us much about the social status of overseas Koreans in the countries where they live. If he had examined these matters more closely, his policy recommendations for the South Korean government would have been very different from those he has actually made.

As for Cheong's policy recommendations, it appears that he wants to recommend to the South Korean government almost everything that the Chinese, Singaporean, and Taiwanese governments have done vis-à-vis overseas Chinese—notwithstanding that there are several critical differences between overseas Chinese and overseas Korean communities. On the whole, overseas Koreans are potentially a far more valuable resource than Cheong realizes. For one thing, proportionally, there are more overseas Koreans than overseas Chinese. On average, first-generation overseas Koreans are far better educated than overseas Chinese. Moreover, it is simply not true that overseas Korean communities account for fewer outstanding business leaders and celebrities than overseas Chinese communities, relatively speaking.

To give just a few examples of outstanding Korean leaders overseas, Shin Kyuk-Ho, chairman of the Lotte Group in South Korea, is a prominent businessman in Japan as well. The late founder of the Poongsan Group was an outstanding businessman in Japan before he made his name in Korea. Son Masayoshi, widely regarded as the Bill Gates of Japan, is a third-generation Korean-Japanese. The late Paik Namjoon was a world-renowned pioneer in what could be called electronic art. The list goes on. And many of the brightest students on leading university campuses in the United States today are from the so-called 1.5-generation Korean-Americans. What all this means is that overseas Koreans can serve as a far more important source of not only capital but also knowledge and expertise for Korea's development in the years to come.

Although Cheong notes that for overseas Koreans to play a more significant role in South Korea's development, the obstacles specific to them must be removed, he fails to spell out what these are. One particular obstacle he could have identified, but did not, has to do with the universal military service obligation that the Korean government forces on many young men of Korean descent whose nationalities are not fully clear once they land in Korea. As long as this is an issue, Korea will not be able to make use of the talents and aspirations of many young Korean-Americans who belong to the 1.5 generation.

There is one obstacle that Cheong does discuss. This has to do with "cold treatment," meaning the low esteem in which Koreans who have emigrated are held by Koreans who have stayed in South Korea. In making this point, he is probably right with respect to those Koreans who emigrated before World War II; for the most part, they were poorer and less educated than the average Korean. However, almost the opposite is true of recent emigrants, who are on the whole better educated than ordinary Koreans.

Moreover, many of these recent emigrants have done very well abroad professionally, as well as in the education they have given their children. If anything, many of them are held in great respect and are the envy of other Koreans. Needless to say, these observations have one very important policy implication: If South Korea wants to attract more foreign investment from overseas Koreans, it needs to make its entire business environment as good as or even better than those that overseas Koreans find in the countries where they live and work. This of course means that Korea should continue with its reform efforts in every sector of its economy and society.

Nonetheless, Cheong says much about the need to extend preferential treatment to overseas Koreans to encourage them to increase their investment in South Korea. He fails, however, to specify what this treatment should be. As far as I am concerned, what overseas Koreans need more than anything else is equal rather than preferential treatment. Foreign investors in Korea in general want to be assured of what is technically called "national treatment" rather than preferential treatment that goes beyond national treatment.

If extending preferential treatment to bona fide foreign investors is not desirable, why should it be extended to overseas Koreans? In this regard, it needs to be noted that designing and implementing preferential policy for any group, including overseas Koreans, is not as easy as Cheong may think, especially in these days when most insist that the economy work on the basis of market principles. For this reason alone, I question the wisdom of establishing special economic zones for overseas Koreans.

To make an observation on one specific recommendation by Cheong: He recommends that the South Korean government organize a "Council of 100" to give recognition to overseas Koreans, as the Chinese government has done. As he notes, overseas Chinese have a "collective character" in the sense that they tend to work together. But overseas Koreans are very individualistic, wherever they are. Moreover, they have taken with them a high dose of regionalism from home. For this reason, instituting a council of 100 would be more likely to further fragment Korean communities abroad.

However, I do not want to conclude my comments on chapter 3 on a negative note. Cheong is absolutely right when he says that South Korean political leaders should be very careful in trying to enlist help from overseas Koreans in connection with domestic political forays. Attempts of this sort will surely worsen the fragmentation of Korean communities overseas. In addition, policymakers should remember that similar attempts have backfired time and again—as in the unhappy episode involving Park Tong-Sun in the 1970s.

In short, chapter 3 has laid a good foundation for formulating government policy toward overseas Koreans. I, for one, would like to ask Young Rok Cheong to further study overseas Korean communities, as well as South Korea as a nation and economy, and then make policy recommendations.

4

The Impact of Korean Immigration on the US Economy

MARCUS NOLAND

Korean migration to the United States has occurred in three distinct phases. The first phase involved a relatively small number of migrants at the beginning of the 20th century; the second consisted mainly of students motivated by educational opportunity in the first decade or so following the Korean War; and the third started in 1965 with the liberalization of the US national quota system.

This chapter examines the economic impact of Korean immigration on the US economy, focusing on the third wave of immigration that began in 1965. This group of Korean immigrants appears to be distinct both from most other national immigrant groups and previous Korean immigrants. They have high levels of educational attainment, with rates of college education nearly twice the US national average. They form businesses at a rate 70 percent higher than the US public at large, and have savings rates of roughly twice the national average. Their children have achieved even higher rates of educational attainment and earn per capita incomes well above the national average. There is a correlation between the presence of Korean immigrants and state economic performance, and if this were interpreted as a causal relation, it would suggest that a doubling of the Korean immigrant population would increase national per capita income growth by 0.1-0.2 percentage points.

Marcus Noland is a senior fellow at the Institute for International Economics. He would like to thank Scott Holladay for excellent research assistance.

Korean Immigration to the United States

The first treaty on immigration between the United States and Korea was signed in 1882, and within a few years a small number of merchants, students, and political dissidents began arriving in America. It would be another 20 years, though, before significant numbers of Koreans came to the United States.

That process began in 1893, when American sugar and pineapple planters in Hawaii engineered the downfall of the Hawaiian royal family and declared Hawaii a republic. Hawaii was annexed by the United States in 1898 and declared a US territory in 1900. At that time, the immigration into the United States of Chinese laborers was prohibited by the Chinese Exclusion Law, so when the Hawaii Sugar Planters Association needed labor to break strikes by Japanese plantation workers, they turned to Korea. In 1902, King Kojong approved the first organized migration to the United States; the beginning of Korean immigration to the United States is conventionally dated January 13, 1903, when about 100 Korean immigrants landed in Honolulu. (Given that they are sometimes called "the Irish of Asia," perhaps it is fitting that the first Koreans in America arrived on a steamer named the *Gaelic*.)

During the next 2 years, more than 7,000 Koreans arrived in Hawaii, most recruited as strikebreakers by the Hawaiian planters. But this predominant channel of Korean immigration to the United States was closed in 1905, when the Japanese government, concerned about the welfare of Japanese workers in Hawaii, successfully pressured the Korean government to halt emigration.[1] The passage in 1926 of the Asian Exclusion Act closed the door from the US side.

With respect to plantation workers, the Japanese could have saved themselves the trouble—the first-wave Korean immigrants, recruited mainly from urban areas, showed a distinct lack of interest and aptitude for plantation work and fled the plantations at a higher rate than any other ethnic group. However, with conditions deteriorating in Korea, few returned home. Instead, many settled in Hawaiian towns, especially Honolulu.[2]

About 90 percent of the Korean immigrants were male, and this immigrant community exhibited behavioral pathologies typical of other almost exclusively male societies. About 400 of the initial immigrants were Christian. The Koreans began to create social and political organizations in Hawaii, leaders of which tended to either be Christian, have a Korean farm background, or be married. The planters subsidized Christian mis-

---

1. For histories of this early immigration, see Choy (1979), and Patterson (1988, 2000).

2. A love of the city lights seems to be an enduring aspect of the Korean experience in the United States; according to the 2000 US census, the Korean rate of urbanization is exceeded only by that of Jews (Jeong 2002).

sionary work among the obstreperous Koreans with the aim of socializing them into better workers. Significant conversion occurred, and churches have remained an enduring part of Korean-American community life.

Due to urbanization and the unbalanced sex ratio (despite the practice of importing brides), the Korean community in Hawaii exhibited a high rate of intermarriage with other ethnic groups. By 1970, Koreans had the highest per capita income and lowest unemployment rate of any ethnic group in Hawaii. By the time the third great wave of immigration began in the 1960s, the process of acculturation had proceeded so far that the newly arriving immigrants did not recognize the thoroughly assimilated third-generation Koreans as distinct from Americans.

Of the Korean immigrants to Hawaii, more than 2,000 continued on the US mainland, settling on the West Coast. Several hundred settled in agricultural communities in central California and established prosperous agricultural businesses there, which were important sources of finance for Korean nationalists in exile. Indeed, the first president of the Republic of Korea, Syngman Rhee, along with other nationalist leaders such as An Ch'ang-ho and Pak Yong-man, emerged from this milieu.[3] Although Koreans faced racial discrimination in the United States, with the advent of World War II, their antipathy toward the Japanese did not go unnoticed, either by the US government authorities or the general American public.

The second wave of immigration occurred in the decade following the Korean War and was dominated by students who came to the United States for graduate education. Some stayed, while many others returned to South Korea; a few such as Nam Duck-Woo, Kim Manh-Jeh, Lee Seung-Yoon, and Chung So-Young played important roles in the development of the Korean economy in the early 1960s.[4] In addition to students, during this period around 3,000 Koreans annually immigrated as the spouses of US citizens (Jasso and Rosenzweig 1990). This group was overwhelmingly female, and presumably many were wives of US servicemen stationed in Korea.

The third wave of Korean immigration to the United States was made possible by the 1965 Hart-Celler Act, which greatly liberalized the National Origin Quota System and opened the door for greatly expanded immigration from non-European countries, including South Korea. The third wave of immigration differed significantly from the first two, in that the immigrants were often college-educated and brought families with them when they immigrated. Indeed, in numerical terms, this third wave and its offspring make up most of the Korean-American community today.[5]

---

3. See Cha (2002) and H.K. Kim (2002) for further discussion.

4. In addition to the immigrants being motivated by educational opportunities, starting in 1955 American couples began adopting Korean babies. Approximately 100,000 Korean adoptees became Americans between 1955 and 1998 (E. Kim 2002)

5. See Jeong (2002) and Y.S. Park (2002) on the third wave of Korean immigration.

Although many third-wave immigrants had a college education and were white-collar workers in Korea, they found that a lack of proficiency in the English language hampered the full exploitation of their Korean qualifications within the American economy. As a consequence, many shifted careers and started small businesses or purchased existing businesses of retiring non-Korean businesspeople, thus coming to dominate certain types of businesses (e.g., green groceries and dry cleaning) in American cities such as New York, Los Angeles, Chicago, and Washington.[6] In this regard, they are part of a long American tradition of successive waves of immigrant businesspeople, following earlier immigrant entrepreneurs. Along with the ever-present churches, a support network of businesses such as restaurants, newspapers, and radio stations grew to cater to this community.

What seems to distinguish these third-wave Koreans from earlier immigrant groups is that a significant number of them were educated members of the middle and upper-middle classes. So while a lack of English language proficiency impeded their ability to continue their previous careers in the United States, they demonstrated a commitment to education and professional attainment, and their current occupational profiles may be a misleading indicator of their underlying capabilities.

The trend in recent years has been toward a growth in the number of Korean professional service providers such as doctors, lawyers, and insurance agents, as the children of these immigrants have obtained professional accreditation in the United States, and some have opened such businesses oriented, at least in part, toward the Korean-American community. Data from the 2000 US census confirm the casual observation of upward mobility among the children of Korean immigrants, as is discussed below.

Statistics on the Korean-American Community

The number of Koreans in the United States has grown dramatically since 1960, when the US Census Bureau first began reporting Koreans as a distinct ethnic group. As is shown in figure 4.1, the number of "foreign-born" Koreans (i.e., immigrants) increased from roughly 11,000 in 1960, to more than 1 million in 2000, or about 0.4 percent of the total US population. According to data from the US Immigration and Naturalization Service, the peak year for Korean immigration to the United States was 1987, when nearly 36,000 Korean immigrants entered the United States (figure 4.2).

---

6. Often these shops are in inner-city neighborhoods, and one of the most memorable images from the 1992 Los Angeles riots was that of rifle-toting Korean retailers guarding their stores. According to Im (2002), the lives of 10,000 Korean immigrants were disrupted when 2,300 businesses were lost at a cost of approximately $500 million during the rioting. See K. Park (2002) for a fascinating look at relations between Korean shopkeepers and their customers in South Central Los Angeles.

Figure 4.1   Korean immigrants living in the United States, 1960-2000

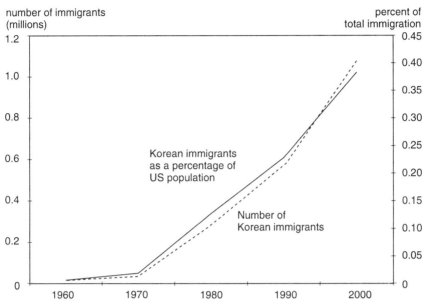

Source: US Census Bureau.

Figure 4.2   Korean immigrants to the United States, 1978-2000

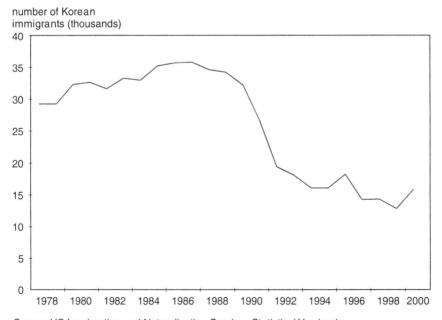

Source: US Immigration and Naturalization Service, Statistical Yearbook.

Since 1987, the number of Korean immigrants has steadily fallen to fewer than half as many, as improvements in the economic, political, and social situation in South Korea have made emigration less attractive. In this respect, the pattern of Korean emigration to the United States has followed the same trajectory of other "sending" countries, such as those in Western Europe.

More than one-third of these Korean immigrants are in California, where they make up about 1 percent of the population. The next most popular destination for Korean immigrants is New York, followed by New Jersey, Illinois, and Washington, DC. In proportional terms, Korean immigrants are most prominent in Hawaii, where they make up nearly 2 percent of the state's population. According to Jeong (2002), if the children of immigrants and undocumented workers are added in, the Korean-American community in the United States is probably on the order of 1.5 million to 1.6 million people.

Census data indicate that Koreans are close to the US population median for household income ($50,000 for Koreans vs. $51,200 for all Americans) and per capita income ($20,000 vs. $26,000), and that the share of the Korean population having attained a college degree or better (49.2 percent) is almost twice the national average (26.8 percent). Jeong reports that an analysis of census data done by the Korean-American Coalition, a nongovernmental organization, found that second-generation Korean-Americans appear to be upwardly mobile, with median incomes of $70,000, nearly 40 percent higher than the national average, and a rate of college degree attainment of 54.7 percent, more than twice the national average.

Korean immigrants exhibit a higher rate of entrepreneurship than the average American, with Korean-Americans in 2000 having a "business density" (i.e., persons per business) of 7.9, compared with 13.5 for the general population (US Small Business Administration 2001, table 12). This is to say that the Korean-American community has been creating businesses at a rate 70 percent higher than the rest of the population.

A Census Bureau survey of minority businesses found that in 1997, Korean-Americans owned 135,571 businesses, generating $45.9 billion in revenue and employing 333,649 workers with wages totaling $5.8 billion (US Small Business Administration 2001, table 11). These figures may be a bit misleading, though. Of the 135,571 businesses mentioned above, more than half (85,495) are sole proprietorships (US Small Business Administration 2001, table A.1). The 50,076 firms that pay employees average nearly 7 workers per establishment with average wages of more than $17,000 annually (US Small Business Administration 2001, table 15).

This, in turn, represents a tremendous intensification of business activity from the already high level documented in the first Census Bureau survey in 1982 (table 4.1). If one applies the 1980 census population figure to the 1982 business formation data reported in table 4.1 (which would

Table 4.1 Korean business survey data, 1982-97

Measure	1982	1987	1992	1997
All businesses (number)	31,769	69,304	104,918	135,571
Gross receipts (thousands of dollars)	2,677,067	7,682,668	16,170,438	45,936,497
Businesses with employees (number)	7,893	21,657	n.a.	50,076
Gross receipts (thousands of dollars)	1,704,762	5,502,006	n.a.	40,745,504
Employees (number)	24,663	70,530	n.a.	333,649

n.a. = not available

Source: US Small Business Administration (2001, table A.4).

tend to lend an upward bias to the business density figure) this would yield a business density of 9.1—already substantially below the national average—which dropped even further to the 7.9 rate in 1997 as mentioned above. As a group, during a 15-year period, Korean-American businesses exhibited a more than 13-fold increase in employment and a nearly 24-fold increase in revenues.

In reality, these figures probably understate Korean-American economic clout. Sole proprietorships and small businesses often understate revenues and even employment. There is no reason to believe that Korean immigrants are atypically accurate in their responses. Ergo, because of their overrepresentation in occupational categories that tend to understate the magnitude of their business transactions, the figures above should be regarded as a floor on actual Korean-American business activity. Korean Americans have come a long way from breaking strikes on Oahu.

The Impact of the Korean-American Community

As the preceding section documented, the Korean-American community is characterized by a high level of economic achievement, entrepreneurial activity, and upward social mobility. It is reasonable to ask what the macroeconomic impact of Korean-American immigration on the United States has been.

Economists have identified a number of channels through which immigration can affect the economy.[7] The most obvious channel is the labor market. Immigrants add to the labor supply, pushing down wages and raising the rate of return on land and capital. In a simulation model of undifferentiated labor demand, Borjas (1994) calculated that for 1994, the

---

7. For a survey, see Borjas (1999).

total gains to the US economy were only about $6 billion—and that the amount of redistribution away from native workers ($114 billion) dwarfed the net gain to the economy. Given uncertainty about the net fiscal effect of immigration (though immigrants pay taxes, they may also go on welfare and their children attend public schools), Borjas's analysis suggests that the net impact on native workers may well be negative.

But this approach seems at once too simple and ill-suited for the specific case at hand. First of all, labor is not an undifferentiated mass, and the particular immigrant group in question appears to be unusually well endowed in human capital. Modern endogenous growth theory suggests that human capital accumulation may be important in forestalling a declining marginal product of capital and a secular decline in growth in high-income economies (Romer 1986; Lucas 1988). Moreover, as the discussion above demonstrated, Korean-Americans have been unusually focused on the formation of rapidly growing new businesses.

This kind of entrepreneurial activity is probably associated with what economist Harvey Leibenstein (1966) described as X-efficiency—a key to the growth of total factor productivity and overall economic prosperity. Immigrant entrepreneurial activity of this sort is also likely to be associated with unusually high savings rates and capital accumulation. Carroll, Rhee, and Rhee (1999), for example, used data from the 1980 and 1990 censuses and found that Korean immigrants had savings and wealth accumulation rates around twice as high as the overall US population. Yet another way in which immigration can have an impact on macroeconomic performance is by contributing to international trade, thus stimulating global ethnic networks (Rauch and Trindade 2002).

So rather than the usual static demand-for-labor approach, a dynamic growth approach would appear to be more appropriate. The standard framework for empirical investigation is the "convergence" approach of Barro and Sala-i-Martin (1992, 1995), derived from the endogenous growth literature. In this approach, long-run per capita growth is a function of an initial starting point, the accumulation of physical and human capital, macroeconomic stability, trade openness, economic and political institutions, and so on. Although this work has spawned a vast literature on the determinants of growth performance across countries, it is particularly well suited for studying growth at the subnational level. This is because many economic phenomena that vary across countries, such as differential rates of inflation or differences in trade policies, can be ignored when examining developments within a single country using data on subnational jurisdictions.

Table 4.2 reports regression results for real per capita growth across the 50 states and the District of Columbia. Following Barro and Sala-i-Martin, the right-hand-side explanatory variables include the log of per capita income in the initial year of the sample and three regional dummy variables to capture regional affects. If poor economies grow faster than rich ones

Table 4.2 Regression results for US real per capita growth

	Dependent variable	
Independent variable	(1) Growth rate, 1950-2000	(2) Growth rate, 1950-2000
Income per capita, 1950	−1.02 (−7.64)[a]	−1.05 (−8.05)[a]
Dummy for Northeast	0.45 (6.48)[a]	0.44 (6.69)[a]
Dummy for South	0.25 (3.52)[a]	0.26 (3.71)[a]
Dummy for Midwest	0.14 (2.06)[b]	0.15 (2.25)[b]
Per capita state government spending, 1950	0 (−2.83)[a]	0 (−2.86)[a]
Percentage of Korean immigrants, 1990	0.46 (3.50)[a]	—
Percentage of Korean immigrants, 2000	—	0.32 (4.04)[a]
Constant	0.11 (9.23)[a]	0.11 (9.68)[a]
R²	0.83	0.84
F	35.09[a]	38.21[a]
n	51	51

a. Significant at the 1 percent level.
b. Significant at the 5 percent level.
Note: Coefficients on all variables have been scaled by 100 for the purposes of presentation.

as predicted by the standard neoclassical growth model, then they are said to "converge," and one would expect the coefficient on initial income per capita to be negative. To these variables we add two: state government expenditure per capita and the share of Korean immigrants in the state's population. State government expenditure is a measure of the size of government, which has typically been found to be negatively associated with economic growth in many cross-national studies. In addition to these variables, a weather variable used by Barro and Sala-i-Martin (1992), state educational spending, and the state murder rate were also tried as right-hand variables, but they did not have any robust explanatory power, and in the interests of brevity, those regressions are not reported.

Because the boom in Korean immigration really began with the Immigration Reform Act of 1965, we would ideally like the sample to extend from 1965 to the present. But real per capita income data were reported only every 10 years from 1950 to 2000. Likewise, Korean immigrants were only identified as a distinct group in the 1990 and 2000 censuses. The decision here has been to use the longest state growth rate sample available (i.e., 1950-2000) because we are really interested in long-run growth performance and want to abstract from transitory effects.

However, this raises a problem: Logically, Korean immigration in 1990 cannot cause differences in cross-state growth performance starting at an earlier date (in technical terms, the right-hand variable is said to violate exogeneity). As a consequence, it is really not proper to claim that Korean immigration caused the differences in state growth performance; rather, it is appropriate to state that Korean immigration is associated with or statistically correlated with these differences.

With that caveat, the results given in table 4.2 show that, as expected, initial-period per capita income is negatively associated with subsequent growth—that is, US states converge. State government spending is also negatively associated with growth. The presence of Korean immigrants, however, is positively associated with growth, with a coefficient of 0.46 in regression 1 and a coefficient of 0.32 in regression 2. This means that a 1-percentage-point increase in the Korean immigrant share of the state's population was associated with an increase of 32 to 46 basis points in the state's real per capita growth rate.

However, it should be kept in mind that Koreans made up only 0.4 percent of the US population in 2000, so percentage points are probably the wrong unit to use in assessing this result. Instead, suppose the Korean immigrant share doubled (i.e., the share of Korean immigrants in the US population increased by 0.4 percent). Then, according to the results in table 4.2, this would be associated with an increase of 0.1 to 0.2 percentage points in the growth rate of per capita income.

Conclusion

This chapter has examined the impact of Korean immigration on the US economy. Korean immigrants have been found to have rates of educational attainment nearly twice the US national average; to create businesses at a rate roughly 70 greater than the general population; and to maintain savings and wealth accumulation rates roughly double the national average. The children of these immigrants exhibit even higher rates of educational attainment and incomes approximately 40 percent higher than the US population as a whole. There is a statistical correlation between the presence of Korean immigrants and state economic performance, and if this statistical correlation were interpreted causally, it would suggest that a doubling of the Korean immigrant population would increase national per capita income growth by 0.1 to 0.2 percentage points.

However desirable this might be, it is unlikely to come to pass. The flow of Korean emigrants peaked in 1987 and has since been falling. Economic, political, and social improvements in South Korea have diminished the lure of emigration, and in this respect the pattern of Korean emigration to the United States follows the same historical trajectory of other sender countries such as those of Western Europe. In addition, the 1992 Los Angeles riots may have reduced the attractiveness of the United States as a destination, though this is not apparent in the date reported in figure 4.2.

An interesting issue for the US economy will be whether the descendents of today's Korean immigrants will reproduce the same process of assimilation and acculturation that previous immigrant groups have experienced. For example, it could well be that the children and grandchildren of today's immigrants will manifest attitudes toward risk and entrepreneurship much closer to the American mainstream than to those of their risk-taking forebears. This could be an interesting topic of investigation at conferences celebrating the bicentennial of Korean immigrants in the United States.

References

Barro, Robert J., and Xavier Sala-i-Martin. 1992. Convergence, *Journal of Political Economy* 100, no. 2: 223-51.

Barro, Robert J., and Xavier Sala-i-Martin. 1995. *Economic Growth*. New York: McGraw-Hill.

Borjas, George J. 1994. The Economic Benefits from Immigration. NBER Working Papers 4955. Cambridge, MA: National Bureau of Economic Research.

Borjas, George J. 1999. The Economic Analysis of Immigration, in *The Handbook of Labor Economics*, Volume III, eds., Orley Ashenfelter and David Card. New York: North-Holland.

Carroll, Christopher D., Byung-kun Rhee, and Changyong Rhee. 1999. Does Cultural Origin Affect Saving Behavior? Evidence from Immigrants. *Economic Development and Cultural Change* 48, no. 1: 33-50.

Cha, Marn J. 2002. The First Korean Towns in the Mainland U.S.A.: Reedley and Dinuba, California. Paper presented at a conference on Korean Americans, past, present, and future, sponsored by the Industrial Council on Korean Studies and Centennial Committee of Korean Immigration to the United States, Falls Church, VA (August 16-18).

Choy, Bong-youn. 1979. *Koreans in America*. Chicago: Nelson-Hall.

Im, Hyepin. 2002. From Marginality to Creativity: Korean American Immigrant Churches Setting Their Own Course. Paper presented at a conference on Korean Americans, past, present, and future, sponsored by the Industrial Council on Korean Studies and Centennial Committee of Korean Immigration to the United States, Falls Church, VA (August 16-18).

Jasso, Guillermina, and Mark R. Rosenzweig. 1990. *The New Chosen People: Immigrants in the United States*. New York: Russell Sage Foundation.

Jeong, Dong K. 2002. Comparative Analysis of Social and Economic Mobility Among Korean, Chinese, and Japanese Americans in the United States. Paper presented at a conference on Korean Americans, past, present, and future, sponsored by the Industrial Council on Korean Studies and Centennial Committee of Korean Immigration to the United States, Falls Church, VA (August 16-18).

Ji, Chueng-Ryoung. 2002. Statistical Analysis of Korean Immigrants for the Last Hundred Years. Paper presented at a conference on Korean Americans, past, present, and future, sponsored by the Industrial Council on Korean Studies and Centennial Committee of Korean Immigration to the United States, Falls Church, VA (August 16-18).

Kim, Eleana. 2002. Korean Adoptees Role in the United States. Paper presented at a conference on Korean Americans, past, present, and future, sponsored by the Industrial Council on Korean Studies and Centennial Committee of Korean Immigration to the United States, Falls Church, VA (August 16-18).

Kim, Han-kyo. 2002. The Korean Independence Movement in the United States—Syngman Rhee, An Ch'ang-ho, and Pak Yong-man. Paper presented at a conference on Korean Americans, past, present, and future, sponsored by the Industrial Council on Korean Studies and Centennial Committee of Korean Immigration to the United States, Falls Church, VA (August 16-18).

Leibenstein, Harvey. 1966. Allocative Efficiency v. X-Efficiency. *American Economic Review* 56, no. 3: 392-415.

Lucas, Robert E. 1988. On the Mechanics of Economic Development. *Journal of Monetary Economics* 21, no. 1: 3-42.

Park, Kyeyoung. 2002. Foundations of Violence: Korean Vendors and Powerless Customers in South Central Los Angeles. Paper presented at a conference on Korean Americans, past, present, and future, sponsored by the Industrial Council on Korean Studies and Centennial Committee of Korean Immigration to the United States, Falls Church, VA (August 16-18).

Park, Yoon-shik. 2002. Challenges and Opportunities for Korean Businesses. Paper presented at a conference on Korean Americans, past, present, and future, sponsored by the Industrial Council on Korean Studies and Centennial Committee of Korean Immigration to the United States, Falls Church, VA (August 16-18).

Patterson, Wayne. 1988. *The Korean Frontier in America: Immigration to Hawaii, 1896-1910.* Honolulu: University of Hawaii Press.

Patterson, Wayne. 2000. *The Ilse: 1st Generation Korean Immigrants in Hawaii, 1903-1973.* Honolulu: University of Hawaii Press.

Rauch, James E., and Vitor Trindade. 2002. Ethnic Chinese Networks in International Trade. Review of Economics and Statistics 84, no. 1: 116-30.

Romer, Paul M. 1986. Increasing Returns and Long-Run Growth. *Journal of Political Economy* 94, no. 5: 1002-37.

US Small Business Administration. 2001. *Minorities in Business, 2001.* Washington: US Small Business Administration, Office of Advocacy.

Comments on Chapter 4

SOOGIL YOUNG

In chapter 4, Marcus Noland tries to assess the impact of Korean immigration on the US economy by quantifying the contribution of Korean immigrants in the United States to the economic growth of the states where they have lived. His hypothesis is that Korean immigrants contribute to the growth of local economies by increasing the productivity of the local capital stock through the human capital they embody as well as by enhancing the X-efficiency of local economies, helping to form productive capital by saving more than the average American, creating many new small local businesses as a result of their strong entrepreneurial ability, and facilitating trade between the United States and South Korea. And though the lack of the necessary census data prevents him from statistically confirming this hypothesis, he does statistically establish that the presence of Korean immigrants is positively associated with the growth of local economies. I have six groups of comments to offer on this chapter.

First, Noland's hypothesis sounds plausible, and we want to believe that Korean immigrants contribute to accelerating the growth of the US economy. But he fails to prove that this is the case. In fact, the actual causation may equally plausibly be the other way: The high growth poles of the US economy, such as New York City and Los Angeles, could be attracting Korean immigrants. I believe that in reality the causal relationship operates in both directions and that the causality from the growth pole to the arrival of immigrants runs stronger than that in the opposite direction.

Second, at a more fundamental level, I believe that Noland's attempt to measure the macroeconomic impact of Korean immigrants on the United States was doomed to fail in any case because the Korean immigrant population's 0.4 percent share of the total US population would have been too small to generate a statistically discernible impact on the performance of the US economy. In contrast, microeconomic analyses could have yielded more meaningful and interesting insights on Korean immigrants' impact on the US economy. To give an example, Noland states that Korean-

Soogil Young is former president of the Korea Institute for International Economic Policy and Korea's former ambassador to the OECD.

Americans are unusually concentrated in the formation of rapidly growing new businesses, such as green groceries and laundries. Accordingly, I believe that Korean-Americans are having a significant impact on local economies in a few specific business sectors.

I have done a rough calculation (using data from the Korean Ministry of Foreign Affairs and Trade) of the number of ethnic Koreans registered at South Korean consular offices in the United States by occupation. It indicates that, as of 2000, "own businesses" accounted for 48 percent of the total, consisting of 20 percent for commerce, 16 percent for services, and 2 percent for manufacturing. I believe that all of these own businesses qualify as small businesses. Let us take green groceries in New York City as an example. (This in fact seems to be the most prominent example that I can cite.) In the city, Koreans have established a 24-hour green grocery on nearly every other corner and have come to claim 80 percent of the market.

The impact of these green groceries on the local economy should be multifaceted: the ready availability of fresh fruits and vegetables and such basic foodstuffs as milk, bread, flowers, and delicatessen items; their lower prices and higher quality (including freshness); much greater consumer surpluses; higher local employment; and revitalization of neighborhoods, including safer and cleaner streets. And there are likely to be other similar benefits from businesses such as laundries.

Third, there is a significant category of Korean immigrants, which should have been examined by the author—that is, professionals, such as medical doctors, nurses, lawyers, accountants, and financial analysts. I believe that a substantial number of Korean immigrants are in these professions. For medical doctors and nurses in particular, I recall that there was a wave of immigration from South Korea to the United States during the Vietnam War, which must have served to alleviate the shortage of these professions in the United States, contributing to lower costs and a higher quality of medical services. I wonder how large the contribution of Korean immigrants has been in these professions. My rough calculation indicates that, as of 2000, professionals accounted for 2.0 percent of Korean immigrants. This figure seems to be rather small, and it may be interesting to find out whether this smallness is due to supply-side constraints or US immigration policy.

Fourth, the author indicates that the community of ethnic Koreans in the United States is about 50 to 60 percent larger than the number of Korean immigrants, which is about 1 million. The children born to Korean immigrants in the United States account for the difference. These second-generation Korean-Americans are doing far better than their parents economically. According to Noland, their median income of $70,000 is 1.4 times the US national median income of $50,000. This is so because their parents have made sure that their children receive a good education so that their college-degree attainment ratio is 55 percent, twice the US national average of 27 percent. This, in turn, means that Korean-Americans work hard to be able to finance concentrated investment in the human capital of the United States. In this way, they contribute to a more knowledge-based, more productive profession and workforce, ultimately contributing to the growth dynamism and vibrancy of the US economy. The Korean-Americans' enduring contribution to the US economy seems to be found here.

Fifth, Noland observes that Korean immigrants come from the middle and upper classes of South Korea, which have very high education levels. His analysis also indicates that once in the United States, despite their hard work, they earn about 30 percent less than what their children earn when they grow up. It would be interesting to try to explain this earnings gap. The answer, however, seems to be obvious. The gap seems to be mostly a composite measure of the lower quality of education and poor English-language teaching available in Korea. By the same token, it shows how much Korea may gain economically by improving its educational system and the English-language proficiency of its people. I regard the latter as an important requirement for efficacious communication with the global community, of which the United States may be taken as a microcosm.

Sixth, Noland mentions the contribution that the Koreans who returned home after their graduate education have made to South Korea's economic development. This is a very important point that should have been treated much more extensively. On the whole, Noland by far understates the contribution made by the US educational system to Korea's economic development.

The number of Korean PhDs educated in the United States—most of them largely funded by US scholarships during the period up to the early 1980s—was very small in the early 1960s. And most of the returnees in the 1960s were readily recruited into important posts in the science and economic policymaking process, rising to the highest-ranking posts in the 1970s under the then-president Park Chung-Hee. The most outstanding case of an economist in this regard has been that of Nam Duck-Woo, who served as minister of finance for a number of years and subsequently as special assistant for economic affairs to President Park during the 1970s and as prime minister under President Chun Doo-Hwan during the 1980s.

However, the number of Korean PhDs educated in the United States has increased steadily since the 1960s. And though they have been spread equally over both natural sciences and social sciences, during the period up to the mid-1980s, there was in fact a marked concentration in engineering and economics, in particular. The number of Koreans seeking a PhD-level education in the United States began to increase rapidly as, with Korea's economic takeoff in the 1960s, the demand for PhD-level thinkers, and for engineers and economists in particular, began to increase rapidly.

This increased demand was especially connected with the establishment of two government-funded think tanks, the Korea Institute of Science and Technology and the Korea Development Institute, in the early 1970s. These two institutes were created by the order of President Park Chung-Hee for the purpose of inducing the return of foreign-educated (mostly in the United States) PhDs in engineering and economics by offering "huge" economic compensation as well as a comfortable research environment. The two institutes were so successful in encouraging Koreans to undertake a PhD-level education in the United States, as well as in inducing the return of US-educated PhDs, that more government-funded think tanks with the same purpose have since mushroomed. As of today, tens of thousands of US-educated PhDs are scattered throughout all disciplines and make up a very large majority of all PhDs in Korea as well as the mainstream of Korea's brainpower.

These PhDs have been making a more and more broadly based, systematic contribution to the sustenance of South Korea's rapid industrialization and high economic growth since the mid-1970s. And their contribution has covered not only economic policymaking but also social policymaking, engineering, and research and development. It should be obvious that the US educational system has contributed to the creation and continuation of Korea's economic miracle through the brainpower of these PhDs and that the US economy in turn has benefited in many ways because Korea's high economic growth has been accompanied by the flourishing of trade and other mutually advantageous economic interactions between the two countries. The Korean students who are studying in the United States—who are now nearly all financed by their parents or employers at home—are doing so to be able to contribute to such relations between Korea and the United States in the future.

5

The Status and Role of Ethnic Koreans in the Japanese Economy

TOSHIYUKI TAMURA

Who really are ethnic Koreans and who are they not in Japanese society? To answer this question is not an easy task. They are sometimes wrongly taken for *Korean-Japanese*, that is, Koreans residing in Japan with Japanese nationality. Actually, these people may or may not be included in the concept of ethnic Koreans, depending on the scope and the context of argument. The overwhelming majority of ethnic Koreans are legally foreigners with foreign passports, and accordingly their legal status should not be considered parallel to that of people in other countries, such as Korean-Americans.

For a closer understanding of the concept, we must retrace the modern history of Korea and Japan and their interrelationships. A smattering of history will convince one how and why the illusion that Japan is ethnically homogeneous—which I have termed the "homogeneity myth"[1]—has spread so widely among Japanese citizens. It was this kind of consciousness that, together with the North-South division of the Korean peninsula, had made the legal status of Korean residents so complicated and peculiar to Japan.

In this chapter, I try to describe the past and the present situations of Koreans in Japan, making utmost use of official statistical data, as well as the results of my own work. In the second and third sections, I

Toshiyuki Tamura is dean of the Faculty of International Politics and Economics at Nishogakusha University.

1. See Tamura (1983b).

introduce my own definition of the concept of Zainichi Koreans. "Zainichi" literally implies people residing in Japan, but customarily the word has been used to designate Korean residents. Because the most appropriate statistical time series that correspond to my definition are the demographic figures in the Japanese census, I put in order the census-based population figures so as to show how Korean immigrants have come to constitute the largest ethnic minority group in Japan.

The fourth section concerns explanations of the complexity of the post-war Japanese immigration control and registration systems, and with the process whereby they have been improved. In my opinion, what distinguishes discrimination from prejudice is the ex stence of acts or the exercise of power from the side of the majority in any sense, ranging from speeches and violence to customs and institutions—and in some cases even the knowledge of the fact that others are discriminated against in one's neighborhood (statistical discrimination!).

Needless to say, prejudice may cause and aggravate discrimination, but the causality also may go the other way around. At any rate, it is my belief that—as far as Koreans in Japan are concerned and apart from psychological elements—their legal status is one of the crucial factors that have enabled the Japanese to segregate these people from daily opportunities. This explains why I am so inclined to examine legal problems in this chapter.

In the fifth section, I show the recent situations in which Koreans are put, again making use of census data. For the convenience of comparison, I try to add the information on the Chinese people living in Japan, whose relative weight has rapidly increased in recent years. In the strata of communities of immigrants, recent Chinese and Korean arrivals are frequently called "newcomers." Even if we count early arrivals and latecomers in a lump, their *ethnic densities* (weights in the total population) cannot be overestimated. Nonetheless, there are political leaders like Shintaro Ishihara, the governor of Tokyo, who in his speeches trifles Korean and Chinese immigrants in contempt, calling them *sangokujin* (people of the third countries), a derogatory phrase once popular among Japanese in the days immediately after the surrender at the end of World War II in 1945.[2]

Finally, the sixth section of the chapter is devoted to conclusions. To my regret, I am forced to fully rely on the official data published by the Japanese government. I know there are plenty of materials and research findings accumulated by local governments, private institutions and groups, and so on. But they do not necessarily provide a good basis

---

2. Ishihara is reported to have said in the *Spiegel*, April 12, 2000, that *sangokujin* may "rise in riot." Again on April 10, 2000, he made a similar warning speech during a ceremony at the Ground Self-Defense Force's garrison.

for the following exposition. In addition, I cannot conduct any analyses in line with standard economic theories (e.g., the economics of discrimination). For these remaining tasks, I have to ask the reader to expect another effort.

Historical Background

One of the most disputable problems in our argument is how to define ethnic Koreans in their historical context. The ethnological definition contradicts the historical fact that Japan as a nation itself was a mixture of people from neighboring nations. Even the emperors Hirohito and Akihito acknowledged that the imperial family was of Korean origin.

Yet the legal definition based on the nationality concept becomes awkward in two senses. First, with the annexation of Taiwan and Korea to Japan in 1895 and 1910, respectively, people in the colonial territories were deprived of their native nationalities and incorporated into the Japanese nation. Legally, therefore, there were no Koreans in the prewar Japanese Empire. Second, the legal definition excludes those who adopted Japanese nationality after the end of World War II in 1945.

To explain the second point more precisely, the postwar Japanese government did not give the people from ex-colonial regions the right to choose their nationalities, on the ground that the Potsdam Declaration of 1945 and the San Francisco Peace Treaty of 1951 treated these people as the subjects of victorious nations, and accordingly Taiwanese and Koreans remaining in Japan were given the residential status of foreigners. It was in 1965 that the Japan-South Korea Treaty and the accord concerning the status of Koreans in Japan were signed. The latter accord first gave Korean residents (only those with South Korean nationality who had been in Japan before the war and their descendents) the legal status of permanent residence. Hence the most realistic and practical way of defining ethnic Koreans in Japan would be to restrict them to Zainichi (people residing in Japan) in the narrower sense.[3]

More concretely, I propose to define Zainichi in the narrower sense as those who fall under any of the following three categories and their descendants: (1) Korean nationals who moved to Japan before the annexation; (2) people who moved to Hondo, or the Japanese Main Islands (Japan Proper), during the colonial period; and (3) those who remained in Japan after the end of World War II either as nationals of victorious countries or with foreign passports, and—especially after the restoration of diplomatic relations with South Korea in 1965—people who landed in Japan with long-run or permanent residential status.

---

3. The meaning of narrowness in this definition will become clear in the succeeding sections.

According to the *Teikoku Tokei Nenkan* (Statistical Yearbook of the Empire), which had been the sole reliable source before the Japanese censuses, there were only 4 Koreans in 1882, and 790 in 1909, the year before the annexation (1910). A common opinion of historians has been that most of them were diplomats, students, and political refugees. Recent research has revealed, however, that there were a variety of muscular laborers in those days, indicating that the Japanese economy started to introduce a Korean workforce at the early stage of industrialization.[4]

Another data source is the research on households and inhabitants conducted by the Naimusho Keihokyoku (Police Bureau, Ministry of Domestic Affairs) for the period 1913-44, which covers the Korean population in Hondo, Japan (henceforth, Police Bureau population) by prefecture and by occupation since 1915, by sex since 1920, and by Joju (usually living) and non-Joju. The censuses in Japan have been conducted since 1920, and accordingly the definition of Joju population in the Police Bureau data seem to correspond to that of the census data, that is, "those persons who had lived or were going to live for three months or more at their respective households at the census date."

The census figures for Joju Koreans (henceforth, the census population) are available for 1920, 1930, and 1940. Unfortunately, the coverage of the Police Bureau population is only 74 percent of the census population in 1920, goes down to 71 percent in 1830, and rises to 96 percent in 1940. This is why I started to estimate the census-based annual Korean population in Hondo, Japan during the whole colonial period (1910-45) by prefecture, sex, and occupation.[5] Figure 5.1 summarizes the results by sex for national totals.

My estimation of the census Korean population in 1910 is 2,600, of which the female population was merely 244. The total population increased to 40,755 in 1920, and to 419,009 in 1930, with the sex ratio gradually improving from 7.65 in 1920 to 2.45 in 1930. The total hit the 1 million mark in 1939, and it was 2,206,541 at the end of World War II, with a sex ratio of 1.64. Needless to say, the whole process of improvement in sex ratios reflects the widening of working opportunities for women and increased family reunions. It should be noted here that the extremely high sex ratios in the early years support the recent findings cited above. This point can be confirmed by my estimates of census Koreans by occupation.

As table 5.1 indicates, a characteristic feature of census Koreans in the early years of the colonial period is their surprisingly high rates of labor participation, centering on physical labor. Although the weight of work-

---

4. Komatsu et al. (1994) and Kimura and Komatsu (1998). See also Tamura and Kunihisa (1982) for the development of Japanese capitalism since the Meiji Era.

5. My work with this estimation problem started in 1977, and after the reestimation of previous results, I published Tamura (1999).

Figure 5.1 Population of ethnic Koreans in Japan, according to the census, 1910-45

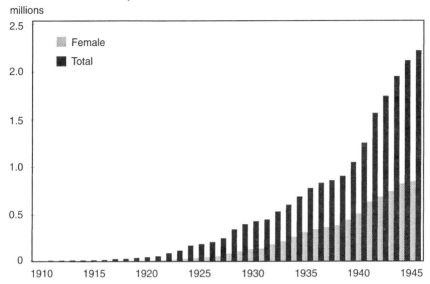

Source: Tamura (1999).

Table 5.1 Population of ethnic Koreans in Japan by occupation, according to the census, 1910-45

Year	Professional	Commerce	Agriculture and fishery	Laborers	Others	Labor force	Total population
1910	0	162	154	1,913	6	2,235	2,600
1915	34	1,052	746	6,687	312	8,831	9,939
1920	137	683	707	31,196	999	33,722	40,755
1925	329	3,056	2,201	137,910	3,327	146,823	179,050
1930	499	13,773	2,251	232538	30120	279,181	419,009
1935	1,474	44,155	5,948	349,486	23,707	424,770	765,947
1940	3,850	73,231	8,821	519,919	31,604	637,425	1,241,315
1945	10,116	68,540	18,255	994,588	35,591	1,127,090	2,206,541

Source: Tamura (1999).

ing people decreases keeping step with *feminization* (the improvement in sex ratios), physical labor maintains the top priority even in the later years. Behind this finding was a dark side of Japanese colonialism and militarism, as we will see below. The number of students and school pupils was 182 in 1910, and it reached 1,000 in 1930, 50,000 in 1935, and roughly 250,000 in 1945.

Geographical proximity outweighed the economic, social, and other factors at the outset. My estimates by birthplace indicate that Cheju Do, a volcanic island off the southern tip of the Korean peninsula, has been the major supplier of immigrants to Japan. In the early years, most of them landed at the ports of the nearest prefectures, such as Fukuoka and Yamaguchi, directly, or via Busan, Korea, the major seaport through which more than 90 percent of emigrants sailed for Hondo. As time passed, however, the range of birthplaces of immigrants went up north, while their main residential places in Hondo, Japan moved eastward up to Osaka.

In 1910, the share of Fukuoka in the distribution of Koreans' residential areas was 15.15 percent, and those of Yamaguchi, Osaka, and Tokyo were respectively 7.27, 9.35, and 15.81 percent. The share of Osaka increased to 22.52 percent in 1925, and those of Fukuoka and Tokyo went shoulder to shoulder at slightly less than 10 percent. This means that attractive economic forces outweighed geographical and the sociopolitical gravity. What is important here is the share of Hokkaido, the extreme northern district of Japan; its share increased from 1.15 percent of 1910 to 3.46 percent in 1945, which again suggests the dark side of the history. In the postwar years, the geographical distribution of Koreans has become stable, in the sense that the Kinki Area with Osaka at its center has been maintaining almost half of the population, followed by the Kanto Area including Tokyo, with a share of about 20 percent.[6]

Let us now reinterpret the above process from the point of view of the immigration control policy of the Japanese government. Until the outbreak of the 3.1 Independence Movement in 1919, the "generous" stance of the Hondo government, contrary to the militaristic rule in the Korean peninsula, helped to attract more and more Koreans to Hondo. While undertaking conciliatory measures in the Korean peninsula, the Hondo government started to force Korean immigrants to carry travelers' certificates.

This policy change could be seen as an immediate consequence of the Independence Movement, but at the same time it reflected the anti-Korean sentiment among the Japanese brought up in Hondo society. The heavy economic slumps after World War I, together with the increasing number of Korean immigrants, touched off Japanese frustrations and paved the way for making Koreans scapegoats for the social unrest, culminating in the massacre of Koreans amid the Kanto earthquake disaster, on September 1, 1923. In many communities (even in police offices), mobs or bands of vigilantes—incited by false rumors intentionally spread by the authority—killed about 6,000 to 10,000 Koreans.[7]

The social unrest after the earthquake put the Hondo government in a position to implement a tighter immigration control policy. Local marshals on the Korean peninsula were given the right to suspend the is-

---

6. See Tamura (1988).

7. Tamura (1983a, 1983b).

suance of the certificates at their disposal. The Emigration Control Office at Busan, which had been set up in 1937, was at the forefront of the so-called Genchi Soshi (On-the-Spot Suspension) Policy. As Japan rushed to the wartime system, however, a switchover of the policy was decided in such a way as to introduce positively the Korean workers to Hondo and other territories for the forced labor, and to send the Korean soldiers and girls (comfort women) to the war fronts.

According to Park Kyung Shik, 725,000 Koreans were drafted for military services and forced labor during the period 1939-45, the last stage of World War II.[8] An increase of the share of Hokkaido indicated above partly testifies to the conscription and concentration of Korean youth in coalmines, construction sites, and so on. About 4,300 Koreans were left discarded at the time of Japanese withdrawal from Sakhalin, an island lying north of Hokkaido and now under Russian rule. Moreover, many Korean Hibakusha (A-bomb victims) are still waiting for medical care and financial aid.

The Postwar Situation

The story does not end with the topics in the previous section. Since 1950, the census has been conducted every 5 years. The population of Joju Koreans according to the 1950 census was 464,277, a sharp decline from 1945, mainly due to the repatriation of 1,100,000 to 1,410,000 Koreans to their homelands, North Korea and South Korea. In accordance with the agreement between the Red Cross of Japan and its North Korean counterpart, 93,444 Koreans were sent back to the North as of 1976.[9] Throughout the 1950s and 1960s, according to the census, the population of Koreans remained stable at about 520,000. It started to increase at an incomparably slower pace than the prewar pace, and then attained its first peak of 570,000 in 1986.

Japan's surrender at the end of World War II gave birth to the *nationality clause problem* concerning the legal status of ex-colonial descents. The Alien Registration Law of 1952 took away Japanese nationality from these ethnic minorities and treated them the same as other foreigners in general. Thus they have been shut out from governmental and semigovernmental organizations, as well as large business firms or professional occupations, because of the nationality clauses inserted implicitly or explicitly in laws, rules, regulations and so on. This type of occupational segregation forced them to rush into the "ethnic" industries, such as restaurants, finance, entertainment, and other service-related businesses.

---

8. Park (1965).

9. Cited by Morita (1996).

Since the 1980s, however, the narrow gate to full participation in Japanese society has been forced open little by little, at the cost of countering the inflow of Japanese nationals and Korean "newcomers" into the ethnic industries. A remarkable change happened in 1982, when public research institutes including universities were allowed to employ foreigners on their permanent staffs. The Nationality Law was amended in 1985 so as to recognize eligibility for Japanese citizenship through either the paternal or maternal line. The New Immigration Control Law of 1990 intended to invite a wider range of newcomers from South Korea, China, Brazil, and countries in other regions.

The mid-1980s were a turning point not only for the Japanese economy but also for Koreans in Japan. Concurrently with the "internationalization" of Japan—that is, the opening up of society to more and more foreign laborers and students—the Zainichi Koreans are now facing a prospective crisis of extinction: the possibility that their community might disappear within several generations. Aside from newcomers, people who had moved to Japan during the colonial period and their direct descendants were aging, and accordingly the memories of the past history were diminishing among younger generations. The number of Koreans who want to be naturalized in Japan has been increasing sharply in recent years. The main reasons for their decisions to apply for naturalization are said to be, among others, job hunting, marriage to a Japanese citizen, and their children starting school.

Although the number of applicants for naturalization is not available, family law specialists compiled annual data for those who acquired Japanese nationality for the period 1952-99. According to their research, only 232 Koreans were naturalized in 1952. After the mid-1970s, however, the number increased to between 4,500 and 6,000, and then went up to nearly 10,000 after the mid-1990s. The total for the whole period is 233,920 (73.6 percent of the total permitted applicants).[10] In comparison, the 1999 census recorded the ethnic Korean population as 530,649 (figure 5.2).

There are two ways of tracing the postwar trends in the Korean population. One is to follow the census data for every 5 years after 1950. Aside from the census, we can make use of the annual data gathered under the Immigration Control Act and the Alien Registration Law. Let us refer to the latter as the *registered* population, which covers all foreign residents, except those persons exempted from registration and those departing from Japan within 90 days from the date of landing, or within 60 days after birth. Among them are long-term residents and permanent residents, and their spouses and children. Because the foreigners' registration system in Japan has been and still is very complicated, we discuss this and related problems further in the next section. Here it suffices to note

10. Research Group on Zainichi's Family Law (2001).

Figure 5.2   Postwar ethnic Korean population in Japan, 1947-2000

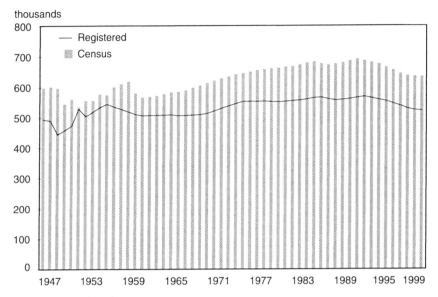

Source: Tamura (1984).

that the registered population is a concept wider than the census population, the latter being slightly smaller numerically than the Zainichi in the narrower sense.

In the same way as I endeavored for the colonial period, I have also put in order the estimated results of the annual census-based Korean population by sex and prefecture for the period 1950-80 (Tamura 1984). In preparing the present chapter, I extended the periods of estimation to 1947-49 and 1981-2000, but only for national totals. I leave the detailed explanation of the estimation procedures to a footnote.[11] The results are summarized in figure 5.2.

According to my estimates, the number of registered Koreans increased until it peaked at 693,000 in 1991, which caused an increase in the census population, with a peak of 572,000 in 1986. The time lag between the two peaks explains the explosive rush of newcomers due to Japan's relaxation of its immigration control policy on one hand, and liberalization of overseas traveling in South Korea on the other. Thanks to the

---

11. This time, I made use of a very simple regression equation: $\ln X(t) = 0.6244 + 0.93295 \ln X(t\text{-}1)$, with t-values respectively (1.145071) and (23.33003), and $X(t)$ being the Police Bureau population in year t. In addition, $N = 53(1948\text{-}2000)$, $R^2(\text{adjusted})=.912648$, $S^2 = .02158$, and $DW = 2.059123$. Although it is easy to improve the regression equation, let us be content with this provisional result for the moment.

newcomers more than compensating for the decrease in the census population, the latter attained the second peak of 575,000 in 1992, but it tended to go down as soon as the new wave of the inflow paused and started declining. Needless to say, the long-lasting slump in the Japanese economy has been the key factor in the recent decrease in registered Koreans.

Nationality and the New Registration System

The institutional basis that allows Japan to treat Zainichi differently from Japanese nationals goes back to a Circular Notice issued in 1952 by a bureau chief of the predecessor agency of the Ministry of Justice. The notice declared that (1) Koreans and Taiwanese, inclusive of those residing in Japan, were deprived of their Japanese nationality, and (2) they had to go through the same formalities as foreigners in general if they were to be naturalized in Japan. The notice was then embodied in the Alien Registration Law of 1952, which, together with the Immigration Control Act of the previous year, paved the way for the establishment of the basic principle of the postwar immigration control and registration systems in Japan. Foreigners thus have been required to be fingerprinted and usually carry a certificate of alien registration.

The first example of the principle was the Law for the Protection of War Victims (1952), which, by means of the nationality and registration clauses, shut out ex-colonial residents from almost all kinds of national indemnities other than those concerning the atomic bomb victims. Then the same clauses came to be inserted in bills or notices, as well as regulations and other forms of rules issued by the government and semigovernmental bodies—both central and local, and public and private institutions, and so on. Even today, many public and private institutions unconsciously imitate the texts of others, and, as it turns out, "contribute" to the exclusion of foreign residents from daily opportunities. In my personal experience, I have found several examples of this kind of exclusion for admission into a city assembly (public!) and membership in a golf club (private!).

What has had a graver impact on Zainichi are the cases of social welfare measures, qualifying examinations, financial transactions, and employment practices. In most welfare measures, such as pension plans and livelihood protections, nationality clauses have been gradually removed with some interim measures, especially after Japan ratified the International Covenants on Civil and Political Rights (1979) and the Convention Relating to the Status of Refugees (1982). However, there are such cases as the national pension scheme, where imperfect interim measures left the elderly and the physically handicapped without relief.

Finally, many lawsuits have been filed by Koreans and Chinese against the Japanese government, local autonomous bodies, and business enterprises that once were committed to using forced labor. Most of the lawsuits have been seeking compensation for damages caused either by nationality clauses in postwar regulations or by conscription during the colonial period. It has been very difficult, however, for the plaintiffs to win their cases.

It is now clear that the New Immigration Control Act (1990) and the amended Alien Registration Act (1992) were to conform to the latest trends in international society. Diplomatically, the new system was the direct result of the agreement between Japan and South Korea on the treatment of the *descendents* of the Permanent Residents by Accord, a legal status originally introduced through diplomatic settlement in 1965 and applied only to South Korean nationals.

By the Accord of 1965, Korean nationals residing in Japan after the colonial period were able to apply for permanent residency. As for their descendents, however, the accord went through further consultations for 25 years from the day it came into effect. Then the two governments arrived at a new agreement in 1991 on the treatment of descendents of the Permanent Residents by Accord, and, corresponding to this, the Japanese government promulgated the Special Law on Immigration Control in 1991, by which those who have continuously resided in Japan since the end of World War II or before and their lineal descendents were classified as Special Permanent Residents (SPRs).

Under the new system, therefore, there are two broad categories of permanent residents, SPRs and General Permanent Residents (GPRs), the latter being applicable to foreigners in general. The new system made SPRs and GPRs free from legal limitations on daily activities, including length of stay and fingerprinting, in exchange for the duty to describe the full list of family members in the application form. But for spouses and children of Japanese nationals and permanent residents, the period of stay is either 1 year or 3 years, depending on their individual situations.

Apart from these, there is another category named Teijusha (Long-Term Residents, or LTRs), indicating those who are authorized to reside in Japan for a period of stay designated by the minister of justice after considering individual circumstances. It follows that Zainichi in the narrower sense correspond to the sum total of people of five status categories: SPRs, GPRs, foreign spouses and children of SPRs and GPRs, Korean spouses and children of Japanese people, and LTRs.

In general, there are 22 categories of nonpermanent residential status, other than the 5 listed above. These nonpermanent residents are not required to describe the family list in the application, but have to comply with fingerprinting if they are 16 years of age or more and if their total period of stay is more than 1 year. Those who come under any of the following 5 categories are exempted from the registration duty: (1) Those who depart from Japan within 90 days from the date of landing or within 60 days of the date of birth; (2) those who have been granted a provisional stay; (3) those granted a transit stay or emergency stay, or crew members; (4) diplomats or officials; and (5) members and civilian employees of the US armed forces. Table 5.2 shows registered Koreans by residential category. The permanent residents in row 1 of the table are the sum of GPRs and SPRs, and Zainichi are the sum of rows 1 through 5.

I have been stressing that my definition of Zainichi in this chapter is "narrower." It is now time to explain in what sense it is narrower. Indeed, the concept in table 5.2 is broader than the permanent resident categories that exclude spouses and children. But the former is narrower in the sense that it does not take into account either of those who have been actually residing in Japan for long with a nonpermanent visa other than the status of LTR, or of those who have been already naturalized, with illegal residents being disregarded.

By definition, we cannot cite the statistical figures for illegal entry. Nor do we know how many Koreans with a formal visa have gone underground after landing legally. According to the records of the Immigration Control Office, roughly 10,000 Koreans are sent back home annually. The annual number of Koreans arrested for working illegally is almost of the same order.

Many students, professors, and business workers have been applying for an extension of stay or a change of residential status. The economic success of South Korea produced a mass exodus of "happy" emigrants, in the late 1980s, to the United States, Canada, Australia, and Japan, with the result of rising "category jumpers" in these countries.[12] The long-term legal residents with a short-term visa who have not been successful with category jumping, renewal, or extension must have been repeating to-and-fro moves between the home and host countries immediately before the expiration of residential permission.

The bottom row of table 5.2 gives the estimated census figures for registered Koreans living in Japan. The slight gaps between the Zainichi and the census data are attributable to the differences in definitions and methods of investigation. In the next section, we describe the status quo of Zainichi Koreans. Observations based on table 5.2 will satisfactorily explain the usefulness of census data for this purpose.

The Economic Role and Status of Koreans

One of the most serious problems Japan is now facing is a prospective decrease in population due to a decline in the birthrate. Government demographic experts are warning that Japan's population will peak at 127

---

12. Tamura and Morita (2001).

Table 5.2   Registered ethnic Koreans living in Japan, by residential category, 1995-2000

Status	1995	1996	1997	1998	1999	2000
Registered	666,376	657,159	645,373	638,828	636,548	635,269
(1) Permanent	580,122	572,564	563,338	554,875	546,553	539,384
(2) Nonpermanent	86,254	84,595	82,035	83,953	89,995	95,885
Spouses and children of						
(3) Japanese	21,385	21,090	20,738	21,078	21,753	22,057
(4) Permanent residents	5,259	4,842	4,522	4,190	3,875	3,560
(5) Long-term residents	12,468	11,855	10,868	10,416	10,028	9,509
(6) Others	47,142	46,808	45,907	48,269	54,339	60,759
Zainichi: (1)+(3)+(4)+(5)	619,234	610,351	599,466	590,559	582,209	574,510
Census	560,414	552,251	545,030	535,769	530,649	528,904

Source: Japan Immigration Association.

million in 2007 and then decrease to 67 million by 2100. The declining birthrate has been requiring the revision and rescheduling of future programs concerning, for example, education, tax system, pension schemes, and the labor market.[13] The Korean community is no exception to this trend, as table 5.3 suggests.

A glance at table 5.3 will convince one how rapidly the Korean community has been aging. One might well be impressed by a slight increase in the share of population in the labor force (those of age 15 to 64 years), but hidden behind this is a sharp decline in the population below age 14.

As of 2000, the share of the elderly population (65 and over) was 14.8 percent for the national total including foreigners, whereas the share of the population 14 years and below is 15.3 percent (these figures are not in the table). In the case of Koreans, a drastic decrease in infants' population within these 15 years has contributed to shaping the lantern-shaped age structure.

The labor participation rates in table 5.4 are defined as ratios of people in the labor force to those above 15 years of age. The older cohort of the Korean community has shown a slight decrease in this rate, but it is not a conspicuous one, in both sexes and in comparison with the national total. Rather than the Koreans' case, an extremely low rate of labor force participation by Chinese residents poses a difficult question. My tentative answer to this is that, because their community is composed of relatively smaller proportions of infants and older people, the remaining young generations are either attending schools and/or universities, or are in workplaces segregated from other ethnic groups.

---

13. Tamura (2002).

Table 5.3   Population of ethnic Koreans in Japan by age group, according to the census, 1985-2000

Age (years)	2000	1995	1990	1985
85 and above	4,528	2,978	2,035	1,271
80-84	7,300	5,899	4,335	3,047
75-79	14,145	10,564	8,918	6,957
70-74	15,646	17,549	13,841	12,131
65-69	20,654	18,328	20,569	16,873
Total (65 and above)	62,273	55,318	49,688	40,279
Percent of total				
Korean population	11.8	9.9	8.8	7.1
60-64	28,484	22,795	20,328	23,683
55-59	34,770	30,606	24,423	22,470
50-54	41,896	37,347	32,057	26,001
45-49	43,328	45,550	39,216	33,742
40-44	42,962	46,666	47,503	40,629
35-39	44,755	46,267	48,818	48,892
30-34	46,356	48,830	48,117	49,358
25-29	49,958	50,461	50,476	46,683
20-24	39,128	50,106	47,450	46,888
15-19	33,038	40,534	49,605	49,286
Total (15-64)	404,675	419,162	407,993	387,632
Percent of total				
Korean population	76.5	74.8	71.9	67.9
10-14	24,924	36,012	42,920	54,106
5-9	20,387	27,626	38,107	46,969
0-4	16,645	22,296	28,890	42,248
Total (0-14)	61,956	85,934	109,917	143,323
Percent of total				
Korean population	11.7	15.3	19.4	25.1
Total Korean population	528,904	560,414	567,598	571,234

Source: Japanese census.

This interpretation is supported by the rates of unemployment in table 5.4. Although the census does not give us information on wages and salaries, incomes, and livelihoods by ethnic group, the low level of unemployment rates of Chinese residents, together with the very large proportion of temporary employed workers in table 5.5, permit us to say that many Chinese are employed in jobs that well-paid Korean workers are reluctant to take. Moreover, why are Koreans' unemployment rates so high, irrespective of sex and time period? My personal observations give me the impression that frequent job switching is not unusual among Korean youth. The difficulty in getting positions in big firms may have discouraged them to hunt for new jobs. And they must have borne the burden of the prolonged slump since the Plaza Accord (1985), which caused the abrupt evaluation of the yen. But, of course, these reasons do not tell the whole story. In any case, this question must be a task left for my further scrutiny.

Table 5.4 Rates of labor force participation and unemployment for ethnic Chinese and Koreans in Japan, 1985-2000 (percent)

Group	Labor force participation[a]	Unemployment
Koreans, 2000		
Total	59.7	8.2
Male	74.6	8.5
Female	46.8	7.8
1995		
Total	61.4	8.5
Male	77.8	8.6
Female	46.3	8.4
1990		
Total	60.8	6.1
Male	77.2	6.3
Female	45.1	5.9
1985		
Total	61.5	7.6
Male	78.5	8.4
Female	44.3	6.3
Chinese, 2000		
Total	46.3	5.2
Male	68.1	5.4
Female	47.8	4.9
National total, 2000		
Total	61.1	4.7
Male	74.8	5.1
Female	48.2	4.2

a. Labor force participation is defined as the ratio of people in the labor force to those above 15 years of age.

Source: Japanese census.

Let us now focus on employment status across industries, as shown in table 5.5. First, contrary to the Chinese case, the high proportion of regular employees, above all in the service industry, attracts our attention. The share of the self-employed is also very high, exceeding the average of the national total. Second, the most popular industry is a marketing-related one, followed by services, manufacturing, and construction. In these industries, many Korean businesspeople are engaged in owner-manager type individual enterprises. This fact may not conform to the general image of Koreans centering on so-called ethnic industries. Third, though not shown in the table, manufacturing comes first in the ranking of popularity among Chinese, followed by marketing, and then services. Reflecting the *postindustrialization* of the Japanese economy, however, the overall employment structure of Japan is shifting toward service industries.

Table 5.5 Employment status of ethnic Chinese and Koreans in Japan by industry, 2000

Industry	Employed persons	Employees				Self-employed[a]		Family workers
		Total	Regular	Temporary	Directors	(1)	(2)	
Koreans								
Total	255,880	157,142	125,701	31,441	27,597	26,047	26,632	18,411
(A) Agriculture	713	280	190	90	19	47	153	214
(B) Forestry	79	40	26	14	6	12	12	9
(C) Fisheries	66	31	22	9		8	14	12
(D) Mining	304	156	147	9	88	16	29	15
(E) Construction	34,891	19,492	16,249	3,243	5,523	4,581	3,498	1,792
(F) Manufacturing	40,544	24,862	20,867	3,995	3,632	3,497	4,698	3,851
(G) Electricity and gas[b]	171	170	150	20	1			
(H) Transport[c]	13,311	10,152	8,765	1,387	1,029	432	1,479	218
(I) Wholesale and retail trade[d]	79,813	42,817	31,399	11,418	5,858	11,848	9,945	9,324
(J) Finance and insurance	8,471	6,757	6,423	334	560	368	631	155
(K) Real estate	6,867	2,738	2,499	239	2,055	654	1,076	343
(L) Services	62,189	42,836	34,569	8,267	8,411	4,189	4,494	2,257
(M) Government[e]	365	365	182	183				
(N) Other establishments[f]	8,096	6,446	4,213	2,233	415	395	603	221
Male	148,086	84,846	72,546	12,300	20,595	19,379	18,771	4,477
Female	107,794	72,296	53,155	19,141	7,002	6,668	7,861	13,934
Chinese								
Total	121,574	105,701	72,167	33,534	6,982	2,666	3,198	3,015
Male	62,669	53,622	39,331	14,291	5,103	1,705	1,874	361
Female	58,905	52,079	32,836	19,243	1,879	961	1,324	265
All Japan								
Total	62,977,960	48,763,386	42,042,051	6,721,335	3,517,151	2,047,417	4,884,000	3,761,408
Male	37,248,770	28,417,698	26,179,128	2,238,570	2,672,669	1,674,021	3,789,757	692,880
Female	25,729,190	20,345,688	15,862,923	4,482,765	844,482	373,396	1,094,243	3,068,528

a. (1) self-employed, employing others; (2) self-employed, not employing others.
b. Electricity, gas, heat supply, and water.
c. Transport and communications.
d. Wholesale and retail trade, and eating and drinking places.
e. Government (and not elsewhere classified).
f. Establishments not adequately reported.

This seems to be the best place to conduct an empirical study making use of a framework provided by economic theories, but again further research is required. My conjecture at this stage of study is that, with a little more side information on labor conditions, I would have been able to estimate the numerical magnitudes of several important concepts in economics, for example, discrimination coefficients as proposed by Becker and Arrow.[14]

I can calculate the Segregation Index (SI) for Koreans and Chinese on the basis of the census. This index is defined by the formula

$$SI = (\sum_i^n |Y(i)/Y - Z(i)/Z|)/2(1 - D)$$

where $Y(i)/Y$ is a share of a minority group's population in the ith industry, Y being its total over n industries, and $Z(i)$ and Z the share and the sum of the national total, respectively. Moreover, $D = Y/Z$ designates the *ethnic density* of the group in question. It is clear that SI assumes 0 when Ys and Zs are identically distributed, while it takes the value of 1 if they are concentrated at the opposite extreme.[15] The segregation indices with respect to Koreans and Chinese employment distributions in 2000 are as shown in table 5.6.

Indeed, though the results do not seem to be of special interest, I can point out two findings. First, skewed sex ratios of the Korean and national totals produced awkward results in ethnic densities. In the Korean case, the high female density compensated for the low male density.

In the Chinese case, however, the density of total Chinese is less than the densities of individual sexes. All in all, Koreans are enjoying a higher share per thousand than Chinese. Second, Segregation Indices reveal that there is no difference between both sexes within each ethnic group, but the Koreans' occupational distribution across industries is more remote than the Chinese one from that of the national total. By definition, Koreans are more "segregated" than Chinese, to the extent that the former's SI is higher than the latter's.

So much for the employment problem. Let us go on to the two other topics. Table 5.7 summarizes an interesting fact concerning the "international" marriages of Korean and Chinese husbands. According to this table, the number of couples with Japanese husbands and Korean wives exceeds, only at the margin of 5,000, the number of those with the opposite combination, which is a sharp contrast to the Japanese-Chinese couples.

---

14. Becker (1971); Arrow (1972a, 1972b).

15. Since Ys are a part of Zs with the same dimensions, it is easy to see that SI in the text is equivalent to the well-known Hoover Index (HI). Make $X(i) = Z(i) - Y(i)$ with $X = Z - Y$. Because $Z(i)/Z = DX(i)/Z + (1 - D)Y(i)/Z$, the expression in SI is reduced to $Y(i)/Y - Z(i)/Z = (1 - D)(X(i)/X - Y(i)/Y)$. Summation over i of the absolute values of both sides gives $SI = HI$. See Tamura (1988) for the application of this index to the Koreans' residential distribution in Japan for the periods 1910-45 and 1950-85.

Table 5.6 Ethnic density and Segregation Index, ethnic Chinese and Koreans in Japan, 2000

Measure	Korean			Chinese		
	Total	Male	Female	Total	Male	Female
Ethnic density	4.06301	3.97559	4.18956	1.93042	2.43572	2.28942
Segregation Index	0.03720	0.03737	0.03769	0.02233	0.02677	0.02658

Source: Japanese census.

Table 5.7 Number of couples by nationality of husband, ethnic Chinese and Koreans in Japan, 2000

	Husband	Wife		
		Japan	Korea	China
Japan	31,135,886	30,981,928	37,625	36,195
Korea	115,022	32,391	82,070	237
China	43,899	9,419	112	34,199
Total[a]	31,394,173	31,054,551	120,082	70,944

a. Includes "statelessness and name of country not reported."

Source: Japanese census.

Incidentally, it is getting more and more difficult for Zainichi youth to find marriage partners within the community. For one thing, their circles of acquaintance tend to contain more Japanese than Zainichi Koreans. For another, they have no or a diluted sense of reluctance to marry Japanese, and elder generations are also realizing that objections based on nationalistic sentiments are of little use. Note here that marriages between Zainichi and "original" Koreans are also increasing, "original" being a self-mocking phrase for "native in the peninsula" frequently used among Zainichi youth.

Finally, table 5.8 informs us of the dwelling conditions, again of Koreans and Chinese. It shows a simple calculation, and we know that, in these 15 years, the number of persons per household has been decreasing from 3.3 to 2.6 in the case of Korean households, whereas the average number of household members have been a little more or fewer than 2 persons in the Chinese case.

The pace of decrease in the Koreans' case can be considered as moving on the same trend line as national totals. In the Chinese case, however, the high proportion of single-person households might have been the main reason for their low averages. Unfortunately, figures concerning the lease-ownership distinction of dwelling sites are not classified according to nationalities. In view of the above observations, however, it may safely be said that the average Koreans' dwelling conditions are not far away from those of the upper half of all foreigners.

Table 5.8   Private households in Japan with ethnic Chinese and Korean members, 1985-2000

Measure	1985	1990	1995	2000
Number of households	281,640	444,141	637,192	611,122
Korean households	146,173	192,820	207,680	190,006
Chinese households	19,134	51,053	82,055	96,034
With own houses	117,550	133,225	154,559	147,858
With rented houses	178,274	102,115	408,944	411,096
With rented rooms	4,536	18,920	28,521	27,737
Household members	875,914	1,137,062	1,532,923	1,473,675
Korean households	487,590	589,351	581,435	487,702
Chinese households	41,812	95,183	150,676	177,691

Source: Japanese census.

Conclusions

"Long, long ago, when tigers were enjoying cigars . . ." is a hackneyed phrase with which Korean folktales begin. I started this chapter with the Zainichi Koreans' history. At that time, tigers would have quit smoking.

When the South Korean government opened the 1988 Olympic Games in Seoul, it had to import a mascot tiger from abroad. As I stressed above, the mid-1980s marked a turning point for Zainichi Koreans, and, at the time of the Seoul Olympics, the Zainichi population began to decline.

Discrimination by the Japanese against Koreans may be "invisible" to outside observers, as well as Japanese. It is very difficult to distinguish the two ethnically and culturally similar nations. Under the old registration system, Zainichi Koreans were "advised" to call themselves by Japanese-style names, which, to my sorrow and regret, was certainly a remnant of the So-shi Kai-mei (Chang-shi Kae-myung in Korean) policy that Japanese colonialists had forced on the people of Taiwan and Korea. This "advice" in turn made the problem all the more "invisible." Even today, many Koreans in Japan prefer to use Tsumei (Japanese-style names) whenever they are afraid of discrimination. It was because of these kinds of invisible discrimination that I emphasized in this chapter the legal side of the problem.

In a 1988 essay, I closed by saying, "The highest barrier to be cleared is the fact that we lack reliable data other than population."[16] There has been little improvement in the situation since then. In this chapter, I again was forced to rely heavily on the census. Indeed, there have been many investigations into the actual conditions of Koreans in Japan, but they are "too much of one thing, and not enough of the other," as the Japanese proverb puts it.[17]

---

16. Tamura (1988, 195).

17. It says "Obi-ni mijikashi, tasuki-ni nagashi." A typical example will be the Employment Security Bureau (1995), where assorted results for foreign workers were not released.

I admit that the findings in the previous section are not fruitful enough. Nonetheless, if I am allowed to pick up some new points, the "riddle" of the high unemployment rate of Koreans comes first, and their value on the Segregation Index next. I must ask the reader again to look forward to my next essay.

Finally, I close this chapter by touching on three topics that seem to help explain the present situation, irrespective of whether they are encouraging or not. First of all, Maihara-cho, a small town in Shiga Prefecture with 12,000 inhabitants, decided to give voting rights to foreign residents in a referendum on March 26, 2002, in balloting for and against amalgamation with neighboring local jurisdictions.

Although the referendum had no legal force with respect to the result, it was an encouraging event for Korean activists and Japanese supporters who have long been demanding the right to vote in the electoral assembly of local jurisdictions. With respect to this demand, the ruling political parties are divided, and the bill has not yet been presented to the Diet.

In the case of Maihara-cho, only 13 persons among the qualified 31 foreigners actually voted. Among the 13, absentee voting amounted to 6. This was because blackmailing letters were sent to the mayor, Toshio Muranishi, and even to the qualified foreigners. The mayor made house-to-house visits to persuade the foreign inhabitants not to be afraid of the threat.[18]

The Lawyers' Association of Zainichi Koreans (LAZAK) was established in July 20, 2002, with 32 members. Historically, this must be a dream-come-true story for those like Kim Kyung Duke and others who had fought for a long time in the courts to qualify Zainichi Koreans who had passed their bar examinations for legal activities. It was reported that the aims of LAZAK were to protect the human rights of newcomers, to alleviate discrimination against Zainichi Koreans, and to promote the movement for the right to vote and participate in the performance of official duties. Except for quite a few local governments, the majority of local bodies have been rejecting foreigners seeking to become permanent staff.

Third, the basic stance of Japanese diplomats seems to have not shown any signs of change. The cruel treatment of a North Korean family by the staffs of the Consulate General in Shenyang, China, on May 8, 2002, sent shock waves among Japanese people. Personally, the news reminded me of the "homogeneity myth" syndrome.[19]

As of September 1997, only 10,241 Indo-Chinese refugees were permitted to reside in Japan. Of the boat people Japan temporarily admitted, 6,816 were deported to Australia, Canada, Norway, the United States, and other countries (the total number temporarily admitted is not available). In addition, during the period 1982-98, there were 1,651 applications for refugee designation, but merely 218 requests were authorized and 23 law-

18. *Toyo Keizai Nippo*, May 5, 2002.

19. See the first section above.

suits were filed. It is clearly because of these poor performances that the Japanese diplomats in Shenyang reacted to the refugees as they did.

It is true, as Gregory Clark suggests, that a more generous asylum policy is beneficial not only for refugees but also for the Japanese.[20] As I think of the above examples together, however, their essence is neither a problem of asylum policy nor Japanese diplomatic principle. The more important thing is to look at what lies deep in the minds of ordinary Japanese. Beneath the reactions expressing reluctance or open antagonism to making Japanese society much more multicultural, there lies an obsessive sentiment that they do not want to face up to their own belief in the "myth" to be torn into pieces.

References

Arrow, K.J. 1972a. Models of Job Discrimination. In *Race Discrimination in Economic Life*, ed. A.H. Pascal. Lexington, MA: Lexington Books.

Arrow, K.J. 1972b. Some Mathematical Models of Race Discrimination. In *Race Discrimination in Economic Life*, ed. A.H. Pascal. Lexington, MA: Lexington Books.

Becker, G.C. 1971. *The Economics of Discrimination*, 2d ed. Chicago: University of Chicago Press.

Employment Security Bureau. 1995. *The Present Situation of Employment Policies of Foreigners* (in Japanese). Tokyo: Employment Security Bureau, Ministry of Labor.

Immigration Control Office. 1999. *Immigration Control: For the Sake of Smooth International Exchange in the 21st Century* (in Japanese). Tokyo: Immigration Control Office.

Kimura, K., and H. Komatsu, eds. 1998. *Koreans and Chinese in Japan Immediately after the Annexation* (in Japanese). Tokyo: Akashi Shoten.

Komatsu, H., Kim Y., and Yamawaki K., eds. 1994. *Koreans in Japan before the Annexation* (in Japanese). Tokyo: Akashi Shoten.

Morita, Y. 1996. *A Numerical History of Koreans in Japan* (in Japanese). Tokyo: Akashi Shoten.

Park, K.S. 1965. *Documents of Forcible Conscription of Koreans* (in Japanese). Tokyo: Miraisha.

Research Group on Zainichi's Family Laws. 2001. *The Family Laws of Zainichi* (in Japanese). Tokyo: Nippon Hyoron-sha.

Tamura, T. 1983a. Income Threshold, Contact Theory, and Korean Immigrants to Japan. *Journal of East and West Studies* 12, no. 2: 51-65.

Tamura, T. 1983b. Korean Minority in Japan: An Overview. *Asian Economies* 46: 5-31.

Tamura, T. 1984. Estimation of Korean population in Postwar Japan (in Japanese). *Keizai-to Keizaigaku* 55: 67-80.

Tamura,T. 1988. Koreans in Japan: A Further Analysis. *The Korean-Japanese Journal of Economics and Management Studies* 4: 173-97.

Tamura, T. 1999. Korean Population in Japan 1910-1945, (1)-(3) (in Japanese). *Keizai-to Keizaigaku* 88-90: (1) 1-45, (2) 17-55, (3) 19-56.

Tamura, T. 2002. Survival Race among Japanese Universities at the Age of Population Decrease. Paper presented at the XIX Pan-Pacific Conference, May 29-31, Bangkok, Thailand.

Tamura, T., and S. Kunihisa. 1982. Education, Transport Capital and Productivity Change: The Case for Japan's Experience Since the Meiji Era. In *Japanese Management: Cultural and Environmental Considerations*, ed. S.M. Lee and G. Schwendiman New York: Praeger Publishers.

Tamura, T., and K. Morita. 2001. Korean Economic Miracle and Migrants in Australia: A "Happy" Stage? *Journal of International Politics and Economics* 9: 1-11.

20. G. Clark, "New Asylum Policy Would Benefit Japan and Refugees," *Japan Times*, July 13, 2002.

Comments on Chapter 5

JANG HEE YOO

Toshiyuki Tamura's chapter reveals many important facts about ethnic Koreans in Japan, particularly with regard to their history, their current social status, and their economic role in Japanese society. The chapter presents four main points:

1. The legal status of ethnic Koreans in Japanese society is not as high as it should be.

2. The informal social status of ethnic Koreans suffers from much invisible prejudice in Japanese society.

3. The major occupational areas of ethnic Koreans in Japan include service businesses, owner-managed small businesses, and marketing businesses.

4. The unemployment rate of ethnic Koreans is much higher than that of any other ethnic community in Japan.

Tamura does not give a detailed analysis of the above findings because of a lack of data or official information. However, intellectuals in the two countries have long known that there are other perceived reasons that ethnic Koreans in Japan have such an unequal status, in addition to historical antagonism.

First, some perceive ethnic Koreans in Japan to be too aggressive, tough, and prone to troublemaking. The Y.H. Industrial Company incident[1] in the late 1970s, the case of war-comfort women, troubles related to history textbooks, the opposition movement against the Yaskuni Shinsha, and so on—these events involving ethnic Koreans are enough to leave ordinary Japanese with strongly negative perceptions of ethnic Koreans.

Jang Hee Yoo, former president of the Korea Institute for International Economic Policy, is a professor of economics and dean of the Graduate School of International Studies at Ewha Women's University.

1. The first overt manifestation of workers' discontent appeared in August 1979 with demonstrations by 200 women employees of the Y.H. Industrial Company, which had just gone bankrupt.

Second, the ethnic Korean workforce in Japan happens to be mainly concentrated in such risky service businesses as Pachinko,[2] gambling, and related businesses. Third, the endless conflict between the Mindan (ethnic Koreans who support South Korea) and the Jochongryun (ethnic Koreans who support North Korea) often causes instability and discomfort in Japanese society.

Fourth, there is a notion in Japanese society that South Korea as a nation and the ethnic Korean community in Japan are two different entities. That is, the Japanese view South Korea as a respectable and highly recognized partner—as has been demonstrated by the two countries' successfully cohosting the World Cup, Korea's rapid growth in information technology industries, and Korea's hosting of the Asian Games. Yet on the contrary, the Japanese tend to view ethnic Koreans in Japan as a group of people who left Korea for a number of different and complicated reasons.

Despite the above-mentioned dark-side stories, the business connection between South Korea and ethnic Koreans in Japan has been quite impressive during the past four decades. Quite a few Japanese businesses run by ethnic Koreans have invested heavily in Korea, and many of them have been rather successful there. Examples include Lotte, Kolon, Shindorico, and Shinhan Bank.

These successful businesses still are deepening their roots in the Korean economy. Also, their contribution to South Korean economic development, particularly in its earlier stages, has also been of enormous value.

Today's ethnic Koreans in Japan may still be viewed by some as aggressive, tough, overly egoistic, and so on. Nevertheless, as the Japanese economy becomes more globalized, open, and outward looking, I am sure that ethnic Koreans in Japan will work for Japan first, and perhaps for South Korea afterward, to make the economy more competitive and dynamic.

---

2. Pachinko is a combination of slot machine and pinball.

6

The Economic Status and Role of Ethnic Koreans in China

SI JOONG KIM

China is a multiethnic country officially composed of 56 nationalities, although the number of nationalities may increase if the definition of "nationality" is changed.[1] The absolute majority of the Chinese population are Han nationals, which account for about 92 percent of the total population according to official population data. The remaining 8 percent of the total population, which is still more than 100 million, are composed of the 55 minority nationalities.

Among the 55 ethnic minorities in China, the Zhuang are the most numerous, with more than 15 million, and the Manchu, Hui, Uygur, Mongol, and Tibetan are relatively well known to the outside world. However, these 55 minority nationalities are quite diverse. Some of the ethnic minorities, such as the Zhuang, Manchu, and Hui, are very much similar to the Han, except for a few cultural aspects. However, other

Si Joong Kim is professor of economics at Yeungnam University. He appreciates beneficial comments and valuable references provided by the people whom he interviewed during his research trip to Beijing, Yanji, and Shenyang from July 30 to August 7, 2002. In particular, consul general Joon-Gyu Lee of the Korean Embassy in Beijing, professor Youfu Huang of Central University for Nationalities, professor Seunghun Park of Yanbian University, and Dequan Lee of Liaoning Chosun Wenbao were of great help in writing this chapter.

1. The Chinese government officially recognized 54 minority nationalities among the 183 nationalities that were registered in the 1964 census. At that time, the unrecognized ones were considered to be part of recognized ones or indeterminate. Afterward, 1 nationality was added to the official list. Still, more than 1 million people are classified as "unspecified and unclassified" minorities.

nationalities are clearly distinguished from the Han in many aspects, such as the Tibetan and Uygur. Some of these distinctive nationalities have staged separation or independence movements, which sometimes have led to bloodshed.

Ethnic Koreans can also be regarded as one of the distinct ethnic minorities in China, although they are not as hostile to Han nationals as Tibetans or Uygurs. That is, they have some particular characteristics that distinguish them from most of the other ethnic minorities in China. Although ethnic Koreans ranked just thirteenth among the ethnic minorities of China in population, they attract attention because of two characteristics.

First, ethnic Koreans migrated to China in the relatively recent past, whereas most of the other ethnic minorities have a long history of residing inside the current Chinese territory. The ancestors of the ethnic Koreans in China migrated to China mostly during the period 1850-1945,[2] particularly from 1910 through 1930s, when the control of the Chinese government (whether it was the Qing Dynasty or the Nationalist Party's Republic of China) over the region was rather weak. They moved to China for diverse reasons, such as to escape famine in their homeland, to stage an independence movement against Japanese invasion and colonial rule, or because of the Japanese regime's policy-induced migration in the late 1930s. In any case, the fact that they have lived in China for a relatively short period implies that they may not have fully assimilated by the Chinese or Han culture.[3]

Second, ethnic Koreans are one of a few ethnic minorities that also have nationals forming an independent country neighboring their clustered resident areas in China. This type of ethnic minority includes Koreans, Mongols, Uygurs, and Thai. Actually, of course, ethnic Koreans in China have two countries in their homeland, North Korea and South Korea. In particular, South Korea is a relatively prosperous country with a higher living standard than China. Furthermore, interactions between ethnic Koreans in China and South Korean people recently have been increasing significantly, as overall exchanges grow between Korea and China with the establishment of diplomatic relations in 1992. It is conjectured that the Chinese government is watching closely over the potential link between ethnic Koreans in China and the South Korean government or several nationalistic groups within South Korea.

---

2. They moved into the Northeastern parts of China, which is next to the Korean peninsula across the Yalu River or Tumen River and was mostly barren at that time. This was the area where the Japanese puppet government of Manchuria functioned in the 1930s and 1940s.

3. At the same time, 100 years is long enough for them to assimilate Chinese culture to a certain extent. Their culture is clearly distinguished from that of their homeland. In particular, the distinction is more evident compared with South Korea, because they had been thoroughly separated from South Korea during the Cold War period of nearly four decades.

From the Korean perspective, conversely, ethnic Koreans in China take the major share of overseas Koreans. It is reported that there exist about 5.7 million ethnic Koreans all over the world, which is more than 10 percent of the population of South Korea. Among them, about 2 million—about 40 percent of all overseas Koreans—reside in China. Furthermore, the role of ethnic Koreans in China vis-à-vis South Korea has grown substantially in diverse ways, including as a source of *foreign* labor and as an intermediary in South Korea's contacts with China and even North Korea. Therefore, ethnic Koreans in China have taken on a certain importance from the perspective of the South Korean government—economically, politically, and diplomatically.

Considering these two aspects, we can see that it is worthwhile to examine the ethnic Korean community in China. This chapter looks into this issue, particularly paying attention to their economic status and role. The second section of the chapter describes the demographic conditions of ethnic Koreans in China, mainly before major change occurred in the 1990s. The third section looks at the economic and social situations of ethnic Koreans in China before reform began, paying due attention to China's policy toward ethnic minorities. The fourth section examines the changes that have occurred in ethnic Korean society during China's reform period, particularly as the interactions with South Korea have increased substantially. This major section is divided into three subsections, which look at demographic changes, changes in ethnic Koreans' economic role and status, and their overall social challenges. The fifth section introduces the newly emerging Korean society in China, which is being formed through increasing de facto immigration from South Korea.

The Population of Ethnic Koreans in China

When the first census of the People's Republic of China (PRC) was conducted in 1953, the population of ethnic Koreans in China was 1.11 million, about 0.19 percent of the total Chinese population of 578 million and about 3.1 percent of the total ethnic minority population (State Ethnic Affairs Commission and State Statistical Bureau 1993, 263). But this population size was smaller than its peak of about 1.7 million in 1945, because about 0.6 million people returned to Korea (North or South) after Korea was liberated from Japanese rule in 1945 (Kim 1992, 233-34). In 1945, at most 20 percent of Koreans residing in China had Chinese citizenship (Kim and Oh 2001, 49). However, most of the remaining ethnic Koreans who decided not to return to Korea had obtained Chinese citizenship by 1952, under the comprehensive policy of the Chinese Communist Party (CCP) toward ethnic Koreans.

The population of ethnic Koreans in China has been growing relatively slowly, so that the share of ethnic Koreans in the total Chinese population has been steadily declining over time. Table 6.1 shows the change of the ethnic Korean population in China and its geographical distribution over time, based on the official PRC censuses of 1953, 1964, 1982, and 1990.[4]

As table 6.1 shows, the population of ethnic Koreans in China increased from 1.11 million in 1953 to 1.92 million in 1990. The population increased 72.8 percent during the 37 years, implying that the annual growth rate was 1.49 percent. This growth rate of the ethnic Korean population was lower than that of Han nationals as well as that of all ethnic minorities, which respectively were 1.78 and 2.62 percent. Although each ethnic Korean family, as a member of an ethnic minority, has been allowed to have two children—in contrast to the compulsory one-child family for Han nationals since the 1970s—most ethnic Korean families have opted to have just one child. Therefore, the share of ethnic Koreans in the total Chinese population decreased from 0.19 percent in 1953 to 0.17 percent in 1990, and the share of ethnic Koreans in the total ethnic minority population decreased from 3.1 percent in 1953 to 2.1 percent in 1990.

There is much evidence that this trend of slow population growth continued or even accelerated during the 1990s. For example, the ethnic Korean population in the Yanbian region, which has the greatest concentration of ethnic Koreans in China, even decreased throughout the late 1990s. There are many reasons for the recent population decrease in the ethnic Korean population in Yanbian or in China as a whole. The key reason for the decrease in Yanbian's ethnic Korean population is that many people migrated out of the region, particularly out of the rural villages, to other regions in China or to South Korea to seek nonagricultural work. The low birth rate of ethnic Korean couples was also a factor. One of the reasons for the decrease in the overall ethnic Korean population in China is that many females of reproductive age migrated to South Korea for marriage or for work.

As is shown in table 6.1, ethnic Koreans lived mostly in three Northeastern provinces, Jilin, Heilongjiang, and Liaoning. This geographical distribution of ethnic Koreans in China had shown a minor but clear direction of change, with the concentration ratio somewhat decreasing over time. Still, the three provinces combined accounted for more than 97 percent of ethnic Koreans in China in 1990. The share of Jilin Province continued to decline, from 68 percent in 1953 to 62 percent in 1990, whereas the respective shares of Heilongjiang and Liaoning increased by 3 and 2 percentage points during the 37-year period.

---

4. The fifth census was conducted in 2000. However, the outcome of the census has not yet been made public, except for some aggregated data. It is regrettable that this chapter should depend on data from the 1990 census and previous ones, even though population mobility increased significantly during the 1990s.

Table 6.1   China's ethnic Korean population (thousands) **and geographical distribution** (percentage of total ethnic Korean population), **by province, 1953-90**

Census year	Total population	Jilin Total population	Jilin Yanbian Prefecture	Heilongjiang	Liaoning	Inner Mongolia	Other provinces
1953	1,111 (100)	756 (68)	551 (50)	232 (21)	116 (10)	7 (1)	1 (0)
1964	1,349 (100)	867 (64)	623 (46)	308 (23)	147 (11)	11 (1)	16 (1)
1982	1,765 (100)	1,104 (63)	755 (43)	432 (24)	198 (11)	18 (1)	14 (1)
1990	1,921 (100)	1,182 (62)	821 (43)	452 (24)	230 (12)	23 (1)	33 (2)

Note: Figures in parentheses are in percent.
Source: Yun (1993, 26); based on the official Chinese census.

Outside the three Northeastern provinces, Inner Mongolia and Beijing had nonnegligible ethnic Korean populations, respectively 17,600 and 3,900 in 1982 and 22,600 and 7,700 in 1990. One notable change between 1982 and 1990 was that the population increase outside the Northeastern provinces was remarkable, from 14,000 to 33,000. This increase mostly occurred in Beijing, Hebei, Shandong, and Tianjin (see table 6.2).

Within the three Northeastern provinces, ethnic Koreans tend to cluster in areas by themselves. In particular, the Yanbian region of Jilin Province has been the largest clustered area of ethnic Koreans in China,[5] with more than 40 percent of the country's total ethnic Korean population. Yanbian has been designated as an ethnic Korean autonomous prefecture since 1952, on the basis of the minority policy of the PRC, which allows regional autonomy for ethnic minorities in their clustered region. At lower administrative levels, there is 1 ethnic Korean autonomous county within Jilin (namely, Changbai autonomous county), and there are 43 ethnic Korean townships (or towns) throughout the three Northeastern provinces. These lower-level Korean autonomous areas, excluding Yanbian, account for a little more than 10 percent of the ethnic Korean population. Furthermore, even when ethnic Koreans live outside Korean-cluster areas, they tend to form a village of their own within the Han-dominated townships or towns.

---

5. Yanbian Prefecture is located at the Northeastern border of China, adjacent to North Korea across the Tumen River and Russia to the north. Yanbian is 42,700 square kilometers in size, which is about a fourth of Jilin Province, or about 40 percent of the size of South Korea.

Table 6.2   Ethnic Korean population of major Chinese cities, 1982 and 1990

City	1982	1990	Percent change
Beijing	3,905	7,689	96.9
Changchun	18,324	27,241	48.7
Dalian	2,042	4,816	135.8
Harbin	30,514	36,562	19.8
Qingdao	83	355	327.7
Qinhuangdao	108	869	704.6
Shanghai	462	734	58.9
Shenyang	69,460	80,539	16.0
Tianjin	816	1,788	119.1
Yanji	100,337	177,547	77.0

Sources: Chinese census, 1982, 1990.

The number of counties (or cities), whose ethnic Korean population exceeds 10,000, was 21 in Jilin Province, 14 in Heilongjiang Province, and 3 in Liaoning Province as of 1990. Eleven cities (or counties) had ethnic Korean populations exceeding 50,000: Yanji City, Longjing City, Hualong County, Hunchun City, Wangqing County, Tumen City, and Antu County, which are within Yanbian Prefecture; Jilin City and Tonghua City, which are within Jilin Province but outside Yanbian; and Mudanjiang City in Heilongjiang Province and Shenyang City in Liaoning Province.

The above description of the regional distribution of the ethnic Korean population is mainly based on the 1990 census. Since then, substantial change must have occurred in the demographic situation of ethnic Koreans in China, because overall population mobility has increased significantly as market-oriented reform has proceeded in China. The mobility of the ethnic Korean population has increased as well, particularly because of increased interaction with South Korean people. However, no official data are available on the size and geographical distribution of the ethnic Korean population in China after 1990, because the 2000 census data have not yet been made public. Nevertheless, an analysis of the ethnic Korean population after 1990 will be attempted below, on the basis of diverse and fragmented documents and evidence.

The Condition of Ethnic Korean Society in China in the Prereform Period

This section looks at the situation of ethnic Koreans in China, before substantial change occurred during its reform period. The section begins with a brief introduction of China's policy toward ethnic minorities and then examines the socio-economic conditions of ethnic Koreans in China in the prereform period.

China's Policy toward Ethnic Minorities

China has a long history of assimilating neighboring nationalities into the Han culture. Even Manchu nationals, who once invaded and ruled the Han people during the Qing Dynasty, have been almost fully assimilated, losing even their languages. A similar appraisal can be applied to Mongols to a certain extent, which also ruled China during the Yuan Dynasty. That is, the Han nationals' dominant population size and advanced culture were powerful enough to assimilate other ethnic groups involved in Chinese history.

The Republic of China's Nationalist Party, led first by Sun Zhongshan and later by Zhang Jieshi, implemented a rather aggressive assimilation policy toward ethnic minorities, which was based on a crude Han nationalism. This might reflect the fact that Han nationals had recovered the ruling position, after more than two centuries of being ruled by an ethnic minority, the Manchu. However, the Chinese Communist Party's (CCP's) policy toward ethnic minorities was much softer from the start, probably because it needed the support and help of minorities in its struggle against the Nationalist Party. It proclaimed equality across nationalities and promised ethnic autonomy in a unified country. In fact, the CCP did absorb many ethnic minorities in its struggle against Japan and later in the civil war against Nationalist Party forces.

This policy line was officially adopted after the PRC was established in 1949, and has been maintained, except for the Cultural Revolution period (1966-76).[6] The Constitution of the PRC explicitly proclaims equality and unity across nationalities, banning discrimination against or persecution of any ethnic group. In principle, it negates both Han nationalism and the nationalism of minorities. That is, on the basis of the same principle, China does not explicitly promote Han nationalism and at the same time does not allow separation movements by any ethnic minority. However, the PRC strongly promotes Chinese (*zhonghwa*) nationalism, which it claims includes all 56 nationalities. Chinese nationalism has emerged as the main PRC ideology in recent years, as the socialist ideology has waned in Chinese society.

The PRC's specific policies toward ethnic minorities have three main aspects. First, ethnic minorities have been given certain political rights to represent their interests. For example, the National People's Congress should have at least one representative of each ethnic minority, and it allots more seats to ethnic minorities than their population shares allow. Also, the State Commission of Ethnic Affairs was established at the ministry level under the State Council, and similar organizations at provincial and local levels of

---

6. During the Cultural Revolution, all the ethnic cultures, including that of Koreans, were criticized as antirevolutionary, and many ethnic minority leaders, including ethnic Koreans, were severely persecuted.

government administer ethnic minorities' affairs. The CCP and the Chinese government also gave importance to fostering the cadres of ethnic minorities that are loyal to the CCP's leadership. They expect these minority cadres to mediate between the government and members of ethnic minorities.

Second, regional autonomy is being implemented for minority-cluster regions. Currently, China has 5 minority autonomous regions at the province level, 30 minority autonomous prefectures, and 120 minority autonomous counties. Forty-four out of 55 ethnic minorities have at least 1 autonomous area at a certain level. The autonomous area, in principle headed by personnel from the corresponding ethnic minority, is allowed certain privileges to self-govern some of its internal affairs within the area. Within these autonomous areas, special consideration is given to the ethnic language, education, and culture.

Third, governments at several levels provide special subsidies for the economic development of ethnic minority regions. The central government and relatively well-off provinces allocate fiscal subsides for minority regions, which are in fact underdeveloped areas. This type of subsidy for ethnic minority regions is most conspicuous in Tibet. The recent policy for developing China's western regions is partially intended to improve the economic conditions of ethnic minorities, because most ethnic minorities live in the western areas. Also, subsides to preserve ethnic culture and foster the education of ethnic minorities are also allocated by governments at various levels.

Although these Chinese policies toward ethnic minorities seem to be quite generous, all of them have a limit. That is, they are implemented subject to the condition that they should not lead to separation movements by minorities. In particular, any potentially political link with foreign countries is under close surveillance. Ultimately, China's policies toward ethnic minorities are assessed to be aiming for the assimilation of ethnic minorities into mainstream Chinese culture, namely, Han culture. But these policies are being pursued for the long term, avoiding trouble as much as possible during the interim period.

Ethnic Korean Society in China during the Prereform Period

When Japan surrendered to the Allied Forces in 1945, Koreans in China had to choose whether to stay in China or to return to Korea—North or South. A few more than 1 million people, which then was more than 60 percent of the Korean population, opted to stay.[7] Most of them, who were

---

7. Han and Kwon (1993, 36) estimate that the ratio of ethnic Koreans returning to South Korea was much lower in Yanbian (about 25 percent) compared with other regions (more than 50 percent). They conjectured that the lives of Yanbian's ethnic Koreans were more deeply rooted in the area due to their longer period of settlement there than those of other regions.

landless or poor peasants, supported the CCP over the Nationalist Party. In particular, the ethnic Koreans enthusiastically welcomed land reform, which was implemented in Northeast China by the CCP even before 1949. Subsequently, during the 1949-52 period, most of them received Chinese citizenship without much difficulty, because they were welcomed by the CCP as well. Finally, ethnic Korean people constituted a stable part of Chinese society with the establishment of the PRC in 1949. They have remained so since then, even though some people returned to North Korea during or just after the 1950-53 Korean War and during the Cultural Revolution.

Ethnic Koreans were welcomed by the CCP mainly because of their contributions to the CCP and to the economy of Northeastern China. The officially recognized contributions of ethnic Koreans in China can be summarized as follows. First, many ethnic Koreans collaborated with the CCP in its war of liberation against Japan, its civil war against Nationalist Party forces, and later in the Korean War (Kim and Oh 2001, 59-77). Most ethnic Koreans then seemed to be sympathetic to the CCP's ideology and policies, having the background of poor peasants and people colonized by Japan. Many ethnic Korean people were sacrificed as they struggled in alliance with the CCP against Japan and the Nationalist forces, and this was well recognized by CCP leaders. Although some Korean revolutionaries returned to North Korea, many remained in China and went on to have successful careers in the military or government.

Second, ethnic Koreans were the people who reclaimed the then barren land in Northeastern China during the late 19th and early 20th centuries. They succeeded in cultivating rice paddies for the first time in these areas, which have rather long and cold winters (Kim and Oh 2001, 81-84). Once the wasted land was developed by Koreans, many Han people migrated to this region from more populous regions of China, such as Shandong Province.

That is, Koreans as an ethnic group were recognized for their contributions in the formation and development of the PRC. Due to these recognized contributions of ethnic Koreans—in combination with the Chinese government's generous policy toward ethnic minorities—ethnic Koreans formed a rather stable minority society under the PRC regime in the pre-reform period. They formed some large ethnic communities, such as the Yanbian Autonomous Prefecture, and many small communities within many rural villages in Heilongjiang or Liaoning Provinces.[8] Because most of them lived in these clustered communities, they were able to maintain their language and culture to a certain extent.

---

8. The ethnic Koreans who lived in scattered villages in Heilongjiang and Liaoning Provinces tend to be from the same region back in South Korea, because their ancestors migrated to China in groups organized by the Japanese authorities, mainly in the 1930s.

Moreover, ethnic Koreans could maintain their identity because the Chinese government under the CCP implemented a generous policy toward ethnic minorities, allowing autonomous administrative regions and fostering ethnic education and culture, except during the Cultural Revolution. This was in sharp contrast to the fate of ethnic Koreans in the then-Soviet Union. Like the ethnic Koreans migrating to China, Russian ethnic Koreans had migrated mostly to the Russian Far East during the late 19th and early 20th centuries. However, Russian ethnic Koreans have almost lost their ethnic language and culture, particularly when compared with their counterparts in China. The main reason was that they were severely persecuted by the Soviet regime and were forced to resettle in Central Asia in the late 1930s.

The economic lives of ethnic Koreans in China in the prereform period were rather monolithic. Most of them resided in rural communities in the Northeastern provinces, concentrating on agriculture, particularly cultivating rice paddies. Mainly on the basis of this rice cultivation, they enjoyed a relatively high living standard for rural China, because rice was a relatively highly valued agricultural product. However, it did not mean that the average living standard of ethnic Koreans was higher than that of Chinese urban residents. This could not be true, because the urban living standard was much higher than the rural one, given the strict control over rural-urban migration.[9]

Another characteristic of ethnic Koreans worth mentioning is that they highly valued the education of their offspring. They mainly held the Confucian belief in the great importance of education, even though they were peasants and their ancestors had mostly been landless people back in their homeland. Their ancestors had already established many schools for ethnic and general education in the early 20th century. As of 1982, the illiteracy rate of ethnic Koreans 12 years of age and above was 10.5 percent, the lowest of the 56 Chinese nationalities and one-third the national average of 32 percent (Yun 1993, 33).

In addition, the share of ethnic Korean people with a college-level education was 19.6 out of 1,000, which was the highest of the 56 nationalities and more than three times that of the national average of 6 out of 1,000 (Yun 1993, 34). Their emphasis on education was one factor in helping ethnic Koreans maintain their language and high culture, such as literature, music, and dance. Their higher level of education also was reflected in their job structure. The share of both specialist-technician and adminis-

---

9. The share of urban population was only about 20 percent until reform began in the late 1970s. The per capita income and consumption of urban residents were respectively 2.4 and 2.9 times as large as those of rural residents in 1978, under strictly controlled population mobility (*China Statistical Yearbook 1998,* 325).

trative workers among ethnic Korean workers was about twice as large as the national average in 1982 (Yun 1993, 35). Along with their higher level of education, some ethnic Korean government officials achieved their positions on the basis of their military service in the war of liberation and/or the Korean War.

The relationship of ethnic Koreans in China with their home country was drastically skewed toward North Korea during the prereform period, which overlaps with the Cold War. Ethnic Korean society in China was thoroughly isolated from South Korea, with any bilateral contact being forbidden by both sides. But ethnic Koreans had relatively close relations and diverse interactions with North Korea, on the basis of geographical closeness and family relations.[10] Therefore, they accepted the North Korean standard in language and culture until the late 1980s, because they had little information on South Korea. However, even relations between the PRC and North Korea showed some fluctuations, going sour particularly during the Cultural Revolution. At that time, some ethnic Koreans returned to North Korea permanently to escape the persecution and famine in China.

To summarize the above discussion, ethnic Koreans formed stable communities in the Northeastern border regions of China. They engaged mostly in agriculture, earning a relatively higher income than the Chinese rural standard by cultivating rice paddies. Some of them entered government or academic careers, with higher education or military experience as a background. They could maintain their language and culture mainly because they formed several geographical clusters, where they emphasized ethnic education for their offspring. Also, they were helped by the Chinese government's rather generous policy toward them.

However, ethnic Koreans were essentially an ethnic minority living mostly in remote border regions. They were too small in number and lived too far away from the center of China to play a major role in Chinese society. Even highly educated ethnic Koreans had difficulty entering the leading group of mainstream Chinese society. One of the main reasons for this may be that they were members of a minority group. That is, they had lived in ethnic Korean communities without much experience of mainstream society and culture, namely, Han society and culture. Also, they had a rather inadequate command of the Chinese language, because most of them received bilingual education that focused on their own language.

---

10. The majority of ethnic Koreans in China, particularly in Yanbian, are originally from North Korean regions, so many of them have relatives in North Korea. In contrast, a substantial portion of ethnic Koreans in Heilongjiang and Liaoning Provinces are originally from the southern part of the Korean peninsula.

Changes in Ethnic Korean Society during the Reform Period

This section looks at the major changes that occurred in the ethnic Korean society in China during the reform period. The section is divided into three parts. The first part examines the population movement of ethnic Koreans in China in the 1980s and 1990s, which has increased remarkably. The second part examines the changes in their economic role and appraises the consequent change in their economic status. The third part examines the emerging challenges faced by the ethnic Korean society in China for maintaining their ethnic identity.

Demographic Changes

The most visible change in ethnic Korean society during China's reform period was the increased mobility of population. Although this was true of Chinese society as a whole, the extent of population movement was more conspicuous for ethnic Korean society. During the first stage until the late 1980s, before their contacts with South Korean people fully materialized, the extent and characteristics of the movement of the ethnic Korean population was similar to that of the other ethnic groups in China. However, as contacts with South Korea increased substantially during the 1990s, there were some particular changes in ethnic Korean society.

The first wave of population movement in the 1980s was mainly toward coastal urban areas or large cities in Northeastern China. That is, rural-urban migration began to materialize as migration control weakened with market reform proceeding in China.[11] Table 6.2 shows the migration of ethnic Koreans to major cities between 1982 and 1990, on the basis of official census data. It shows first that the growth rate of ethnic Korean migration to major coastal cities was remarkable. The ethnic Korean populations of such cities as Beijing, Tianjin, Dalian, and Qinghuangdao, where it used to be rather small, increased by substantial percentages.

Second, table 6.2 shows that Shenyang, Changchun, Harbin, and Yanji, the major cities in Northeastern China, substantially added to their already large ethnic Korean communities. Even within Yanbian Prefecture, movement to Yanji, the capital city of Yanbian, was observed. That is, rural-urban migration within the ethnic Korean communities also began during this period.

The motive for this migration was mainly to take advantage of new opportunities that emerged as China's economic reform proceeded. That is,

---

11. The household registration (*hukou*) system, which distinguishes the rural or urban status of each individual, has been maintained. However, abolition of food rationing and market transactions for housing made rural-urban migration much easier than in the prereform period.

many people left the ethnic community in rural areas of Northeastern China, looking for new nonagricultural activities mostly in urban areas. Some of them had accumulated a certain amount of capital for starting small businesses, with China's successful rural reform as a background. They set up individual businesses (*getihu*, in Chinese terminology) with fewer than eight employees, mostly in the cities.[12] Initially, many of them were engaged in retailing kimchi, Korean-style pickled cabbage. But many other people without the minimum capital needed to start their own business sought work opportunities in those cities, where the demand for unskilled labor was increasing.

The second wave of massive migration occurred with the reopening of contact between China and South Korea. The first momentum came in 1988, when South Korea was publicized in China for the first time because it hosted the Olympic Games. Ethnic Koreans in China were exposed to diverse types of information about South Korea, which were quite different from Chinese government or North Korean propaganda. Some ethnic Koreans were able to visit South Korea to see relatives, even though the two countries did not yet have formal diplomatic relations.

Economic transactions between South Korea and China also began to increase—a substantial portion of which then was made through a third economy (mainly Hong Kong). The second and major momentum came when the two countries established formal diplomatic relations in August 1992. Since then, bilateral economic exchanges between South Korea and China have increased very rapidly in diverse forms, including commodity trade, direct investment, and tourism.

First, bilateral trade has increased by almost 20 percent a year since 1992, reaching $31.5 billion in 2001, with South Korean exports being $18.2 billion and imports being $13.3 billion, according to Korea's trade statistics (see appendix table 6A.1). According to China's customs statistics, the volume of bilateral trade was even larger, reaching $36.0 billion in 2001, with China's imports from Korea being $23.4 billion and China's exports to Korea being $12.5 billion. Consequently, either economy has become the other's third largest trading partner, if Hong Kong is excluded as one of China's trading partners.

Second, South Korean direct investment in China has been growing steadily, albeit with some fluctuations. Currently, the second boom is in full swing; the first boom was in the period 1993-96. The cumulative number of Korean direct investment projects in China reached 6,600 with an investment value of $6 billion by July 2002, according to Korean official statistics compiled by the Korea Export-Import Bank (see appendix tables 6A.2 and 6A.3 for details). However, according to Chinese statistics, Korean direct investment in China reached $12 billion by

---

12. The new businesses were opened not just in urban areas but also in rural ones. Rural residents set up many township and village enterprises during the 1980s.

2001—more than double the Korean statistics.[13] According to the Chinese statistics, South Korea has become China's fifth largest source of foreign direct investment, following the United States, Japan, Taiwan, and Singapore.[14]

The number of South Korean visits to China, including business trips, tourist visits, and student visits, also increased substantially throughout the 1990s, surpassing 1 million in 2000 and reaching 1.3 million in 2001. At last, China became the number one foreign country chosen by Korean travelers during the first five months of 2002, surpassing Japan for the first time. The number of South Korean visitors to the PRC is estimated to reach 1.6 million in 2002, extrapolating the data for the first five months. Furthermore, the number of Korean people staying long term has increased to a substantial degree; it is estimated to reach 130,000 in mid-2002 (Embassy of the Republic of Korea in China 2002). The number of Chinese visiting Korea has been gradually growing as well, reaching 482,000 in 2001.

As bilateral economic transactions increase, the demand in China for ethnic Korean residents of China who are needed to help with these transactions also has visibly increased. They have played the roles of translator, tourist guide, information provider, and even business partner for South Korean people, particularly during the early period of bilateral contact. This phenomenon has been accompanied by a massive migration of ethnic Koreans within China toward the areas where the activities of South Korean people are concentrated. Consequently, the ethnic Korean population of such cities as Beijing and Tianjin, of several coastal cities on the Shandong peninsula (Qingdqo, Weihai, and Yantai), of Dalian and Shenyang in Liaoning Province, and even of Shanghai has increased substantially. Although we do not have formal data on ethnic Korean populations in China after 1990, we can provide several types of data from scattered sources on this recent population movement.

According to the State Ethnic Affairs Commission (2001, 171), the ethnic Korean population of Beijing was reported to reach more than 60,000 in 1998, which was almost eight times that of 1990. The same source reported that the ethnic Korean population of Shanghai increased by 60 percent from 1990 to 1995. In Tianjin, the ethnic Korean population was reported to be more than 15,000 in 1996, which was more than eight times that of 1990 (Cho and Park 1997, 1073). Also, many ethnic Koreans moved to coastal areas of Shandong Province, where Korean direct investment,

---

13. The discrepancy between the two statistics reflects the investment of many small-scale investment projects not reported to the Korean authorities, investment via a third economy, and locally financed investment.

14. This ranking excludes Hong Kong.

particularly by the small and medium-sized enterprises, is heavily concentrated.[15] That is, following the massive inflow of South Korean investments to Shandong, ethnic Koreans moved to Shandong from Northeastern areas as well. According to Pan and Huang (2002, 758), the ethnic Korean population of Shandong reached about 70,000 in 2000 (including temporary residents).

Within the Northeastern provinces, the ethnic Korean population increased in major cities in such Liaoning Province cities as Dalian and Shenyang, as Koreans firms' investment was concentrated in these areas. An ethnic Korean newspaper published in Shenyang reports that the ethnic Korean population of Dalian reached 15,000, tripling the number in 1990 (*Liaoning Chosun Wenbao*, May 29, 1997). Shenyang's ethnic Korean population was reported to have reached 120,000 in 1999, an increase of 50 percent from about 80,000 in 1990.

Conversely, the ethnic Korean population in rural areas all over Northeastern China has decreased substantially. Even the official ethnic Korean population of Yanbian Prefecture reached its peak of 860,000 in 1995, steadily decreasing afterward to reach 842,000 in 2000 (*Yanbian Statistical Yearbook* 2001, 66). However, the ethnic Korean population of Yanji City, the capital of Yanbian, continued to increase throughout the 1990s from 171,000 in 1990 to 228,000 in 2000 (*Yanji Statistical Yearbook* 2001, 85). Also, there are many reports that the ethnic Korean population of rural villages in Jilin and Heilongjiang Provinces decreased substantially during the 1990s (Huh 2001, 262).

Another major destination of ethnic Korean population movement has been South Korea. At first, starting in late 1980s, ethnic Koreans in China visited relatives in South Korea, also selling miscellaneous products from China on the street. Subsequently, they made diverse kinds of visits to South Korea. The major type was official or unofficial labor export. That is, many ethnic Korean residents of China came to South Korea seeking work, which pays much higher than in China.

Because foreigners by law are allowed to work only on limited occasions in South Korea, most of the ethnic Koreans from China work there illegally. Actually, most of them entered Korea legally as official industrial trainees, or for visits to relatives, study, or even tourism. But many of them have become illegal workers by seeking jobs, which is not allowed under their entry conditions. And these illegal *foreign* workers get jobs

---

15. According to the Korea Export-Import Bank, which publishes official data on Korea's overseas direct investment, Korean firms had invested in 2,230 projects with a value of $1.74 billion in Shandong Province as of July 2002 (http://www.koreaexim.co.kr). This is more than one-third the total number of projects with Korean investment in China (6,641), and the share in the total invested amount was 28.7 percent. According to Chinese statistics, about 3,000 enterprises with Korean investment were registered in Shandong Province by the end of 2000 (Pan and Huang 2002, 742).

mostly in "3-D" (dirty, difficult, and dangerous) positions, which average Korean people avoid.

Another type of migration of ethnic Koreans from China to South Korea has been through marriage, typically with the female coming from China. Some of the marriages have been real, whereas others have been fakes used as a channel to enter Korea. The number of visas issued for marriage by the Korean consular offices in China has been about 6,000 to 7,000 a year since the mid-1990s.[16] Even this type of an immigrant cannot get South Korean citizenship right away, because the Korean government has set a 2-year probation period due to many fake marriages. In any case, Huang (2002) points out that such a massive outflow of young ethnic Korean women of reproductive age will jeopardize the reproduction and long-term survival of the ethnic Korean society in China.

As of March 2002, there were officially 116,000 ethnic Koreans from China residing in South Korea, among whom 76,000 were staying illegally (*Kookmin Daily*, May 26, 2002). However, these statistics are only for the ethnic Koreans who entered South Korea legally, and many entered Korea illegally, mainly on smuggling ships. Although the number of these illegal immigrants is difficult to estimate, it is not negligible; the total number of ethnic Koreans from China currently in South Korea ranges from 150,000 to 200,000, according to some media reports.

To summarize the above discussions, we can see that a substantial number of ethnic Koreans migrated from rural Northeastern China to South Korea and many Chinese coastal cities during the 1990s. Besides, many ethnic Koreans of China actually migrated to Japan through diverse channels, such as tourist visits, student programs, and trade. According to Pan and Huang (2002, 72), about a quarter of ethnic Koreans have left their hometowns during the reform period. This has been a major shock to the ethnic Korean society in China, changing lives across the board— mainly from rural to urban, from closed to open, from static to dynamic.

Changes in Economic Role and Status

The population movement of ethnic Koreans in China examined above was closely linked with the changes in their economic activities. That is, both migration within China and migration to South Korea have been associated with a shift in the economic activities of the ethnic Koreans involved. Broadly speaking, they were moving out of agricultural

---

16. The number of marriage visas issued by the Korean consulate in Beijing was 7,693 in 1995, 6,139 in 1997, 6,555 in 1998, and 7,543 in 2001. In 1999 and 2000, the visa-issuing job was shared with the consular office in Shenyang, whose data cannot be obtained. (Data obtained from the Embassy of the Republic of Korea, Beijing.)

production, mainly toward industry and service sectors. This shift, in turn, entailed higher income for them and their family back home. Let us look at these issues more closely.

The intra-China migration of ethnic Koreans has been associated with at least three types of economic activities. The first type is working directly for South Korean companies or the people in China. That is, ethnic Korean people have become employees of enterprises with Korean investment or of branch offices of Korean companies in China, as translators, regular workers, or occasionally business partners.[17] The business sectors of the Korean or Korean-invested companies in China are diverse, comprising manufacturing and services.

The second type of economic activity is ethnic Koreans' having their own businesses or being employed in businesses run by other ethnic Koreans. They are mostly service-sector businesses, such as restaurants, tourism-related business, nightclubs, and motels. Most of them have at least indirect relations with South Korean people or companies. But the business sectors of ethnic Koreans in China have recently diversified, to include information technology ventures and real estate development. The third type is that some ethnic Koreans have found jobs with major Chinese companies or public agencies of diverse levels, on the basis of their ability to help with Korea-related activities.

That is, ethnic Koreans in China have been playing the role of intermediary between South Korea and China in diverse ways for the past 15 years. In particular, their ability to speak both Korean and Chinese has been their main asset. However, the assessment on their performance for this role has not always been positive. Although there have been many success stories, there have also been many failures ending in serious conflict between South Koreans and ethnic Korean-Chinese residents. The key problem in these failures seems to have been the differences between expectation and reality. Often, South Korean businesspeople expected quite high levels of performance from their ethnic Korean workers or partners which were not met—such as a high proficiency in the Chinese language, sufficient understanding of Chinese government and laws, and even loyalty to the South Korean firm.

Conversely, many ethnic Korean-Chinese residents working for South Koreans expected to receive a special reward for their contributions at a similar level as did South Koreans, which was not possible. Also, the subtle differences between the two forms of the Korean language—particularly the use of foreign-language terminology by South Korean people

---

17. According to my interview with professors at Yanbian University of Science and Technology, which is a private university founded by a Korean-American in Yanbian Prefecture to educate ethnic Koreans, about 80 percent of their graduates are recruited by Korea-related companies.

that ethnic Koreans mostly do not understand—became a source of miscommunication and/or mistranslation.

As many conflicts arise between the "two" Korean languages and South Korean people's understanding of Chinese language and society improves, South Korean people and companies tend to depend less on ethnic Korean residents of China. In particular, some large Korean companies strategically employ Chinese of Han nationality rather than Korean nationality as part of their localization effort. That is, they think employing Han nationals with strong credentials would be beneficial for them to do business with major Chinese companies or deal with Chinese bureaucrats. In that sense, the role of intermediaries between China and South Korea as played by ethnic Koreans in China recently has been seriously challenged.[18] However, the demand for capable ethnic Koreans by Korean companies is still strong, but under the condition that they compete with other Chinese workers. Also, many small and medium-sized Korean companies still urgently need ethnic Koreans' help to do business in the Chinese market.

Yet ethnic Korean migrants from China are engaged mostly in 3-D jobs in South Korea, such as that of construction worker for men and waitress or factory worker in labor-intensive industries for women. That is, most of them are filling the positions that most domestic workers avoid. Actually, many ethnic Korean workers from China have experienced industrial accidents in Korea leading to serious injury or even death, reflecting their poor working conditions. Also, their employers often treat them unfairly, taking advantage of their status as illegal immigrants.

Under normal conditions, however, these workers earn an income almost 10 times higher than they would earn in China. At the same time, many of them learn the know-how to operate small businesses or industrial techniques for small-scale workshops while they are working in South Korea. Actually, many of them set up their own business after returning to China, using the capital they accumulated in Korea and following the business model they learned from their Korean experiences.

We can cite another role ethnic Koreans in China have played for the past decade, namely, as intermediaries between South and North Korea. Though there are many barriers for South Koreans to contact North Koreans, ethnic Koreans in China can access North Korea rather easily. Therefore, there is demand from South Korean people or companies for ethnic Koreans to provide information on North Korea or to link them with North Korean counterparts. The demand from the South Korean side is very diverse, including the search for the whereabouts of separated family members, information on tradable goods between the two Koreas, and

---

18. Both South Korean business circles and ethnic Korean leaders in China agree that the potential role of ethnic Koreans in linking China and South Korea has not been fully realized. But each side tends to think that the main blame should go to the other side.

the situation of the North Korean economy. Sometimes, ethnic Koreans play a critical role in helping separated family members to meet somewhere in China or in providing up-to-date information on North Korea.

As the economic activities of ethnic Korean residents of China change as described above, ethnic Korean entrepreneurs have appeared. The first generation of ethnic Korean entrepreneurs, who began their business in the 1980s, had mostly rural backgrounds, without much formal education. They grasped business opportunities arising from China's reform process, particularly founding and managing township-village enterprises under freer conditions than state-owned enterprises. Some of them entered the business circle, taking advantage of opportunities arising from the rapidly increasing contacts between South Korea and China in the early 1990s. Some of them were successful enough to have large-scale enterprises by the early 1990s. However, most of them did not have the ability to manage a large business organization, and soon sank. Currently, only a fraction of the first generation of businesspeople has achieved modest success managing medium-sized enterprises.

However, a new generation of ethnic Korean entrepreneurs has emerged since the late 1990s. They are distinguished from the earlier generation of entrepreneurs in several aspects. First, they tend to have more formal education, with most of them having at least a bachelor's degree. Second, many of them have worked as government officials or visited foreign countries, typically South Korea or Japan as students, before starting their businesses. Currently, their business sectors are centered on trading, developing and/or managing real estate, construction, and information technology ventures. It seems that this new generation has a better understanding of how markets function, how modern enterprises operate, and how the outside world is changing. They might have more of a potential to manage their current businesses as large-scale modern enterprises than the previous generation.

However, not even one business run by ethnic Koreans is successful enough to enter the list of the 500 largest private enterprises in China. According to my interviews with ethnic Korean entrepreneurs and academicians, at most 1 or 2 ethnic Korean businesses belong to the top 100 private enterprises in some municipalities, such as Dalian and Shenyang. That is, ethnic Korean businesses could not yet enter China's national private business circle. Even the most successful ethnic Korean business is just a local trader. Also, no one with an ethnic Korean background is the chief executive of any of the large-scale state-owned enterprises that account for the lion's share of China's large enterprises.

We can conclude that ethnic Koreans are at the periphery of the Chinese economy. They are engaged mostly in the consumption-oriented services sector, though they have come out of their closed ethnic communities in Northeastern China during the past more than 20 years of China's reform.

The question then is: why could they not enter the main stage of the Chinese economy? According to the ethnic Korean academicians and entrepreneurs I interviewed, there are several reasons. First, they point to the lack of business talent among ethnic Koreans in China. Although ethnic Koreans put great emphasis on education, they have used their top talents to enter academic or government careers reflecting their traditional Confucian values. They have produced some top-level scientists, many professors and researchers, and even a few high-ranking officials in the party or government hierarchy. However, they have not produced chief executives of either state-owned or private enterprises. Recently, though, some of their top talents have begun to enter the business circle, suggesting that they may have some successful businesses in the future.

Second, ethnic minorities have many hurdles to success in China's mainstream business circle. It is widely known that the network of connections (*guanxi*) with government or bank officials is a key factor in doing successful business in China. Ethnic minorities, including ethnic Koreans, are relatively weak in establishing networks of connections in China, compared with Han nationals. Additionally, ethnic Koreans' command of the Chinese language in general does not reach a high level, because most of them were brought up under bilingual environments until high school. However, fluency in the Chinese language and a shared Han culture would be key factors for establishing connections with mainstream Chinese communities.

We have already seen that contacts with South Korea, which began in the late 1980s, were a major shock to the ethnic Korean society in China. How, then, should the influence of South Korea on the ethnic Korean economy in China be assessed? There are two contrasting evaluations. The overall evaluation is very positive, in the sense that ethnic Koreans in China could have opportunities to earn income and intangible know-how for diverse economic activities through their contacts with South Korean people, directly or indirectly. By utilizing these favorable conditions, ethnic Koreans could have achieved a relatively higher living standard in China on average,[19] and many of them have accumulated a certain level of wealth. Therefore, it is difficult to deny the economic benefits of South Korea and its people for ethnic Koreans in China.[20]

According to another evaluation, however, in the long run South Korea might constitute a serious barrier for ethnic Koreans in China seeking to

---

19. There are no publicly available data showing average incomes of diverse nationalities in China. However, we can get several types of anecdotal and indirect evidence, which suggest that ethnic Koreans' average income is higher than the overall average income of Chinese people. This is mainly due to the extra opportunities related to South Korea, which are only accessible to ethnic Koreans.

20. It may be compared with the contribution of overseas Chinese to the economy of their hometowns in southern China, although the extent of their contribution might be less.

become an independent and affluent ethnic group. That is, ethnic Koreans have become much too dependent upon South Korea, thereby making themselves vulnerable to shocks from South Korea. Actually, when the South Korean economy went through a financial crisis in the period 1997-98, the ethnic Korean economy in China had a difficult time as well. At the microeconomic level, some ethnic Korean elders worry that many talented ethnic Koreans choose a relatively easier career connected with Korean companies rather than seeking a risky but potentially much more rewarding career in mainstream Chinese society. This concern seems to be legitimate to a certain extent, although it should not be exaggerated.

Can Ethnic Identity Be Maintained?

As we have seen in the above descriptions, China's deepening economic reform and increasing contacts with South Korea have brought major changes to the ethnic Korean society in China during the past 20 years. These changes have been and will become even larger challenges to ethnic Koreans in China as they seek to survive as a distinct ethnic group. The changes are very serious in the sense that the ethnic Koreans' ethnic identity, which they have kept for the past century under highly unfavorable conditions, may be in jeopardy in the long run.

The key question is whether ethnic Koreans will be able to keep their ethnic language and culture in the long run, even when many of them leave their rather isolated ethnic communities and mix with and are outnumbered by Han people in scattered cities all around China. Many rural ethnic Korean villages in the three northeastern provinces have already been hollowed out, with only the elderly and some children remaining. Subsequently, many ethnic elementary and intermediate schools have been closed due to decreasing enrollment and/or a lack of qualified teachers.[21] There are also many broken families, with a family member living far away in South Korea or somewhere in China. After all, the traditional rural ethnic Korean communities in northeastern China have disintegrated to a certain degree, and this disintegration is impossible to reverse.

Yet ethnic Koreans have moved to many cities all around China. Some cities where ethnic Koreans are clustered, particularly in Northeastern

---

21. According to Huang (2002, 29), the number of ethnic Korean elementary schools in Yanbian Prefecture decreased from 419 in 1985 to 177 in 1995, and the number of ethnic middle and high schools decreased from 118 in 1985 to 49 in 1995. The situation is even worse in other regions. The number of ethnic Korean elementary schools in Heilongjiang Province decreased from 382 in 1990 to 51 in 1997, and the number of ethnic middle and high schools decreased from 77 to 15 during the same period.

China (e.g., Yanji, Shenyang, and Changchun), will be able to maintain ethnic Korean education and culture even under these rapidly changing situations. For example, in Shenyang, where the ethnic Korean population has been increasing, there has been a movement to construct new ethnic Korean towns in the suburbs. It is likely that these northeastern urban areas with relatively large ethnic Korean populations will continue to constitute centers for maintaining the ethnic Korean identity.

However, many ethnic Koreans are now living in rather small numbers in many other cities, where many are separated from their families. The governments of these cities with a small number of *temporary* ethnic Korean populations do not provide any preferential treatment for them.[22] Therefore, these scattered ethnic Koreans face difficulties in forming communities or establishing schools to teach their language and culture. Some leaders of the ethnic Korean communities in these cities are making efforts to establish such private schools.[23] However, they lack the funds and labor to foster these unofficial schools as systematic educational institutions. Therefore, it is uncertain whether ethnic Koreans can form communities to maintain their language and culture in the cities where they have moved in recent years, such as Beijing, Tianjin, Shanghai, and Indio.

Furthermore, more fundamental questions arise as to what constitutes ethnic Koreans' ethnic identity and how it will be maintained. Actually, it has become a trend for some ethnic Korean parents to send their children to Han national schools rather than ethnic schools, seeking a better education, particularly in the Chinese language. Thus, some ethnic Koreans are opting to assimilate the Chinese majority culture by identifying themselves as Chinese citizens rather than emphasizing their ethnic minority identity. But some others are attempting to learn and copy the culture of South Korea as much as possible, giving up many peculiar aspects of ethnic Koreans in China.

Some others, however, still claim the necessity of their peculiar culture and the worth of their potential role. Actually, in China there is a big debate among ethnic Korean intellectuals on the real identity of ethnic Koreans in China (Kim and Oh 2001; Huh 2001; Cho and Park 1997, 397-420). The ethnic Koreans in China, not just common people but also their leaders, seem to be confused about their identity. Therefore, it is quite uncertain how ethnic Koreans will be changing over time. But it is at least quite evident that they are in the midst of a major upheaval.

---

22. Most of the ethnic Korean people living in major Chinese cities are officially temporary migrants or illegal migrants who have not had their household registration (*hukou*) transferred to these cities.

23. E.g., the ethnic Korean community in Beijing was established in an ethnic school open on weekends and managed mostly by volunteers.

The Emerging Korean Society in China:
Immigrants from South Korea

As bilateral contacts have increased between South Korea and China (briefly described in the previous section), a growing number of South Koreans has actually migrated to China. Although official migration is not allowed, a substantial number of South Koreans stay in China for a prolonged period. The reasons for these long-term stays are very diverse, including business, social service, and study. Consequently, in many parts of China, new Korean communities are emerging, which are distinct from the traditional ethnic Korean communities.

A majority of the de facto immigrants has come to China for business purposes. In particular, each direct investment by South Korean companies requires that a certain number of expatriate managers and technicians come to China. Actually, there are more than 10,000 Korean direct investment projects in China—many more than the official Korean number of more than 6,000. Assuming that each investment project needs 5 expatriate workers on average, the number of Koreans in China associated with direct investment would only reach 50,000.

The Embassy of the Republic of Korea in China (2002) indicates that as of June 30, 2002, about 35,000 South Koreans were issued official residential permits by the Chinese public security authorities. The Korean Embassy estimates that the total number of long-term residents in China with Korean citizenship had reached 130,000,[24] including more than 35,000 with residential permits (table 6.3). This aggregated estimate was based on the regional estimates made by associations of Korean people established in many localities in China. Further, it estimates that the number of long-term residents has been growing about 40 percent annually since 1998, on the basis of the same sources.

The regional distribution of South Korean de facto immigrants is closely related to the locations of Korean businesses in China. Table 6.3 shows the regional distribution of South Koreans in China. Let us first look at the distribution of Koreans with official residential permits, as shown in the first column of table 6.3. Beijing leads, with 7,995 people, followed by Shandong (6,947), Tianjin (4,850), Liaoning (3,637), Jilin (2,893), Shanghai (2,676), Jiangsu (2,232), and Heilongjiang (1,034). Among the 31 provincial-level regions of China, 30 regions (except Tibet) have a certain number of South Koreans with an official residential permit. The regional distribution of the long-term residents from Korea shows a shape similar to that of the people with residential permit. Some visible differences are that Shanghai's Korean population (7,500) was estimated to be larger than

---

24. In my interview at the Korean Embassy in Beijing, the consul said that this estimate is a conservative one, suggesting that the real number of Koreans in China might be higher.

Table 6.3　Regional distribution of South Korean residents in China, June 2001

City	People with residential permit	Percentage share	Long-term residents (estimate)	Percentage share
Beijing	7,995	22.7	30,000	23.1
Shandong	6,497	18.5	30,000	23.1
Tianjin	4,850	13.8	20,000	15.4
Liaoning	3,637	10.3	11,200	8.6
Jilin	2,893	8.2	6,600	5.1
Shanghai	2,676	7.6	7,500	5.8
Jiangsu	2,232	6.3	4,000	3.1
Heilongjiang	1,034	2.9	1,600	1.2
Zhejiang	696	2.0	2,000	1.5
Guangdong	568	1.6	5,700	4.4
Fujian	315	0.9	500	0.4
Shaanxi	302	0.9	n.a.	n.a.
Sichuan	289	0.8	n.a.	n.a.
Hunan	223	0.6	n.a.	n.a.
Other cities	969	2.8	11,000	8.5
Total	35,176	100	130,100	100

n.a. = not available

Source: Embassy of the Republic of Korea in China (2002).

that of Jilin (6,600), and Guangdong's share (4.4 percent) was much larger than that of people with a residential permit (1.6 percent).

This regional distribution is quite different from that of ethnic Koreans of China. The number of Korean long-term residents in northeastern China, particularly in Jilin and Heilongjiang Provinces, is relatively much smaller compared with the ethnic minority Koreans of China. In contrast, the new de facto immigrants from South Korea tend to cluster in Shandong Province and in the major cities, namely, Beijing, Tianjin, and Shanghai. Among the Northeastern provinces, Liaoning attracted the largest number of Koreans, mainly because it has a better environment for business, being located in the coastal area. As is shown above, ethnic Koreans are moving toward those areas where people from South Korea cluster.

Also, "Koreatowns"—which are similar to Koreatowns in Los Angeles and New York—have been emerging in several cities in China with substantial Korean populations. For example, Wangjing, which is in the northeastern suburbs of Beijing, has become a major Koreatown with more than 10,000 residents, many Korean-style stores, and prevalent Korean ways of life. These Koreatowns around China attract ethnic Korean-Chinese people as well, because they can find many business opportunities there, mostly in service sectors.

Considering the current trend of economic exchanges between South Korea and China, we can easily predict that the number of Korean residents in China will continue to rise. They will certainly form *new* Korean communities in many cities of China, with their own characteristics being established over time. They will play the key role in Korea-China economic exchanges, which are expected to increase further in the future. They will interact with the *old* ethnic Korean society in China through diverse channels, sometimes helping each other and sometimes conflicting.

Conclusions

This chapter has looked at the situation of ethnic Koreans as a minority group in China, mainly from an economic perspective. We have found that ethnic Korean society in China has been undergoing major changes for more than 10 years. China's economic reform set the stage for these changes, and increasing contacts with South Korea have provided major impetus.

Ethnic Koreans have been migrating out of the rural ethnic communities in northeastern China to many of the urban areas in China and South Korea. Consequently, traditional ethnic Korean villages have been hollowing out, while the ethnic Korean populations of major Chinese and South Korean cities have increased significantly. At the same time, ethnic Koreans' economic activities have been diversifying into secondary and tertiary sectors out of agriculture. Consequently, their average income level has been rising along with the overall income strata in China.

South Korea has contributed much to the transition process of these ethnic Koreans in China by providing many economic opportunities. However, some conflicts have arisen between the two "Koreans" in this process, thereby constraining the full realization of the potential role of the ethnic Koreans. Furthermore, the ethnic Koreans have not been able to enter the main stage of the Chinese economy, which has shown remarkable success as well for more than 20 years. Some researchers suggest that the existence of South Korea might be a factor hindering the ethnic Koreans from entering mainstream Chinese society.

Yet, it is questioned whether the ethnic Korean society in China can maintain its identity in the long run. That is, as ethnic Koreans migrate from the rural ethnic villages in northeastern China, they are mixing with and being outnumbered by the Han population of major Chinese cities— or by South Koreans in that country. Their ethnic education has been collapsing in rural northeastern China, signaling the loss of their language and the shrinking of their culture in the future. Furthermore, some ethnic Koreans are even raising questions about their identity itself. Therefore, the future of the ethnic Korean society seems to be quite uncertain.

Finally, a growing number of South Korean people have settled in China. As China achieves rapid economic growth, Koreans are moving to China, regarding China as a land of opportunity adjacent to the Korean peninsula. This trend will certainly continue in the near future. Consequently, new Korean communities—which have characteristics distinct from ethnic Korean society—are emerging in many Chinese cities. It is certain that the role of this new Korean society in China will be increasing. The relationship between the *new* Korean society and the *old* ethnic Korean-Chinese people will be complementary to a certain extent but competitive in some aspects.

Appendix 6.1: Tables

Table 6A.1 South Korea's trade with China (millions of dollars; percent of Korea's total exports or imports)

| Year | Exports to China | | Imports from China | | Trade balance |
	Millions of dollars	Percent of total exports	Millions of dollars	Percent of total exports	
1980	15	0.09	26	0.12	−11
1985	40	0.15	478	1.8	−438
1988	372	0.6	1,387	2.9	−1,015
1990	585	0.9	2,268	3.2	−1,683
1992	2,654	3.5	3 725	4.6	−1,071
1993	5,151	6.2	3,929	4.7	1,222
1995	9,144	7.3	7,401	5.5	1,743
1996	11,377	8.8	8,539	5.7	2,838
1997	13,572	10.0	9,975	6.9	3,597
1998	1,944	9.0	6,484	7.0	5,460
1999	13,685	9.5	8,667	7.2	5,018
2000	18,455	10.7	12,799	8.0	5,656
2001	18,190	12.1	13,302	9.4	4,888

Source: Korea Trade Association KOTIS Database.

Table 6A.2 The flow of South Korean direct investment in China, 1992-2002

| Year | Approval | | Implementation | |
	Number of projects	Amount (millions of dollars)	Number of projects	Amount (millions of dollars)
1992	269	221.5	171	141.2
1993	630	622.7	378	264.0
1994	1,065	820.5	841	632.1
1995	880	1,239.8	740	823.5
1996	917	1,678.9	730	835.6
1997	742	906.4	623	633.2
1998	308	802.9	242	619.8
1999	541	482.6	431	308.1
2000	850	667.2	668	310.2
2001	1,068	885.1	990	466.1
2002[a]	714	790.5	610	356.6
Cumulative balance	7,573	9,188.5	6,641	6,045.9

a. January through July 2002 only.

Sources: Ministry of Finance and Economy (up to 1998); Korea Export-Import Bank (from 1999 and cumulative balance).

Table 6A.3 Regional distribution of South Korean investment in China, 2002

Province	Number of projects	Investment amount (millions of dollars)
Shandong	2,230	1,735.8
Tianjin	610	782.5
Liaoning	1,172	593.3
Jiangsu	365	715.5
Shanghai	299	519.1
Beijing	375	454.6
Guangdong	159	240.5
Zhejiang	166	232.8
Jilin	625	187.3
Heilongjiang	259	171.3
Hunan	10	102.2
Hebei	166	78.4

Note: Cumulative balance as of July 2002.

Source: Korea Export-Import Bank.

References

Cho, Ryongho and Moonil, Park, ed. 1997. *A Study of the Development Strategy of Ethnic Korean People Staging into the 21st Century* (in Korean). Shenyang: Liaoning Ethnic Press.

Embassy of the Republic of Korea in China, Consular Section. 2002. *The Present Status of Long-Term Korean Residents in China.* Bejing: Embassy of the Republic of Korea in China, Consular Section.

Han, Sang Bok, and Tae Hwan Kwon. 1993. *Ethnic Koreans in Yanbian, China: Social Structure and Its Change* (in Korean). Seoul: Seoul National University Press.

Huh, Myungchul. 2001. A Thought on Maintaining the Identity of Ethnic Koreans in China. In *Cultural Advantage and Development Strategy of Ethnic Korean Society in China* (in Korean), ed. Kangil Kim and Myungchul Huh. Yanji: Yanbian Peoples Press.

Huang, Youfu. 2002. Recent Changes and Tasks of Ethnic Korean Education in China (in Korean). *China Ethnicity* 3: 26-29.

Kim, Byungho, and Sangsun Oh. 2001. The Status of Ethnic Korean Society in China. In *Cultural Advantage and Development Strategy of Ethnic Korean Society in China* (in Korean), ed. Kangil Kim and Myungchul Huh. Yanji: Yanbian Peoples Press.

Kim, Wonsuk. 1992. A Study on the History of Immigration of Ethnic Koreans in China. In *East Asian Studies* 25 (in Korean). Seoul: Institute of East Asian Studies, Sogang University.

Pan, Longhai, and Youfu Huang, eds. 2002. *Ethnic Koreans in China: Getting into the 21st Century* (in Chinese). Yanji: Yanbian University Press.

State Ethnic Affairs Commission, ed. 2001. *Chinese Nationalities (Zhongguo Minzu)* (in Chinese). Beijing: China Nationalities Press.

State Ethnic Affairs Commission and State Statistical Bureau, ed. 1993. *Economy of Chinese Nationalities (Zhongguo Minzu Jingji)* (in Chinese). Beijing: China Statistical Press.

Yun, Ho. 1993. Population Trend of Ethnic Koreans in China (in Korean). *Journal of the Population Association of Korea* 16, no. 1: 19-36.

Comments on Chapter 6

BYONG HYON KWON

Si Joong Kim's chapter basically describes the evolution of the economic status and role of ethnic Koreans in China. Because there have not been many studies on ethnic Koreans from an economic perspective, we could name his essay as one of the pioneering works on this subject. He makes three main points.

First, Kim points out that the Chinese Economic Reform and Open Door policy in the late 1970s had been working as a dynamic force changing the community of ethnic Koreans. Many rural ethnic Koreans started to migrate unofficially to urban areas, seeking economic profits from the new policy. And in the late 1980s, many of them even migrated to remote areas of large cities, such as Beijing, Shandong, Shanghai, and Tianjin, to help local governments promote economic interactions between China and South Korea.

Second, this trend was reinforced by the diplomatic normalization between China and South Korea in 1992. Many qualified ethnic Koreans now migrated to focal points of Korean direct investment. Qingdao, Weihai, and Yantai in Shandong Province are three key cities that have absorbed many of these ethnic Koreans to work as facilitators between Korean and Chinese business activities.

Third, though Kim emphasized the new Chinese policy and diplomatic normalization as key factors for change vis-à-vis the ethnic Korean community in China, his overall evaluation of ethnic Koreans is that they are still relatively low in economic status—they are outside the mainstream Chinese society, which is dominated by people of Han nationality. He mentions—as key clues supporting his arguments—that no ethnic Korean company is in the top 500 Chinese companies and that no chief executive of a major Chinese state-owned enterprise is an ethnic Korean. Though it is not vividly described, his prediction for the future of ethnic Koreans seems to be a gloomy one, as they possibly gradually lose their identity.

Byong Hyon Kwon is chairman and president of the Overseas Koreans Foundation and former South Korean ambassador extraordinary and plenipotentiary to Australia, China, and Myanmar.

Basically, I agree with Kim's three major points. Yet his chapter has gaps in a couple of interesting areas—to be investigated in his follow-up research. First, he does not mention much about the origin of ethnic Koreans in China, which would have explained their later economic status. Most diasporas start with turbulence in the source country; many overseas Chinese left China in the midst of extreme instability during the late Qing Dynasty. Likewise, ethnic Koreans in China left the Korean peninsula to escape famine and colonial Japanese dictatorship—and even because of a Japanese "Migration Project" that was intended to reclaim a barren area so that it could be run more efficiently by the Japanese puppet regime in Manchuria.

As such, ethnic Koreans are more interested in sectors related to food production than to manufacturing ones. In this regard, ethnic Koreans selected to remain in China would have tried to stay in peasant communities rather than move to areas oriented toward industry, even after the end of World War II. In addition, the deep-rooted Confucianism of ethnic Koreans reinforced their desire to remain in the less productive agricultural sector.

Second, though general education was stressed by ethnic Koreans in China, it is doubtful whether it included the type of practical technical and professional training that stresses the importance of businesses and manufacturing. It could also be surmised that most education would have been handled not at the advanced national level but by mediocre local administrations lacking an understanding of the importance of business skills and modernization.

This situation raises the fundamental question of the quality of education. Many data show a high ratio of ethnic Koreans concentrated in administrative and public service jobs. Conversely, it would be very rare to find talented and promising ethnic Koreans serving as government officials at the national level, except in a couple of symbolic positions. In my interviews, many ethnic Korean businesspeople in China who had originally been government officials confided that they had turned to small and medium-sized businesses rather than continue seeking careers in government because they had become frustrated by invisible discrimination from the core group of Han people.

Judging from these examples, I agree that ethnic Koreans in China have gloomy future prospects. It might be true that minorities are useful coalition groups in the midst of internal conflicts like civil war. But after stabilization, the role of minorities diminishes with the stronger role of mainstream, dominant nationalities. As a matter of fact, ethnic Korean celebrities made strong contributions to the initial stage of the founding of the People's Republic of China and afterward were promoted to membership in Chinese high society; examples include General Zhao Nanqi and Minister Li Dezhu.

There are really few options for ethnic Koreans to elevate their economic status in the context of China's rapid economic development, which is mostly dominated by the majority of Han people. Key activities are observed in the coastal south, where many overseas Chinese millionaires seize most economic opportunities. These phenomena could not be corrected when we investigated personnel mobility between China and South Korea. Most ethnic Koreans working in Korea have their jobs in the so-called 3-D—dirty, difficult, and dangerous—occupations in which it is difficult to accumulate capital.

If the situation is like this, it would be easy to forecast ethnic Koreans losing their identity, either by being fully assimilated into Chinese society or through increasing intermarriage with the Chinese in future. In recent years, the South Korean government seems to have paid much more attention to taking better care of ethnic Koreans in China. Legally speaking, however, those ethnic Koreans already have adopted China as their mother country, and the Korean government has no option to support them directly without infringing on the sovereignty of China. More seriously, many ethnic Koreans who originated in North Korea rather than South Korea have sympathy for North Korea.

Another interesting situation that Kim examines is that of new Korean residents in China. He uses Korean investment in China as a starting point for estimating this population. If 50,000 Koreans are assumed to work in China, their total population should be at least 150,000, assuming an average family size of about 3. In addition, if we add 20,000 students studying in China, then the population of new Korean residents in China would be estimated at up to 200,000, which means that they will become a more critical factor than expected in changing ethnic Korean society in diverse ways in the future.

Kim's research could be developed further with more clear-cut explanations of various aspects of the subject, such as why many ethnic Korean women marry Koreans, whether the relatively slower population growth of ethnic Koreans will continue, how ethnic Koreans are less talented in business, and why new ethnic Koreans do not create another cluster in the cities of Chengdu, Kunming, and Wuhan, which have direct flights from South Korea. Though, as was mentioned above, Kim's chapter has a couple of shortcomings, its overall contribution to the study of the ethnic Korean diaspora cannot be underestimated.

7

The Global Economic Outlook and Business and Investment Opportunities for Overseas Koreans

C. FRED BERGSTEN, MARCUS NOLAND, AND IL SAKONG

This final chapter discusses the global economic outlook with a particular focus on business and investment opportunities for overseas Koreans. Having, in the rest of the book, discussed overseas Koreans and their impact on both host and home economies, here we address the outlook for those economies and what opportunities might be presented as a result for overseas Koreans.

In the first section of this chapter, C. Fred Bergsten briefly discusses the United States. In the second section, Marcus Noland discusses Japan and North Korea. And in the third section, Il SaKong comments on the South Korean economy.

SaKong's experience particularly qualifies him to make observations on the South Korean economy. He was South Korea's minister of finance in the late 1980s and senior secretary to the president for economic affairs. More recently, he has served as Korea's ambassador for international economy and trade, and he has been a member of the President's Council of National Economic Affairs. He has had a series of major international responsibilities over the years as consultant to the IMF. He was chairman of the ASEM Vision Group, which provided advice to the Asia-Europe economic meetings. This group brought together 26 representatives from

C. Fred Bergsten is the director of the Institute for International Economics. Marcus Noland is a senior fellow at the Institute for International Economics. Il SaKong is chairman of the Institute for Global Economics.

the ASEM countries and tried to envision what that new international institution could do.

SaKong also chaired a very innovative group a few years ago called the Emerging Markets Eminent Persons Group. There have been many eminent persons groups, but most of them have been among representatives of industrial countries and most of the discussion of the international financial architecture has been among industrial countries. SaKong put together a group to bring into that debate the perspectives of the emerging-market economies. Thus SaKong has had a very wide and active series of roles. He and C. Fred Bergsten have also for the past 8 years cochaired the Korea-United States 21st Century Council, which brings together top government and former government officials, private-sector leaders, and intellectuals from the two countries to help chart the relationship both between the countries bilaterally and their joint responsibilities in the international economy on an ongoing annual basis.

The United States

Because the purpose of this chapter is to offer thoughts that might be helpful to overseas Korean businesspeople, this section focuses less on the short run and more on the medium- to long-term outlook for the United States. It seems likely that any businessperson—in considering whether to do business and make investments in various parts of the world, or in choosing among the alternative locations—would be particularly interested in the medium- to long-term outlook and in the fundamental prospects for the various economies that are being considered.

In thinking about the United States, and in fact most countries, probably the single most important variable is the outlook for productivity growth. The main driver of any country's economic progress, in terms of output growth and particularly in terms of real incomes and standards of living, is its productivity. If it can achieve steady and rapid growth in productivity, then the outlook is rather good, and investments are worthwhile. The United States during the past 5 to 10 years has experienced a dramatic increase in its annual productivity growth. In fact, the major reason why the US economy did so well in the late 1990s, and in fact had quite a shallow recession and has had such a strong recovery in 2002, is the rapid growth of productivity.

That productivity growth is a fairly new phenomenon for the United States. From the early 1970s until the early 1990s, the United States in fact had very poor productivity performance. Its productivity was growing only at about 1 percent a year, and that was the underlying reason that there were so many doubts about the strength of the US economy all through the 1970s, 1980s, and into the early 1990s. It is hard to remember, but only 10 or 15 years ago, there were great doubts about the competitiveness and capabilities of the US economy. Many people around the world thought that Japan was not only far superior to the United States but also becoming a dominant force in the world. That of course has all reversed during the past decade.

In the cases of both Japan and Europe, productivity growth has actually been cut in half during the course of the past decade compared with the previous period, whereas the opposite has happened in the United States. US productivity growth has doubled or tripled, depending on how one measures it, during the past decade, particularly since the mid-1990s, compared with the previous 20 years. That pickup in US productivity growth was not unique to the boom of the late 1990s, during which its economy was growing so strongly. In fact, US productivity continued to grow rapidly right through the recession of 2001, and it continued very strongly during the first three quarters of 2002, when—despite press and other comments sometimes to the contrary—the US economy grew strongly and bounced back rapidly from the recession of a year earlier.

As was noted, productivity had grown by only about 1 percent a year in the 1970s and 1980s. During the period starting in about 1995, US productivity has grown between 2 and 3 percent a year, probably averaging about $2\frac{1}{2}$ percent. Virtually every American economist who studies these issues now agrees that US productivity growth has experienced this dramatic increase and is likely to continue at this much higher level. There is some debate whether it is $2\frac{1}{2}$ or 3 percent, but that is the range widely considered as the ongoing underpinning for the US economy.

Why is productivity growth so important? The simple reason is that economic growth, the expansion of output, is a simple sum of productive growth, which is labor productivity in most definitions, and the expansion of the labor supply. In the case of the United States, productivity is growing $2\frac{1}{2}$ to 3 percent a year and the labor supply is growing between 1 and $1\frac{1}{2}$ percent, so the prospect for medium- to long-run economic expansion in the United States is something like $3\frac{1}{2}$ to 4 percent a year. That is rather impressive for a mature, high-income industrial economy like the United States. It is about double the rate of growth the country's economists and policymakers thought it was capable of back in the 1970s and 1980s and even in the early 1990s. At that time, the conventional wisdom was that output potential in the United States was only able to expand at about 2 percent a year. Now, the consensus is that the number is closer to $3\frac{1}{2}$ to 4 percent, meaning that the prospects for the United States over the longer run are quite good.

It must be stressed that this is a supply-side picture of the economy, which does not mean that the United States will grow $3\frac{1}{2}$ to 4 percent every year; the business cycle has not been repealed, and there still are recessions, as we saw in the United States a year ago. But as a medium- to long-run proposition, the crucial variable is productivity growth—what it implies for the expansion of the economy's output capacity—and in the

United States, that number has jumped quite sharply and is about $3\frac{1}{2}$ to 4 percent a year.

The interesting question is why that improvement happened all of a sudden in the United States, and even economists who study it closely are not really sure. There are different theses, but the broad picture is that it is a combination of two elements. One is of course the output of information technology (IT) products and the IT revolution. Investment in that sector of the economy expanded very rapidly in the second half of the 1990s and was a major element in the sharp pickup in total factor productivity and therefore the overall prospects for the US economy. However—and this is the important point—the IT revolution and the increased production of new technologies, were *not* the major reason why US productivity growth increased so sharply.

It was not the production of the new technologies that made the major difference; rather, it was the *utilization* of new technologies by a whole range of traditional industries—housing, automobiles, financial services, retail trade, and wholesale trade. Essentially, the "old" economy was learning to adjust to a new situation and use new tools—the computer revolution, the Internet, and the computer software applications that became so widespread in the 1990s. The ability of a whole range of US industries to adapt and apply these new technologies led to this sharp increase in overall US productivity and output growth. Indeed, if the main factor in productivity growth had been IT production, the country would not have gotten too much improvement in its overall economy, because the IT sector is a very small share of the total US economic picture (probably less than 10 percent of the economy as a whole). Rather, it was the transfer of those new technologies to the traditional sectors—a transfer that, for some reason, all of a sudden began to proliferate in the mid-1990s—that led to this sharp improvement in the productivity of the economy as a whole.

We do not fully understand why this technology transfer proliferated at this particular time, much less how much longer it is going to continue and at what pace. We do know, as we look back at the history of other technological revolutions, that new inventions of a fundamental nature, going back to the steam engine and the telephone and the airplane, take quite a long time to be commercialized and adapted to daily economic reality. But once they are applied in an economically meaningful sense, their impact is rather long-lasting and pervasive, and indeed the previous technological revolutions have often led not to just years but decades of better performance, as industry after industry learns how to use them, further refines the adaptation of the new technology, and fuels a continuing economic expansion of rather impressive dimensions. That is why many believe that the evidence for the widespread adaptation of new technologies in the United States in roughly the past 10 years may in fact result in a continuation of higher productivity growth and may even further accelerate that growth.

The main spokesperson for that point of view perhaps has been US Federal Reserve Chairman Alan Greenspan. Already by the mid-1990s, Greenspan was speaking more actively than probably anyone else, at least in US public life, about the productivity revolution and the increased potential for rapid economic growth that it provided in the United States. He in fact based monetary policy largely on that view, letting US unemployment rates decline very substantially below levels at which previous Federal Reserve Boards would have tightened monetary policy because of a fear of inflation. But he believed that the pickup in productivity growth would turn out to be lasting and that the US economy could run at a higher rate of growth and a lower level of unemployment without jeopardizing price stability and undermining the economic picture. It turned out that he was correct—fortunately so—and therefore the United States saw sharp economic growth and much lower unemployment in the late 1990s.

Of course, as with many new technology developments and periods, part of it was overdone. The IT sector itself became hugely overinvested, excess capacity developed, equity prices ran far beyond what was justified, and the bubble burst, leading to the sharp decline in the stock market. Despite that decline, however, the US economy has picked up very sharply in 2002.

In conclusion, it simply needs to be stressed that the United States has had three quarters of very strong economic growth in 2002. This needs to be noted because, if one listens to some media presentations, one would think that the United States was still in a recession. In fact, however, in 2002 its economy grew at an annual rate of 5 percent in the first quarter, domestic demand grew at an annual rate of 3 percent in the second quarter, and economic growth was probably about 4 percent in the third quarter. So for 2002 as a whole, the US economy has bounced back with an economic expansion of something like 4 percent. It may not continue quite at that level in the fourth quarter and going into 2003, but it will probably be at least in the range of 3 to 3½ percent going forward.

Yet the basic point is that the United States has experienced a sharp increase in productivity growth, which likely provides the basis for very promising economic performance during the coming years. The unemployment rate—which in the past tended to have a floor of about 6 percent; when the economy dropped below that level, inflation did tend to pick up and interest rates had to be raised—during this last expansion dropped to 4 percent and stayed there for a couple of years, and no inflation came into sight (and still has not). So it may be that the United States has moved—at least for a prolonged period—to a considerably lower level of unemployment, reflecting the higher productivity growth that underpins the performance of the economy as a whole.

For an international investor contemplating where to put his or her money during the next decade, it would therefore be good to give a fairly high priority to the United States. This is certainly not to suggest that the US economy is without problems. Its savings rate is too low, its public school system is far too weak, it is running a massive trade deficit (which is unsustainable), and the exchange rate of the dollar will have to come down further. But the basic underlying prospect for the US economy is strong, and as international investors, including overseas Koreans, consider what they might do with their own economic fortunes, it is a worthy country to consider.

Japan and North Korea

Japan faces four challenges. It has a weak banking system, it is experiencing deflation, it has fiscal problems, and there is a need for structural change. With regard to the banking system, estimates vary widely, but if one looks at private-sector estimates, the proportion of nonperforming loans in the Japanese banking system may be something of the order of 25 to 35 percent of GDP. If one assumes a recovery rate of about 50 percent, that means that the net cost of cleaning up the Japanese banking system— if that is ever undertaken—will be something on the same order of magnitude as has been experienced in South Korea. So far, Japan has not dealt with these things; instead it has experienced a provisioning-out profits pattern for a decade. With regard to Japanese bank supervision of more than 60 trillion yen in nonperforming loans—a figure greater than the size of the South Korean economy, the Canadian economy, or the Dutch and Belgian economies combined—unlike in South Korea, nonperforming loans in Japan continue to grow.

The second problem is monetary policy. Japan, as was mentioned, is experiencing deflation. It is the first major industrial country since the Great Depression to do so. The deflation that Japan is experiencing is not of the same magnitude as, say, that in the United States during the Great Depression, where the price level fell by 25 or 30 percent; nevertheless, it makes dealing with banking problems and other problems more difficult. The probable solution is inflation targeting. Unfortunately, there is disagreement within the Japanese government about the advisability of that policy, and the finance minister very recently once again made one of his periodic statements against such a policy.

The third problem is fiscal policy. Japanese fiscal policy is fundamentally opaque; that is to say, it is hard to understand. There is a small cottage industry in Tokyo that does nothing but try to figure out Japan's actual fiscal position. The IMF estimates that the ratio of gross debt to GDP will soon reach 150 percent. Unfortunately, Japan has a very extensive network of public-sector financial institutions that make loans to so-called third-sector projects. It has a number of underfunded liabilities and so on, and if all these are added together, and a guess is made as to how many of them are really bad, some researchers estimate that the actual fiscal burden is as high as 250 percent of GDP.

Japan thus faces a nasty squeeze. In the short run, to get the economy going again, one wants to spend money; however, spending on public funds will simply make the long-run problem of the fiscal deficit worse. Much has been made of the fact that, due to this fiscal deficit problem, Japanese sovereign debt today carries a rating lower than that of Botswana, a sub-Saharan African country with an HIV infection rate of about 25 percent in the adult population. But this is misleading. Botswana is a stable, well-governed country with enormous natural resource wealth. It is basically a big desert with a lot of minerals underneath it. One could think of it as a kind of sub-Saharan Saudi Arabia, except with better politics.

Rather than comparing Japan to Botswana, a more apt comparison is to South Korea. In this comparison between Japan and Korea, the ratings for the past few years show a stair-step coming down, which is Japan, and another stair-step going up, which is Korea (see figure 7.1). If one simply extrapolates the past year's experience, one would find that at the end of this year, the two lines cross. Now this is not to predict that, at the end of this year, South Korean sovereign debt will be rated more highly than Japanese sovereign debt, but it is simply to make the point that the trend is going in that direction. Having pointed out that the final challenge the Japanese face is a need for structural change, space precludes saying any more about that.

Having laid out these four challenges, or reasons to be gloomy about the Japanese economy, there are also two reasons for optimism. First, at least parts of official Japan are no longer in denial. For example, Japanese people engaging in professional conversations with Marcus Noland now are willing to state in front of other Japanese people something like this: "We have a real problem. We cannot compete against China in agriculture. How did you [meaning the United States] deal with agriculture adjustment issues?" Or, "In the Kansai region, we have many small and medium-sized enterprises. We simply cannot compete against low-cost Chinese manufacturers; how do you handle these kind of adjustment issues?" So the people, at least in the hinterlands, are not in denial. The problem is that politicians, or a significant part of the Liberal Democratic Party, still are in denial. And as one moves closer and closer to Tokyo and goes higher and higher in the power structure, the denial gets worse.

The second reason for optimism is that there are reasons to believe that, at least in part of the government, such denial is no longer prevalent. Recently, Japanese prime minister Junichiro Koizumi appointed Takenaka Heizo, who had been his economic adviser, to be head of the financial supervisory administration. And so there is hope that with Takenaka, a devout reformer in charge, there may be real action on these issues. And indeed, the fact that Japanese bank stocks fell by about 15 percent during

Figure 7.1 Japan and South Korea: Converging debt ratings

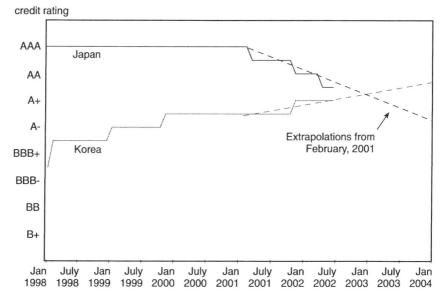

Source: Standard & Poor's sovereign credit rating list.

one week after Takenaka's appointment suggests that the markets seem to think that Takenaka may actually do something. That is a reason to be optimistic.

How can overseas Koreans make profitable investments in this situation? If Japan actually addresses these problems, there will be tremendous economic turmoil in Japan. And turmoil will create winners and losers. As is mentioned below, South Koreans have done rather well in many aspects of information technology. In particular, in certain software niches, there are actually Korean firms today that have penetrated the Japanese market and are making lots of money in Japan. And as Japan reforms its economy—generating in the long run both more growth and much structural change—those Korean firms are poised to benefit. However, in the short run, the crisis in Japan will push the yen down—to 160, 180, or 200 to the dollar—and that is going to cause problems for export-related Korean firms that are competing against Japan either in Japan, in Korea, or in third markets like the United States.

North Korea has challenges that are on a far greater scale than those facing Japan, and North Korea in the past few months has put on the table an economic reform package that basically has four policy components. (The comments here are basically taken from a more detailed paper by Marcus Noland, "Westbound Train Leaving the Station: Pyongyang on the Reform Track," which is available at http://www.iie.com.) The four components are marketization, inflation (if Japan has a deflation problem, North Korea is going to create an inflation problem), special economic zones, and aid seeking.

With regard to marketization, most people agree that it is a good thing. North Korea has announced a series of policies that appear to imitate the Chinese policies of the 1980s of essentially maintaining a dual price system, keeping the central plan in place but having marginal growth occur outside it according to market dictates. The problem is that it is not at all clear to what extent the North Korean government is truly committed to this policy. It is unclear, for example, whether managers will be able to hire, fire, and promote workers; whether failing enterprises will be allowed to close; and, if so, in the absence of any social safety net, how current and former workers in those enterprises will survive.

The second policy—inflation—is one that is a much less obviously desirable thing and has surprisingly attracted less attention, so let us look at it in a little more detail. North Koreans have announced what amounts to tremendous increases in administrative prices, far larger than, say, what China did when it began its reforms in November 1979. For example, at that time, the Chinese raised grain prices by about 25 percent. In comparison, North Koreans have announced price increases for grain on the order of 4,000 percent.

This policy is less likely to be successful in the North Korean case than in the Chinese or the Vietnamese cases. There are about half as many as people in the agriculture sector in North Korea today as there were in China in 1979 or Vietnam in 1989. In those two countries, more than 70 percent of the labor force was employed in agriculture; in North Korea, it is about half as much. That means that the part of the population that is going to benefit directly from the increase in relative prices of agriculture products is much smaller in North Korea.

Moreover, this policy means that it is also less likely to generate a large positive supply response, as it did in China and Vietnam. Agriculture was liberalized, relative prices were increased, and farmers began producing a lot more. The characteristics of North Korean agriculture is that it is much more input intensive; that is, North Korean agriculture relies much more on such factors as chemicals, fertilizers, and electrically driven irrigation, and it is a smaller part of the economy. Thus, one is less likely to get a massive positive supply response. As a consequence—and this is the important point—unlike in China or Vietnam, reform in North Korea is likely to create a substantial number of losers, that is, people who actually do not benefit from reform. And indeed, given the stressed nature of North Korean society, it would not be at all surprising if mortality rates in North Korea increase significantly. And there may be a real possibility of social unrest.

So why pursue this kind of inflation policy? The first reason is what economists call "money illusion." The North Korean government may be banking on the fact that, especially in North Korea, with people relatively unfamiliar with market economics, in the short run at least, pumping a lot of money into the economy and causing inflation will cause money illusion—meaning that people will think they are richer, even if they are not, and will begin in engaging in a lot of activity. That is to say, it will give a short-run boost to the economy but could have a detrimental impact in the long run. As John Maynard Keynes said, in the long run, we are all dead, and from the standpoint of a North Korean policymaker, that long run may have a rather short time horizon.

The second reason is politics. The inflation policy is a way for Kim Jong Il to reward his friends and punish his enemies. It is unnecessary, if one simply wants to change relative wage rates in North Korea, to have a high inflation rate. If policymakers think it is important to give government officials, military officials, or coal miners higher wages, that is easy to do: Just give them a 20 percent or 40 percent raise. One does not need to increase their salaries by a factor of 14 and increase the price level by a factor of 10. It is unnecessary, why do it? The generation of high inflation, and we are talking about really large numbers, hurts people who hold *won*. In socialist governments in the past, including in North Korea, this kind of administered inflation and its cousin, currency reform, have been used to attack traders and black marketeers who engage in economic activity outside state control and are thought to be people having large holdings in *won*.

The problem with this is that, having gone through this—this would be the fourth time in the history of North Korea that this has happened—the country's traders are not gullible. They get out of *won* as soon as they can into dollars, yen, or yuan. Indeed, even in rural areas on the agriculture cooperatives, people would prefer to hold trinkets purchased from Chinese peddlers to the local currency. So this blow, which can be seen to be aimed at people engaged in economic activity outside state control, is actually probably not going to hit the traders or the elites; it is going to hit the masses. Again, the result would be an increase in social differentiation, and potentially social unrest.

The final reason for the inflation policy is ignorance. As an economist, one is taught not to base arguments on the idea that people are not rational, but here is a reason for believing this; in the case of China, Marcus Noland's conversations with Chinese officials, in the early stages of Chinese economic reform, led him to believe that some officials, especially older, more senior ones, literally did not understand the very basis of a market economy. They thought a price or demand or supply was something fixed, that it was a point. They did not understand that demand and supply are schedules that relate quantities to prices.

For example, North Korean policymakers observe a price in the farmers' market for, say, rice and believe that they can administratively raise the price to that level and then simply provide people with lots more *won* to compensate them, without the original farmers' market price changing, they seem to actually believe this—though any economist knows that if one increases the price level by a factor of 10, and no additional supply comes on to the market, one has simply administratively created 900 percent inflation. This is something that they do not seem to understand. And in a political system as hierarchical as North Korea's, where the penalties for being on the wrong side of a political dispute could be quite severe, even people who have reservations about such a policy, or may understand the very basic economics through which one is simply creating inflation, may engage in what is called preference falsification. That is to say, they keep their heads down, and they do not say anything if that is what their bosses have decided to do.

With regard to the third component of the reforms, special economic zones, the one that has been in the news, especially in South Korea, is in the North Korean city of Sinuiju. In some sense, we should not be surprised by this; the North Koreans have been talking about doing something there since 1998, but this initiative seems to have been derailed, at least in the short run, by the selection of a somewhat shady Chinese businessman named Yang Bin as the head of it. He has now been placed under arrest by the Chinese government, and without Chinese government cooperation, obviously a special economic zone on China's border is not going to work. But if it did—suppose that those responsible can get a sort of Hong Kong North version of Tung Chee Hwa to run the zone, instead of Yang—then what would be the effects in Sinuiju? First would be the direct impact. The North Korean economy is so far down that even economic integration with a relatively backward part of the Chinese economy, such as the city of Dangdong, would actually be an improvement. So there would be some local progress.

In addition, if developments in that special economic zone were to be generalized to the rest of the economy, one could look at it as kind of pilot project or experiment, and then that would be another benefit. Finally—and this may actually be the most important part, given the political culture of North Korea—there is a reluctance to get ahead, because if policy changes and policymakers are on the wrong side, the penalties could be very, very severe. As a consequence, even if Kim Jong Il decided that he wanted to reform the economy, it could well be that he would have trouble getting the bureaucracy or the party to actually implement the reforms because the bureaucrats are risk-averse. They literally do not want to lose their heads if policy changes. Because the special economic zone has been established in Sinuiju, a city associated with the Kim family, and because such a big production has been made of Kim's personal connection to it, the zone may well be regarded within North Korea as a political gesture or signal that reform is acceptable, and it may in fact unlock the state apparatus, which has basically been reluctant to engage in reform for political reasons.

The fourth part of the plan is aid seeking, or passing the hat to Japan. The conventional wisdom is that, after the normalization of relations between Japan and North Korea, the Japanese government will make a financial transfer to North Korea on the order of $10 billion. And the issue, from the standpoint of North Korea, is whether that money can start coming in fast enough to put goods on the shelves as the dislocations of the marketization of the economy begin to bite. Unfortunately for the North Koreans, the public reaction in Japan to the recent revelations of the 1979 abductions and the probable killings of some of the abductees has been public revulsion; as a consequence, the process of normalization of relations between Japan and North Korea may be more protracted than either government expected. As a consequence, that $10 billion may be a long time coming, and it may not get to North Korea in time.

The bottom line is that North Korea has now moved from the realm of elite to mass politics. Unlike the diplomatic initiatives the North Koreans have engaged in for roughly the past four years, which only really affect a handful of elite officials, these economic changes affect every single person in the country and affect social and political realities on the ground. So internally, what is at stake now is far, far greater than what has been put at stake in the diplomatic initiatives.

The upside is that if the reforms work, there could be a significant improvement in North Korea's internal situation. Indeed, these reforms ultimately could lead to a process of political liberalization and modernization and to North Korea becoming a more normal country, more like South Korea. Of course, the negative outcome of the reforms could generate social unrest and ultimately political instability and the end of the regime. The bottom line is that the train has left the station, but it is unclear whether the engineer knows where the train is headed and whether he can keep it on the track. Overseas Koreans thinking about investing in North Korea therefore ought to be ready for some real turbulence along the way. This train may ultimately derail.

South Korea

South Korea watchers must have been surprised when the country ran into a serious financial crisis in late 1997. Then, adding to their surprise, Korea came out of the crisis faster than had generally been expected. After suffering a severe setback in 1998 when GDP shrunk by 6.7 percent, Korea's GDP grew by 10.9 percent in 1999. Then, in 2000, Korea continued its rapid recovery with GDP growth of 9.3 percent.

This section briefly touches on the recovery process and seeks to shed light on South Korea's future prospects and investment opportunities. As can be easily imagined, it was the Korean people themselves who were shocked the most by the crisis. Consequently, they had a sense of the crisis and they were ready to take bitter pills. The Korean government took advantage of this general atmosphere in implementing rather painful restructuring measures. In addition, an IMF rescue loan came with conditionalities of various structural adjustments. They also helped in implementing these painful measures in the sense that they depoliticized politically sensitive issues, such as labor and the *chaebol*.

Broadly speaking, the Korean economic recovery since the financial crisis has been primarily driven by an expansion of domestic demand, especially rapidly rising private consumption, which was facilitated by rapid increases in household debt. In 2001, for example, household debt increased by 28 percent.

The expansion of domestic demand was aided by expansionary monetary and fiscal policies that began in the second half of 1998. Monetary aggregates, such as M3, have increased by 14 percent annually. Interest rates were kept at low levels. At the same time, fiscal expenditures increased by 9.6 percent in 1999.

Because the South Korean recovery relied heavily on domestic demand expansion, Korea suffered less than other economies in the region in 2001 when the global economy slowed. In 2001, for example, while Korea grew by 3 percent, the Asian "tiger economies" of Singapore and Taiwan experienced negative growth, and Hong Kong had a zero growth rate.

Obviously, there are some downward risk factors for South Korea's short-term economic performance. Internationally, the weak US economic recovery and a possible war in Iraq, with its negative impact on oil prices, are two such factors. Domestically, the rapid rise in household debt is a concern. Korea's ratio of household debt to income is now reaching Western household averages. The ratio of household debt to financial assets is already higher than that for US households. Unless appropriate measures are taken, nonperforming household debt may become a problem for Korean financial institutions. Despite these downward risk factors, the Korean economy in 2003 is expected to grow by nearly 6 percent.

There are two main reasons why one can be very optimistic about the intermediate to long-term prospects for the South Korean economy. First, thanks to structural adjustments implemented since the 1997-98 financial crisis, the Korean economy today is fundamentally much stronger. There has been literally a sea change in Korea's economic structure. The financial crisis, although painful for most Koreans, was a blessing in disguise for the Korean economy. The crisis forced Korea to accelerate necessary economic structural adjustments. As a result, Korea's corporate and financial sectors today are much more efficient and competitive. The labor market, though still in need of further reform, is much more flexible, and the public sector has become much leaner.

The second reason for optimism is that the South Korean economy is already well attuned to the age of knowledge-based society. It is well known that Korea's broadband access and general Internet usage are already well ahead of many countries that belong to the Organization for Economic Cooperation and Development.

More important, for the first time in its history, South Korea is well positioned to face international competition. In the past, Korea suffered from a lack of arable land and limited natural resources. But in the age of the knowledge-based society, when knowledge is the most important strategic factor for a nation's competitiveness, Korea is well endowed with people who have the highest zeal for education. This gives Korea a competitive edge in the coming decades. For these two simple reasons, one can be bullish on Korea's future.

About the Contributors

Taeho Bark is dean of international affairs and dean of the School of International and Area Studies (SIAS) at Seoul National University. He is also commissioner of the Korea Trade Commission. After a teaching assignment at Georgetown University (1983-87), he returned to Korea and became actively involved in trade and investment policymaking as a senior research fellow at the Korea Development Institute (KDI) and the Korea Institute for International Economic Policy (KIEP). He went on to become the vice president of KIEP. He was economic adviser at the Office of the President of the Republic of Korea; adviser and consultant to the International Monetary Fund and the World Bank; and chair of the Asia Pacific Economic Cooperation's Investment Experts Group. He has written extensively on international trade and investment, including a widely used textbook titled *Theory of International Trade*.

C. Fred Bergsten has been director of the Institute for International Economics since its creation in 1981. He was also chairman of the Competitiveness Policy Council, which was created by Congress, throughout its existence from 1991 to 1995 and chairman of the APEC Eminent Persons Group throughout its existence from 1993 to 1995. He was assistant secretary for international affairs of the US Treasury (1977-81), assistant for international economic affairs to the National Security Council (1969-71), and a senior fellow at the Brookings Institution (1972-76), the Carnegie Endowment for International Peace (1981), and the Council on Foreign Relations (1967-68). He is the author, coauthor, or editor of numerous books on a wide range of international economic issues, including *No More Bashing: Building a New Japan-United States Economic Relationship* (2001), *Whither APEC? The Progress to date and Agenda for the*

Future (1997), *Global Economic Leadership and the Group of Seven* (1996), *The Dilemmas of the Dollar* (second edition, 1996), *Reconcilable Differences? United States-Japan Economic Conflict* (1993), *Pacific Dynamism and the International Economic System* (1993), and *America in the World Economy: A Strategy for the 1990s* (1988).

Inbom Choi, former visiting fellow at the Institute for International Economics, is chief economist at the Federation of Korean Industries. He was assistant secretary to the president for economic affairs and director of international economic policy in the Office of the President of Korea (1995-96). He has been a research fellow at the Korea Institute for International Economic Policy since 1990. He has also been a consultant to the World Bank and a visiting professor at Georgetown University. In 1998 and 1999, he was selected by the Asia-Europe Meeting (ASEM) as one of the Next Generation Leaders of Asia. He is coauthor of *Free Trade between Korea and the United States?* with Jeffrey J. Schott (2001). He is the author of *Competitiveness of Korean Products in the U.S. Market* (1993, in Korean), *Trade Barriers in Government Procurement Practices of Developed Countries* (1992, in Korean), and *Effects of FDI on Productivity in the Manufacturing Industries of Korea and Taiwan* (1991, in Korean), among others.

Young Rok Cheong, former president of the Korean Association for Contemporary Chinese Studies, is a professor of economics in the School of International and Area Studies at Seoul National University. He was research fellow at the Korea Institute for International Economic Policy (1990-98). He was adviser to the ambassador at the Korean embassy in China (1993-95). His major publications include *Entry Mode of Overseas Chinese Foreign Direct Investment in China* (2000) and *The Impact of China's Entrance to the WTO on Neighboring East Asian Economies* (2000), and *The Huaqiao Community in Korea: Its Rise, Demise, and Reemergence* (2002).

Kihwan Kim is chairman of the Seoul Financial Forum and the Korean National Committee for the Pacific Economic Cooperation Council. He also serves as an international adviser to Goldman Sachs. He was chairman and CEO of Media Valley, Inc., a joint initiative between the government and private sector to accelerate the development of information technology industries in Korea. During the 1997-98 Asian financial crisis, he was Korea's ambassador-at-large for economic affairs. Other government positions he had held include chief trade representative, vice minister of trade and industry, and chief delegate to the South-North Inter-Korea Economic Talks. In the early 1980s, he served as president of the Korea Development Institute. He was a member of the Monetary Board, the governing body of Korea's central bank. Prior to his return to Korea in 1976, he taught economics for more than 13 years at a number of American universities, including the University of California, Berkeley.

Si Joong Kim is professor in the department of economics at Yeungnam University, Kyungsan, Korea. He was research fellow at the Korea Institute for International Economic Policy (KIEP). He is the coauthor of *Current Status of Ethnic Koreans in China and Their Role for Korea-China Economic Cooperation* (KIEP, 1994) with Tae Hong Kim.

Byong Hyon Kwon is chairman and president of the Overseas Koreans Foundation and former ambassador extraordinary and plenipotentiary to Australia, China, and Myanmar. In December 1992, he became deputy minister for policy planning of the Asia-Pacific Economic Cooperation forum. He was chief of the Korean delegation for normalization of relations with China (May-August 1992). He joined the Ministry of Foreign Affairs (MOFA) in June 1965 and rose to the position of director-general of MOFA's Asian Affairs Bureau in October 1985. He was decorated with the Order of Merit for Outstanding Diplomatic Performance in May 1987 and the Order of Merit for Excellent Civil Service (Yellow) in December 1992.

Marcus Noland, senior fellow at the Institute for International Economics, was a senior economist in the Council of Economic Advisers and held research or teaching positions at the Johns Hopkins University, the University of Southern California, Tokyo University, Saitama University, the University of Ghana, the Korea Development Institute, and the East-West Center. He received fellowships sponsored by the Japan Society for the Promotion of Science, the Council on Foreign Relations, the Council for the International Exchange of Scholars, and the Pohang Iron and Steel Corporation. He won the 2000-01 Ohira Masayoshi Award for his book *Avoiding the Apocalypse: The Future of the Two Koreas* (2000). He is the author of *Pacific Basin Developing Countries: Prospects for the Future* (1990); coauthor of *No More Bashing: Building a New Japan-United States Economic Relationship* with C. Fred Bergsten and Takatoshi Ito (2001), *Global Economic Effects of the Asian Currency Devaluations* (1998), *Reconcilable Differences? United States-Japan Economic Conflict* with C. Fred Bergsten (1993), and *Japan in the World Economy* with Bela Balassa (1988); coeditor of *Pacific Dynamism and the International Economic System* (1993); and editor of *Economic Integration of the Korean Peninsula* (1998).

Il SaKong is chairman & CEO of the Institute for Global Economics, a private nonprofit research institute based in Seoul. He served in the government of the Republic of Korea as minister of finance (1987-88), senior secretary to the president for economic affairs (1983-87), senior counselor to the minister of the Economic Planning Board (1982) and senior economist of the Presidential Council on Economic and Scientific Affairs (1979-80). He is coauthor of *Government, Business, and Entrepreneurship in Economic Development: The Korean Case* (Harvard University, 1980) and

Korea in the World Economy (1993), and coeditor of *The Korea-United States Economic Relationship* (1997).

Toshiyuki Tomura is dean of the faculty of international politics and economics at Nishogakusha University, Chiba, Japan, where he is also a professor of economics. He is also Professor Emeritus in economics at Tokyo Metropolitan University. He is the author of *Economic Analysis of Market Societies* (1976, in Japanese).

Jang Hee Yoo, former president of the Korea Institute for International Economic Policy, is a professor of economics and dean of the Graduate School of International Studies at Ewha Women's University. He was member of the Presidential Commission for Science and Technology, member of the APEC Eminent Persons Group (EPG), former president of the Korea-America Economic Association, and member of the executive board of the American Committee on Asian Economic Studies. He is the author of numerous articles and books, including *Macroeconomic Theory* (1975) and *APEC and the New World Order* (1995).

Soogil Young is senior adviser and policy analyst at Kim & Chang Law Office in Seoul. He is research adviser at the Korea International Trade Association, National Strategy Institute of Korea, and Institute for Global Economics. He is the vice chairman of the Korea National Committee for Pacific Economic Cooperation; coordinator of the Pacific Economic Cooperation Council Finance Forum; and member of the US-Korea 21st Century Council and the Seoul Financial Forum. He has served as president of the Korea Institute for International Economic Policy and as Korea's ambassador to the OECD. He was senior fellow at the Korea Development Institute for 14 years. Since the early 1980s, he has been advising the Korean government on economic policy matters, with a focus on trade, industrial, macroeconomic, and international issues. He has written extensively on developmental and international policy issues with a Korean perspective.

Index

acculturation
  Korean-American community, 63, 71
  Korean-Chinese community, 102*n*, 108, 122
adoption, Korean-United States, 63*n*
African diaspora, 12, 13
agriculture sector
  China, 110, 125, 139
  North Korea, 139-41
  Vietnam, 139
aid seeking, North Korea, 139, 142
Akihito, Emperor, 79
Alien Registration Law of 1952 (Japan), 83, 84, 85, 87
alumni groups, overseas Chinese, 39
Argentina, 6, 13*n*, 18
Armenian diaspora, 12, 12*n*, 20
ASEM Vision Group, 131
Asian Exclusion Act, 62
Asian financial crisis, 32
Asian Games, 99
Asian "tiger economies," 143
Asia-Pacific Economic Cooperation forum (APEC), 1
assimilation. *See* acculturation
Association of Southeast Asian Nations (ASEAN), 7
asylum policy, Japanese, 96-97
atomic bomb victims, 83, 86
Australia, 35

bamboo network, 20
bang (secret societies), 37-39
banking system, Japanese, 136
Bark, Taeho, 28
Basic Construction Plan for National Information and Communication (Taiwan), 45
Beijing (China), 105, 106*t*, 112, 114, 122, 122*n*, 123-24, 128
Bergsten, C. Fred, 131-32
bilateral negotiations, 7
biotechnology, 49, 53
boat people, 96-97
borders, impact on economic development, 4-5
Botswana, 137
brain drain, 25, 27, 75-76
Busan (Japan), 83
business density, Korean-American community, 66-67, 67*t*
business networks
  Chinese (*See* Chinese business networks)
  created by diasporas, 19-20, 26, 28-29, 52-55
business opportunities, for overseas Koreans, outlook for, 131-144
business sectors
  Korean-American community, 74
  Korean-Japanese community, 83, 91,

92t, 99
business talent
  Chinese, 52
  Korean, 57, 120, 128, 130

California (U.S.). *See also* Los Angeles
  (U.S.)
  Korean-American community in, 66
Canada, 4-5, 21, 35
  Koreans in, number of, 18, 18t
Cape Verde, 14
capital accumulation
  Chinese diaspora, 35-37
  Korean-American community, 68, 70,
    73
Caribbean diaspora, 11n
category jumpers, 99
Changbai autonomous county (China),
  105
Chang-shi Kae-myung policy, 95
Cheju Do (South Korea), 81-82
Chen Qichen, 32
Cheong Young Rok, 31, 56, 59, 128
Chiang Ching-kuo Foundation for
  International Scholarly Exchange, 54
Chiang Mai Initiative, 7
Chile, 13n
China. *See also* Taiwan
  agreements with ASEAN nations, 7
  agriculture sector, 139
  competition with Taiwan, 41-44
  economic status of, 31, 35, 36t
    role of Chinese diaspora in, 41, 45-49,
      57
  employment statistics, 89-91, 91t-92t
  entry into United Nations, 31
  ethnic minorities in, 101n, 101-02, 108,
    110 (*See* also Korean-Chinese
    community)
    policy toward, 103, 107-08
  foreign investment in, 23, 23n, 26, 46-
    49, 47t, 53
  fund transfers to, 23-24, 24t, 27
  General Office of Overseas Chinese
    Affairs, 45
  Korean Embassy in, 123, 123n
  minority autonomous regions in, 105,
    108, 110, 121, 121n
  nationals abroad (*See* Chinese
    diaspora)
  Northeastern, Korean-Chinese
    community in, 109, 110, 112, 113, 115,
    121-22, 124
  one child policy, 104

  regional autonomy in, 108
  registration system, 112n, 122n
  relations with South Korea, 113-14,
    126t, 128
    role of Korean-Chinese community
      in, 102-03, 111, 117-19, 118n, 128
  relations with United States, 39, 44
  sanctions against, 31
  South Korean investment in, 113n, 113-
    14, 115n, 123, 126t-127t
  State Ethnic Affairs Commission, 107,
    114
  trade flows, 48
Chinatowns, 36, 38
Chinese Academy of Science, 49
Chinese business networks, 20, 31-59
  and competition between China and
    Taiwan, 41-44
  and cultural characteristics, 35-39, 59
  evolution of, 33-45, 56
  and hometown background, 38
  impact on Korean diaspora, 50-55, 57
  international conferences, 42
  Internet, 44-45, 49
  role in modernizing China, 41, 45-49, 57
  status of, 33-36
Chinese Communist Party (CCP), policy
  toward ethnic Koreans, 103, 107, 109-
  10
Chinese diaspora, 12-14, 16, 19
  attitude toward home country, 52-53
  capital accumulation, 35-37
  cultural characteristics of, 35-39, 59
  division of, 33
  geographic distribution of, 33-34, 35t
  government policy toward, 32, 39-41,
    40-41, 44, 48, 52-53, 56
  investment in China, 23, 23n, 26, 45-49,
    46-49, 47t, 53
  versus Korean diaspora, 52, 57
  networks created by (*See* Chinese
    business networks)
  political situation and, 39-40
  population, 16n, 33-34, 35t
Chinese Education Committee, 33
Chinese Exclusion Act of 1882, 35, 62
Chinese language, 38, 40, 111, 117, 120
Christianity, 62-63
Chun Doo-Hwan, 75
Chung Jinchul, 50n
Circular Notice (1952) (Japan), 85
"collective character," of overseas
  Chinese, 35-39, 59
colonial diaspora, 12-14, 13t

comfort women, 83, 98
commerce diaspora, 12, 13*t*, 19
Commonwealth of Independent States
    (CIS), Koreans in, 17, 18*t*
community associations
    ethnic Chinese, 45, 45*n*
    ethnic Korean, 16, 17, 51
Confucianism, 129
conscription, 58, 83, 87
Convention Relating to the Status of
    Refugees (1982), 86
convergence approach, 68-69
Council of 100, 44, 44*n*, 54, 58-59
cross-border migration, 10. *See also*
    diaspora
cultural diaspora, 11*n*
cultural exchanges
    Chinese, 44
    Korean, 54
Cultural Revolution (China), 107, 107*n*,
    109, 110
culture
    of Chinese diaspora, 35-39, 59
    Korean, 29
currency reform, 140
current transfers, impact of diaspora on,
    23-24, 27

Daeduk, 25
Dalian (China), 112, 114, 115, 119
Dangdong (North Korea), 141
debt rating
    Japan, 137
    South Korea, 137, 138*t*
deflation, in Japan, 136, 139
Deng Xiaoping, 52, 53
development strategy, South Korea, 1-2
dialects, Chinese, 38
diaspora. *See also* Korean diaspora;
    specific type of diaspora
    definition of, 9-11
    existence of, criteria for, 11
    history of, 3-4
    networks created by, 19-20, 26, 28-29,
        52-55 (*See* also Chinese business
        networks)
    types of, 11-14, 13*t*
diaspora communities, nation-states
    created from, 14
discrimination, 63, 78, 78*n*, 95, 96-97, 98,
    129
discrimination coefficients, 93
"3-D" (dirty, difficult, and dangerous)
    jobs, 25-26, 116, 118, 130

domestic demand, South Korea, 143
Dong, Nelson, 44*n*
dual nationality, 40-41
dual price system, 139
dwelling conditions, Korean-Japanese
    community, 94, 95*t*

East Asian countries, cooperative
    agreements among, 6-7
East Asian economic miracle, 36
economic policymaking, and ignorance of
    economics, 140-41
education. *See also* schools
    Korean-American community, 4, 61, 64,
        66, 70, 74-75
    Korean-Chinese community, 110-11,
        119-20, 129
    of overseas Koreans, 57
    South Korean, 19, 144
    United States, 25, 33, 63, 75-76, 136
Emerging Markets Eminent Persons
    Group, 132
English language, proficiency in, 64, 75
entrepreneurship
    Korean-American community, 61, 64,
        66-68, 67*t*, 70, 73
    Korean-Chinese community, 113, 113*n*,
        117-20, 129
    Korean-Japanese community, 91, 92*t*
ethnic community associations
    Chinese, 45, 45*n*
    Korean, 16, 17, 51
ethnic densities, Korean-Japanese
    community, 78, 93, 94*t*
ethnic industries, in Japan, 83-84, 91
ethnic minority regions, in China, 105,
    108
Europe
    migration from, 3
    national borders in, impact on
        economic development, 5
    productivity growth, 133
    trade with China, 48
exchange rate
    development of, 2
    Japanese yen, 138
    US dollar, 136
export development strategy, South
    Korea, 32
exports, of manufactured goods, 2

Federal Reserve (US), 135
feminization, Korean-Japanese
    community, 81

financial sectors, 25
   foreign investment in, 22-23
fiscal policy, Japanese, 136-37
Fok, Henry, 32, 32n
food, imported, 20-21
forced labor, 87
foreign direct investment (FDI). *See*
   investment
Formosa Plastic, 46
"four dragons" of Asia, 36
free trade agreements, 7. *See also specific*
   agreement
Fujian (China), 34, 38, 48
Fujian Secret Society, 38-39
Fukuoka (Japan), 82
fund transfers, impact of diaspora on, 23-
   24, 27

Genchi Soshi (On-the-Spot Suspension)
   Policy, 83
General Office of Overseas Chinese
   Affairs, 40, 45
General Permanent Residents (GPRs), 87-
   88, 89t
German diaspora, 13n
Germany, 5
getihu (individual businesses), 113
Global Chinese Business Network
   (GCBN), 45
Global Economic and Trade Meeting, 42
globalization
   and economic outlook for overseas
      Koreans, 131-44
   impact of national borders on, 4-5
   importance of, 2
   migration and, 3-4, 14
   role of Korea in, 5-7
Gongsuo, 40
graduate education, in United States, 25,
   33, 63, 75-76
gravity model, 21, 21n
green groceries, 74
Guangdong (China), 34, 38, 48, 124
Guangdong Secret Society, 38-39
guanxi (network of connections), 36, 46,
   49, 53, 120
Guomingdang, 39, 40
Guyana, 14

Han nationalism, 101, 107, 118, 120, 125,
   129
Hart-Celler Act (1965), 63
Hawaii
   Japanese immigration to, 13-14, 62

Korean immigration to, 17-18, 62-63, 66
Hawaii Sugar Planters Association, 62
Hebei (China), 105, 106t
Heilongjiang Province (China), 104, 106,
   109, 109n, 111n, 115, 121n, 123-24
Heizo, Takenaka, 137-38
Hibakusha (A-bomb victims), 83, 86
Hirohito, Emperor, 79
Hokkaido (Japan), 83
homogeneity myth, 77, 96-97
Hondo (Japanese Main Islands), 79, 82
Hong Chaesik, 51
Hong Kong, 23, 36, 47
Hoover Index (HI), 93n
household debt, South Korea, 143
hui (associations), 38
Huiguan, 40
hukou system (registration), 112n, 122n
hybrid diaspora, 11n

illegal entry
   into Japan, 99
   into South Korea, 115-16, 118
Illinois (US), 66
Immigration Control Act (Japan), 84, 85
immigration control system, Japanese, 78,
   82-83
Immigration Reform Act of 1965, 69
imperial diaspora, 12-14, 13t
income level. *See* per capita income
Independence Movement (Japan), 82
India, fund transfers to, 23-24, 24t, 27
Indian diaspora, 13, 16, 19
   investment in India, 23, 23n
   population, 16n
Indonesia
   Chinese in, 34, 35, 35t, 37
   trade with China, 48
inflation
   North Korea, 139-41
   United States, 135
information technology (IT)
   and economic performance, 134, 143-44
   foreign investment in, 22-23, 28, 53-54
   Korean involvement in, 99, 143-44
   overseas Chinese involvement in, 43, 49
Inner Mongolia (China), 105
Institute for International Economics, 1, 3
international conferences. *See also specific*
   conference
   overseas Chinese, 38, 42, 53-54
   overseas Koreans, need for, 54
International Covenants on Civil and
   Political Rights (1979), 86

"internationalization" of Japan, 84
International Monetary Fund (IMF), 131,
    136, 143
International Network of Korean
    Entrepreneurs, 51
Internet network, of Chinese
    businesspeople, 44-45, 49
investment
    by Chinese diaspora, 23, 23n, 26, 37, 45-
        49, 46-47, 46-49, 47t, 53
    in Japan, 138
    outlook for, 131-44
    South Korean, impact of Korean
        diaspora on, 19-23, 26, 28, 53, 58, 99
    in United States, 135-136
Irish diaspora, 12, 12n, 15, 16
"Irish of Asia," 62
Ishihara, Shintaro, 78, 78n
Israel, 14

Jang Hee Yoo, 98
Japan
    agreements with ASEAN nations, 7
    aid to North Korea, 142
    asylum policy, 96-97
    banking system, 136
    Chinese community in, 78
    debt rating, 137, 138t
    deflation, 136, 139
    economic status of
    outlook for, 136-38
        versus South Korea, 6
        versus United States, 133
    fiscal policy, 136-37
    foreign direct investment in, 138
    illegal entry into, 99
    immigration and registration systems,
        78, 82-88
    "internationalization" of, 84
    Korean Chamber of Commerce, 51
    Koreans in (See Korean-Japanese
        community)
    "lost decade" in, 6
    migration of Korean-Chinese to, 116
    "Migration Project," 129
    monetary policy, 136
    population of, 6
    postindustrialization of, 91
    productivity growth, 133
    trade with China, 48
    welfare and pension schemes, 86
Japanese diaspora, 13-14, 15
Japan-South Korea Treaty, 79
Jewish diaspora, 12

Jiang Mianheng, 46
Jiangsu (China), 123
Jiang Zemin, 32, 46
Jilin Province (China), 104, 106, 115, 123-
    24
Jing Shuping, 32n
job switching, Korean-Japanese
    community, 90
Jochongryun, 99
joint-venture companies, 20, 48

Kanto earthquake (Japan), 82
Keynes, John Maynard, 140
kimchi, 113
Kim Deog Ryong, 50
Kim Jae-ik, 63
Kim Jong II, 140, 141
Kim Kyung Duke, 96
Kinki Area (Japan), 82
knowledge-based society, South Korea,
    143-44
knowledge transfer, 25, 27, 75-76
Koizumi, Junichiro, 137
Kojong, King, 62
Kolon, 99
Korea Development Institute, 76
Korea Export-Import Bank, 114, 115n
Korea Institute of Science and
    Technology, 25, 76
Korean American Commerce and
    Industry Federation, 51
Korean-American community, 61-76
acculturation, 63, 71
    Annandale (Virginia), 2
    business sectors, 74
    capital accumulation, 68, 70, 73
    economic outlook for, 132-36
    educational level, 4, 61, 64, 66, 70, 74-75
    entrepreneurship, 61, 64, 66-68, 67t, 70,
        73
    1.5-generation, 57-58
    history of, 15, 61-64
    impact on U.S. economy, 67-70, 69t, 73
    income level, 4, 61, 66, 70, 74
    population, 17-18, 18t
    savings rate, 61, 68, 70, 73
    second-generation, 74-75
    statistics on, 64-67, 65t
    upward mobility, 64, 66
    urbanization of, 62n, 62-63, 64n
Korean autonomous areas, in China, 105,
    108-10, 121, 121n
Korean Chamber of Commerce in Japan,
    51

Korean Chinese Business Association, 51
Korean-Chinese community, 17, 101-30
  acculturation, 102n, 108, 122
    changes in, during reform period,
      112-22
    as cheap labor supply, 26-27, 115-16,
      118, 130
    Chinese government policy toward,
      103, 107-18, 111
    economic role and status of, change
      in, 116-21, 128
    educational level, 110-11, 119-20, 129
    entrepreneurship, 113, 113n, 117-20,
      129
  ethnic identity of, 121-122, 125, 128
  ethnic Korean schools, 121-22, 121n-
    122n, 125
  geographical distribution of, 104-06,
    105t-106t, 123-24, 124t
  history of, 102, 106-11, 108-11, 129
  influence of South Korea on, 120-21
  migration to Japan, 116
  new immigrants from South Korea,
    123-26, 130
  in Northeastern China, 109, 110, 112,
    113, 115, 121-22, 124
  population, 18, 18t
  population of, 103-106, 105t, 116, 123,
    130
    mobility of, 106, 110n, 112-16, 121-22,
      125, 128
  relations with South Korea, 102-03, 111,
    113-14, 117-19, 118n, 123
  returning to Korea, 108n, 108-09, 111,
    111n, 115-16, 130
  role in development of China, 109-10,
    129
  sex ratio, 104
  urbanization, 110n, 112-13, 121-22, 125,
    128
Korean diaspora. *See also* Korean-
  American community; Korean-
  Chinese community; Korean-
  Japanese community; *specific country*
  attitude toward home country, 52-53
  versus Chinese diaspora, 52, 57
  existence of, 9-16, 26
  geographic distribution of, 18t, 18-19,
    26
  impact of Chinese business networks
    on, 50-55, 57
  impact on Korean economy, 19-26, 58
  making of, 15-16
  networks created by, 52-55

political situation and, 59, 99
population, 15-17, 18t, 26, 103
South Korean attitude toward, 32, 50,
  58
status of, 16-19, 18t, 28
Korean-Japanese community, 77-99
  business sectors, 83, 91, 92t, 99
  definition of, 77
  dwelling conditions, 94, 95t
  economic role and status, 88-94
  employment status across industries,
    91, 92t
  entrepreneurship, 91, 92t
  geographical distribution of, 82, 98
  government policy toward, 96-97
  history of, 15, 79-85
  hometown background, 81-82
  investment in Korea, 22, 99
  Japanese attitude toward, 82, 95-98
  labor participation rate, 89, 91t
  legal status, 77-79, 83-88, 89t, 96, 98
  marriage partners, 88, 93-94, 94t
  population, 18, 18t, 80, 81t, 83, 85, 86t
    by age group, 89, 90t
    by residential category, 87-88, 89t
    Segregation Index (SI), 93, 93n, 94t, 96
    sex ratio, 80-81, 81t, 93, 94t
    unemployment rate, 90, 91t, 96, 98
Korean Japanese Credit Association, 51
Korean language, 29, 117-118
Korean Ministry of Foreign Affairs and
  Trade, 74
Korean National Economic Community
  Meeting, 51-52
Korean peninsula. *See also* North Korea;
  South Korea
  population of, 6
  unification of, 5-6
Korean War, 109
Koreatowns, 124
Korea Trade and Investment Promotion
  Agency (KOTRA), 50-51
Korea-United States 21st Century
  Council, 132

labor, forced, 87
labor diaspora, 12-13, 13t, 15
labor market
  impact of diaspora on, 25-26
  and Korean-American community, 67-
    68
  and Korean-Japanese community, 80-
    81, 81t, 89-91, 91t-92t
labor shortages, 25-27

language
  Chinese, 38, 40, 111, 117, 120
  English, proficiency in, 64, 75
  Korean, 29, 117-118
Latin America. *See also specific country*
  Koreans in, 18
laundries, 74
Law for the Protection of War Victims
  (1952) (Japan), 86
Lawyers' Association of Zainichi Koreans
  (LAZAK), 96
Learning Contemporary Korea: Gateway
  to East Asia, 29
Lebanese diaspora, 13
Lee Kuan-Yew, 42, 44, 53
legal status, of Korean-Japanese
  community, 77-79, 83-88, 96, 98
Liaoning Province (China), 104, 106, 109,
  109n, 111n, 115, 123
Liberal Democratic Party (Japan), 137
Liberia, 14
Li Dezhu, 129
Li Kashing, 46
loans, nonperforming, in Japan, 136
Long-Term Residents (LTRs), 87
Los Angeles (US), 17, 64n, 71
Lotte Group, 22, 57, 99
Lu Sunlin, 41n

Macao, 48
Maihara-cho, 96
Malaysia
  Chinese in, 34, 35, 35t, 37
  trade with China, 48
Manchuria, 15
manufactured goods, exports of, 2
Mao Ze-dong, 52
March Fong Eu, 44
marketization, North Korea, 139
market promotion, by diaspora
  networks, 20, 48
marriage
  Japanese-Chinese, 93-94, 94t
  Korean-Chinese, 93-94, 94t, 116, 116n,
  130
  Korean-Japanese, 88, 93-94, 94t
  Korean-United States, 63
Mauritius, 14
Ma Yo-Yo, 44n
medical personnel, Korean-American
  community, 74
migration. *See also* diaspora
  forced, 12
  and globalization, 3-4, 14

military service, 58, 83, 87
Mindan, 99
minorities of superiority, 13n
monetary policy, Japanese, 136
money illusion, 139-140
Muranishi, Toshio, 96
Myanmar, 34, 35t

Naimusho Keihokyoku, 80
Nam Duck-Woo, 75
Nanyang, 34, 34n
national borders, impact on economic
  development, 4-5
Nationalist China. *See* Taiwan
nationality
  Chinese policy on, 40-41, 41n, 101-03,
  107-10
  Japanese policy on, 79, 83-88
Nationality Law (Japan), 84
National Origin Quota System, 63
National People's Congress, 107
National Returned Overseas Chinese
  Association, 40
"national treatment," 58
naturalization, Korean-Japanese
  community, 84
network economies, 32-33
New Immigration Control Law of 1990,
  84, 87
New Jersey (US), 66
newspapers, Chinese language, 39, 49
New York (US), 17, 66, 74
New Zealand, Korean emigrants in, 18-
  19, 24
Nixon, Richard, 39
North African diaspora, 13
Northeast Asian free trade agreements, 7
North Korea
  agriculture sector, 139-41
  aid seeking, 139, 142
  economic status of
    outlook for, 138-42
    versus South Korea, 3
  inflation, 139-141
  Korean-Chinese returning to, 111, 111n,
  130
  marketization, 139
  political situation, 140-41
  special economic zones, 139, 141
  unification with South Korea, 5-6

Olympic Games (Seoul), 95, 113
one child policy (China), 104
Organization for Economic Cooperation

and Development, 144
Osaka (Japan), 18, 82
Overseas Chinese Affairs Commission, 40*n*, 42, 44, 45
Overseas Korean American Businessmens' Association, 51
Overseas Korean Foundation, 27, 50, 51
Overseas Korean Traders Association (OKTA), 50

Pachinko, 99, 99*n*
Paik Namjoon, 57
Pak Yong-man, 63
Palestinian diaspora, 12
Park Chung-Hee, 75, 76
Park Kyung Shik, 83
Park Tong-Sun, 59
pension scheme, Japanese, 86
People's Republic of China (PRC). *See* China
per capita income
    Korean-American community, 4, 61, 66, 70, 74
    South Korea, 6
    United States, 68-70, 69*t*, 74
Permanent Residents by Accord, 87
Philippines, 35
    trade with China, 48
Plaza Accord (1985), 90
political situation
    and Chinese diaspora, 39-40
    and Korean diaspora, 59, 99, 109-10, 129
Poongsan Group, 57
Potsdam Declaration of 1945, 79
preference falsification, 141
preferential treatment, 45*n*, 45-46, 58, 122
prejudice. *See* discrimination
President's Council of National Economic Affairs, 131
price increases, in North Korea, 139-141
productivity growth
    importance of, 133
    South Korea, 143
    United States, 132-35
professional services sector
    foreign investment in, 23
    Korean-American community in, 74
Protection Law on Returned Overseas Chinese and Overseas Chinese Relatives, 41
provisioning-out profits pattern, 136

Qinghuangdao (China), 112

Red Cross, 83
refugee diaspora, 12, 13*t*, 15
regional trade agreements, 6-7
registration system
    Chinese, 112*n*, 122*n*
    Japanese, 78, 83-88
religion, 62-63, 129
research and development, 25, 27, 75-76
residential category, Korean-Japanese community by, 87-88, 89*t*
restaurants, 26
Rhee Syngman, 63
riots. *See* social unrest
rural-urban migration, Korean-Chinese community, 112-13, 121-22, 125, 128
Russia, 18, 110

Sakhalin, 15, 16, 83
SaKong Il, 63, 131-32
San Francisco Peace Treaty of 1951, 79
sangokujin (people of the third countries), 78, 78*n*
savings rate
    Korean-American community, 61, 68, 70, 73
    United States, 136
schools, ethnic Korean, in China, 121-22, 121*n*-122*n*, 125
science and technology capacity, 25, 27, 75-76, 143-44. *See also* information technology (IT)
secret societies *(bang)*, 37-39
Segregation Index (SI), 93, 93*n*, 94*t*, 96
Seoul National University, 29
Seoul Olympics, 95
service diaspora, 12-13, 13*t*, 15
service sector, 25
    foreign investment in, 22-23, 28
    Korean-Chinese community in, 117, 119
    Korean-Japanese community in, 91, 92*t*, 99
sex ratio
    Korean-Chinese community, 104
    Korean-Japanese community, 80-81, 81*t*, 93, 94*t*
Shandong Province (China), 105, 106*t*, 114-15, 115*n*, 123-124, 128
Shanghai (China), 114, 122, 123-24, 128
Shenyang (China), 96-97, 114, 115, 119, 122
Shindorico, 99
Shinhan Bank, 99
Shin Kyuk-ho, 22, 57
Siberia, 15, 16

Sie, Charlie, 44*n*
Singapore, 14, 35, 36, 56
as economic model, 43, 49
trade with China, 48
Singaporean Chinese Business
Association, 43, 45
Sinuiju (North Korea), 141
Sixth World Chinese Entrepreneurs'
Convention, 32
small business. *See* entrepreneurship
social networks, created by diasporas, 19-
20, 26, 28-29
social status, of Korean-Japanese
community, 82, 95-98
social unrest
in China, 43
in Japan, 82
in Los Angeles, 64*n*, 71
in North Korea, 140, 142
Softbank, 22
software development, 22
outsourcing of, 19
Son Masayoshi, 22, 57
So-shi Kai-mei policy, 95
Southeast Asian free trade agreements, 7
South Korea
debt rating, 137, 138*t*, 143
development strategy, 1-2
economic status of, 36
impact of Korean diaspora on, 19-26,
58
versus Japan, 6
versus North Korea, 3
outlook for, 142-144
educational system, 19, 144
exchange rate, development of, 2
export development strategy, 32
financial crisis (1997), 142-43
foreign investment in, 22-23, 28, 58, 99
fund transfers to, 23-24, 24*t*, 27
in globalization process, 5-7
government policy toward Koreans
abroad, 29, 50, 52-53
growth potential, 6, 142-44
household debt, 143
illegal entry into, 115-16, 118
influence on Korean-Chinese
community, 120-21
investment in China, 113*n*, 113-14, 115*n*,
123, 126*t*-127*t*
labor shortages, 25-27
new immigrants to Korean-Chinese
community from, 123-26, 130
per capita income, 6

relations with China, 113-14, 126*t*, 128
role of Korean-Chinese community
in, 102-03, 111, 117-19, 118*n*, 128
return of Korean-Chinese to, 108*n*, 108-
09, 111, 115-16, 130
science and technology capacity, 25,
143-44
trade relations
with China, 48
with United States, 4, 28-29
unification with North Korea, 5-6
universities in, 29
Soviet Union, 110
special economic zones (SEZs), 46, 46*n*,
48-49, 54, 58
North Korea, 139, 141
Special Law on Immigration Control
(Japan), 87
Special Permanent Residents (SPRs), 87-
88, 89*t*
Sun Zhongshan, 107

taidu (independence of China), 47
Taiwan, 36
Basic Construction Plan for National
Information and Communication, 45
Chamber of Commerce, 41*n*
Chinese in, 34, 38-40
policy towards, 39-40, 44, 45, 56
competition with China, 41-44
investment in China, 23, 47
Overseas Chinese Affairs Commission,
42, 44, 45
trade with China, 48
Tang, Henry S., 44*n*
taste effect, 20
technology transfer, 134-35. *See also*
knowledge transfer
Teijusha (Long-Term Residents-LTRs), 87
Teikoku Tokei Nenkan (Statistical Yearbook
of the Empire), 80
Thailand
Chinese in, 34, 35, 35*t*
trade with China, 48
think tanks, government-funded, 76
Tiananmen Square incident, 31, 43, 44
Tianjin (China), 105, 106*t*, 112, 114, 122,
123-24, 128
Tien Chang-Lin, 44*n*
Tokyo (Japan), 82
trade agreements, regional, 6-7
trade deficit, United States, 136
trade diaspora, 12-14, 13*t*, 19
trade flows

China, 48
    impact of Chinese diaspora on, 37-38
    impact of diasporas on, 20-22
South Korea, 4
    impact of Korean diaspora on, 19-23, 26
Tsumei (Japanese-style names), 95
Tung Chee Hwa, 141

unemployment rate
China, 89, 91t
    Korean-Japanese community, 90, 91t, 96, 98
    United States, 135
unification
    of China and Taiwan, 40
    of Korean peninsula, 5-6
United Nations, 31
United States
    Chinese in, 34-35, 35t
    Department of State, 1
    economic status of
    impact of Korean-American community on, 67-70, 69t, 73
    versus Japan, 133
    outlook for, 132-36
    educational system, 136
    education of immigrants in, 25, 33, 63, 75-76
    foreign direct investment in, 135-36
    impact of Korean diaspora on, 4, 61-76
    inflation, 135
    Koreans in (*See* Korean-American community)
    National Origin Quota System, 63
    per capita income, 68-70, 69t, 74
    productivity growth, 132-35
    recession (2001), 132-33, 135
    relations with China, 39, 44
    savings rate, 136
    state government expenditures, 69t, 69-70
    stock market, 135
    trade deficit, 136
    trade relations
        with China, 48
        with South Korea, 4, 28-29
    unemployment, 135
universal military service, 58
universities, South Korean, 29
upward mobility, Korean-American community, 64, 66
urbanization
    Korean-American community, 62n, 62-

63, 64n
    Korean-Chinese community, 110n, 112-13, 121-22, 125, 128
US California Bank, 42
Uzbekistan, 18

Venetian diaspora, 13
victim diaspora, 12-13, 13t, 15
Vietnam, agriculture sector, 139

Wangfujing, 46n
Wangjing (China), 124
Wang Yong Qing, 46n
Wang Yongxiang, 46
Washington, DC (US), 66
welfare measures, Japanese, 86
wig exports, 20, 20n
World Chinese Entrepreneurs' Convention (WCEC), 42-44, 53-54
World Cup, 99
World Federation of Korean Commerce (WFOKC), 50-51
World Trade Organization (WTO), 46
World War II, 15
Wu, Dennis, 44n

X-efficiency, 68, 73

Yamaguchi (Japan), 82
Yanbian Autonomous Prefecture (China), 104, 105, 105n, 106, 109, 111n, 112, 115, 121n, 122
Yanbian University of Science and Technology, 117n
Yang Bin, 141
Yang Zhenning, 32, 32n
Yaskuni Shinsha, 98
Y.H. Industrial Company incident, 98, 98n

Zainichi Koreans, 78-79. *See also* Korean-Japanese community
Zhang Jieshi, 107
Zhao Nanqi, 129
zhonghwa nationalism, 107
Zhu Rongji, 32

)ther Publications from the nstitute for nternational Economics

= out of print

OLICY ANALYSES IN NTERNATIONAL ECONOMICS Series

The Lending Policies of the International Monetary Fund*   John Williamson
August 1982   ISBN 0-88132-000-5

"Reciprocity": A New Approach to World Trade Policy?*   William R. Cline
September 1982   ISBN 0-88132-001-3

Trade Policy in the 1980s*
C. Fred Bergsten and William R. Cline
November 1982   ISBN 0-88132-002-1

International Debt and the Stability of the World Economy*   William R. Cline
September 1983   ISBN 0-88132-010-2

The Exchange Rate System,* Second Edition
John Williamson
Sept. 1983, rev. June 1985   ISBN 0-88132-034-X

Economic Sanctions in Support of Foreign Policy Goals*
Gary Clyde Hutbauer and Jeffrey J. Schott
October 1983   ISBN 0-88132-014-5

A New SDR Allocation?*   John Williamson
March 1984   ISBN 0-88132-028-5

An International Standard for Monetary Stabilization*   Ronald L. McKinnon
March 1984   ISBN 0-88132-018-8

The YEN/Dollar Agreement: Liberalizing Japanese Capital Markets*   Jeffrey A. Frankel
December 1984   ISBN 0-88132-035-8

10 Bank Lending to Developing Countries: The Policy Alternatives*   C. Fred Bergsten, William R. Cline, and John Williamson
April 1985   ISBN 0-88132-032-3

1 Trading for Growth: The Next Round of Trade Negotiations*
Gary Clyde Hufbauer and Jeffrey R. Schott
September 1985   ISBN 0-88132-033-1

2 Financial Intermediation Beyond the Debt Crisis*   Donald R. Lessard, John Williamson
September 1985   ISBN 0-88132-021-8

3 The United StatesJapan Economic Problem*
C. Fred Bergsten and William R. Cline
October 1985, 2d ed. January 1987
ISBN 0-88132-060-9

4 Deficits and the Dollar: The World Economy at Risk*   Stephen Marris
December 1985, 2d ed. November 1987
ISBN 0-88132-067-6

15 Trade Policy for Troubled Industries*
Gary Clyde Hufbauer and Howard R. Rosen
March 1986   ISBN 0-88132-020-X

16 The United States and Canada: The Quest for Free Trade*   Paul Wonnacott, with an Appendix by John Williamson
March 1987   ISBN 0-88132-056-0

17 Adjusting to Success: Balance of Payments Policy in the East Asian NICs*
Bela Balassa and John Williamson
June 1987, rev. April 1990   ISBN 0-88132-101-X

18 Mobilizing Bank Lending to Debtor Countries*   William R. Cline
June 1987   ISBN 0-88132-062-5

19 Auction Quotas and United States Trade Policy*   C. Fred Bergsten, Kimberly Ann Elliott, Jeffrey J. Schott, and Wendy E. Takacs
September 1987   ISBN 0-88132-050-1

20 Agriculture and the GATT: Rewriting the Rules*   Dale E. Hathaway
September 1987   ISBN 0-88132-052-8

21 Anti-Protection: Changing Forces in United States Trade Politics*
I. M. Destler and John S. Odell
September 1987   ISBN 0-88132-043-9

22 Targets and Indicators: A Blueprint for the International Coordination of Economic Policy
John Williamson and Marcus H. Miller
September 1987   ISBN 0-88132-051-X

23 Capital Flight: The Problem and Policy Responses*   Donald R. Lessard and John Williamson
December 1987   ISBN 0-88132-059-5

24 United States-Canada Free Trade: An Evaluation of the Agreement*
Jeffrey J. Schott
April 1988   ISBN 0-88132-072-2

25 Voluntary Approaches to Debt Relief*
John Williamson
Sept.1988, rev. May 1989   ISBN 0-88132-098-6

26 American Trade Adjustment: The Global Impact*   William R. Cline
March 1989   ISBN 0-88132-095-1

27 More Free Trade Areas?*
Jeffrey J. Schott
May 1989   ISBN 0-88132-085-4

28 The Progress of Policy Reform in Latin America*   John Williamson
January 1990   ISBN 0-88132-100-1

29 The Global Trade Negotiations: What Can Be Achieved?*   Jeffrey J. Schott
September 1990   ISBN 0-88132-137-0

30 Economic Policy Coordination: Requiem or Prologue?*   Wendy Dobson
April 1991   ISBN 0-88132-102-8

31 The Economic Opening of Eastern Europe*
John Williamson
May 1991 ISBN 0-88132-186-9

32 Eastern Europe and the Soviet Union in the World Economy*
Susan M. Coffins and Dani Rodrik
May 1991 ISBN 0-88132-157-5

33 African Economic Reform: The External Dimension* Carol Lancaster
June 1991 ISBN 0-88132-096-X

34 Has the Adjustment Process Worked?*
Paul R. Krugman
October 1991 ISBN 0-88132-116-8

35 From Soviet disUnion to Eastern Economic Community?*
Oleh Havrylyshyn and John Williamson
October 1991 ISBN 0-88132-192-3

36 Global Warming The Economic Stakes*
William R. Cline
May 1992 ISBN 0-88132-172-9

37 Trade and Payments After Soviet Disintegration* John Williamson
June 1992 ISBN 0-88132-173-7

38 Trade and Migration: NAFTA and Agriculture* Philip L. Martin
October 1993 ISBN 0-88132-201-6

39 The Exchange Rate System and the IMF: A Modest Agenda Morris Goldstein
June 1995 ISBN 0-88132-219-9

40 What Role for Currency Boards?
John Williamson
September 1995 ISBN 0-88132-222-9

41 Predicting External Imbalances for the United States and Japan*William R. Cline
September 1995 ISBN 0-88132-220-2

42 Standards and APEC: An Action Agenda*
John S. Wilson
October 1995 ISBN 0-88132-223-7

43 Fundamental Tax Reform and Border Tax Adjustments* Gary Clyde Hufbauer
January 1996 ISBN 0-88132-225-3

44 Global Telecom Talks: A Trillion Dollar Deal*
Ben A. Petrazzini
June 1996 ISBN 0-88132-230-X

45 WTO 2000: Setting the Course for World Trade Jeffrey J. Schott
September 1996 ISBN 0-88132-234-2

46 The National Economic Council: A Work in Progress * I. M. Destler
November 1996 ISBN 0-88132-239-3

47 The Case for an International Banking Standard Morris Goldstein
April 1997 ISBN 0-88132-244-X

48 Transatlantic Trade: A Strategic Agenda*
Ellen L. Frost
May 1997 ISBN 0-88132-228-8

49 Cooperating with Europe's Monetary Union
C. Randall Henning
May 1997 ISBN 0-88132-245-8

50 Renewing Fast Track Legislation* I. M.Destl
September 1997 ISBN 0-88132-252-0

51 Competition Policies for the Global Economy
Edward M. Graham and J. David Richardson
November 1997 ISBN 0-88132 -249-0

52 Improving Trade Policy Reviews in the Worl Trade Organization Donald Keesing
April 1998 ISBN 0-88132-251-2

53 Agricultural Trade Policy: Completing the Reform Timothy Josling
April 1998 ISBN 0-88132-256-3

54 Real Exchange Rates for the Year 2000
Simon Wren Lewis and Rebecca Driver
April 1998 ISBN 0-88132-253-9

55 The Asian Financial Crisis: Causes, Cures, and Systemic Implications Morris Goldstein
June 1998 ISBN 0-88132-261-X

56 Global Economic Effects of the Asian Currency Devaluations
Marcus Noland, LiGang Liu, Sherman Robinson, and Zhi Wang
July 1998 ISBN 0-88132-260-1

57 The Exchange Stabilization Fund: Slush Money or War Chest? C. Randall Henning
May 1999 ISBN 0-88132-271-7

58 The New Politics of American Trade: Trade, Labor, and the Environment
I. M. Destler and Peter J. Balint
October 1999 ISBN 0-88132-269-5

59 Congressional Trade Votes: From NAFTA Approval to Fast Track Defeat
Robert E. Baldwin and Christopher S. Magee
February 2000 ISBN 0-88132-267-9

60 Exchange Rate Regimes for Emerging Markets: Reviving the Intermediate Option
John Williamson
September 2000 ISBN 0-88132-293-8

61 NAFTA and the Environment: Seven Years Later Gary Clyde Hufbauer, Daniel Esty, Diana Orejas, Luis Rubio, and Jeffrey J. Schott
October 2000 ISBN 0-88132-299-7

62 Free Trade between Korea and the United States? Inbom Choi and Jeffrey J. Schott
April 2001 ISBN 0-88132-311-X

63 New Regional Trading Arrangements in the Asia Pacific?
Robert Scollay and John P. Gilbert
May 2001 ISBN 0-88132-302-0

64 Parental Supervision: The New Paradigm for Foreign Direct Investment and Development
Theodore H. Moran
August 2001 ISBN 0-88132-313-6

The Benefits of Price Convergence:
Speculative Calculations
Gary Clyde Hufbauer, Erika Wada,
and Tony Warren
December 2001 ISBN 0-88132-333-0
Managed Floating Plus
Morris Goldstein
March 2002 ISBN 0-88132-336-5
Argentina and the Fund: From Triumph
to Tragedy
Michael Mussa
July 2002 ISBN 0-88132-339-X
East Asian Financial Cooperation
C. Randall Henning
September 2002 ISBN 0-88132-338-1

OOKS

MF Conditionality* John Williamson, editor
83 ISBN 0-88132-006-4
rade Policy in the 1980s* William R. Cline, editor
)83 ISBN 0-88132-031-5
ubsidies in International Trade*
ary Clyde Hufbauer and Joanna Shelton Erb
)84 ISBN 0-88132-004-8
iternational Debt: Systemic Risk and Policy
esponse* William R. Cline
)84 ISBN 0-88132-015-3
rade Protection in the United States: 31 Case
tudies* Gary Clyde Hutbauer, Diane E. Berliner,
nd Kimberly Ann Elliott
)86 ISBN 0-88132-040-4
oward Renewed Economic Growth in Latin
merica* Bela Balassa, Gerardo M. Bueno, Pedro-
ablo Kuczynski, and Mario Henrique Simonsen
)86 ISBN 0-88132-045-5
apital Flight and Third World Debt*
onald R. Lessard and John Williamson, editors
)87 ISBN 0-88132-053-6
he Canada-United States Free Trade Agreement:
he Global Impact*
ffrey J. Schott and Murray G. Smith, editors
)88 ISBN 0-88132-073-0
Vorld Agricultural Trade: Building a Consensus*
Villiam M. Miner and Dale E. Hathaway, editors
)88 ISBN 0-88132-071-3
apan in the World Economy*
ela Balassa and Marcus Noland
)88 ISBN 0-88132-041-2
merica in the World Economy: A Strategy for
ie 1990s* C. Fred Bergsten
)88 ISBN 0-88132-089-7
Managing the Dollar: From the Plaza to the
ouvre* Yoichi Funabashi
)88, 2nd ed. 1989 ISBN 0-88132-097-8

United States External Adjustment and the World
Economy* William R. Cline
May 1989 ISBN 0-88132-048-X
Free Trade Areas and U.S. Trade Policy*
Jeffrey J. Schott, editor
May 1989 ISBN 0-88132-094-3
Dollar Politics: Exchange Rate Policymaking in
the United States*
I.M. Destler and C. Randall Henning
September 1989 ISBN 0-88132-079-X
Latin American Adjustment: How Much Has
Happened?* John Williamson, editor
April 1990 ISBN 0-88132-125-7
The Future of World Trade in Textiles and
Apparel* William R. Cline
1987, 2d ed. June 199 ISBN 0-88132-110-9
Completing the Uruguay Round: A Results-
Oriented Approach to the GATT Trade
Negotiations* Jeffrey J. Schott, editor
September 1990 ISBN 0-88132-130-3
Economic Sanctions Reconsidered (2 volumes)
Economic Sanctions Reconsidered:
Supplemental Case Histories
Gary Clyde Hufbauer, Jeffrey J. Schott, and
Kimberly Ann Elliott
1985, 2d ed. Dec. 1990 ISBN cloth 0-88132-115-X
ISBN paper 0-88132-105-2
Economic Sanctions Reconsidered: History and
Current Policy
Gary Clyde Hufbauer, Jeffrey J. Schott, and
Kimberly Ann Ellio
December 1990 ISBN cloth 0-88132-140-0
ISBN paper 0-88132-136-2
Pacific Basin Developing Countries: Prospects for
the Future* Marcus Noland
January 1991 ISBN cloth 0-88132-141-9
ISBN paper 0-88132-081-1
Currency Convertibility in Eastern Europe*
John Williamson, editor
October 1991 ISBN 0-88132-128-1
International Adjustment and Financing: The
Lessons of 1985-1991* C. Fred Bergsten, editor
January 1992 ISBN 0-88132-112-5
North American Free Trade: Issues and
Recommendations*
Gary Clyde Hufbauer and Jeffrey J. Schott
April 1992 ISBN 0-88132-120-6
Narrowing the U.S. Current Account Deficit*
Allen J. Lenz
June 1992 ISBN 0-88132-103-6
The Economics of Global Warming
William R. Cline/*June 1992* ISBN 0-88132-132-X
U.S. Taxation of International Income: Blueprint
for Reform* Gary Clyde Hutbauer, assisted
by Joanna M. van Rooij
October 1992 ISBN 0-88132-134-6

Who's Bashing Whom? Trade Conflict in High-Technology Industries   Laura D'Andrea Tyson
November 1992   ISBN 0-88132-106-0
Korea in the World Economy*   Il SaKong
January 1993   ISBN 0-88132-183-4
Pacific Dynamism and the International Economic System*
C. Fred Bergsten and Marcus Noland, editors
May 1993   ISBN 0-88132-196-6
Economic Consequences of Soviet Disintegration*
John Williamson, editor
May 1993   ISBN 0-88132-190-7
Reconcilable Differences? United States-Japan Economic Conflict*
C. Fred Bergsten and Marcus Noland
June 1993   ISBN 0-88132-129-X
Does Foreign Exchange Intervention Work?
Kathryn M. Dominguez and Jeffrey A. Frankel
September 1993   ISBN 0-88132-104-4
Sizing Up U.S. Export Disincentives*
J. David Richardson
September 1993   ISBN 0-88132-107-9
NAFTA: An Assessment
Gary Clyde Hufbauer and Jeffrey J. Schott/ rev. ed.
October 1993   ISBN 0-88132-199-0
Adjusting to Volatile Energy Prices
Philip K. Verleger, Jr.
November 1993   ISBN 0-88132-069-2
The Political Economy of Policy Reform
John Williamson, editor
January 1994   ISBN 0-88132-195-8
Measuring the Costs of Protection in the United States
Gary Clyde Hufbauer and Kimberly Ann Elliott
January 1994   ISBN 0-88132-108-7
The Dynamics of Korean Economic Development*   Cho Soon
March 1994   ISBN 0-88132-162-1
Reviving the European Union*
C. Randall Henning, Eduard Hochreiter, and Gary Clyde Hufbauer, editors
April 1994   ISBN 0-88132-208-3
China in the World Economy   Nicholas R. Lardy
April 1994   ISBN 0-88132-200-8
Greening the GATT: Trade, Environment, and the Future Daniel C. Esty
July 1994   ISBN 0-88132-205-9
Western Hemisphere Economic Integration*
Gary Clyde Hufbauer and Jeffrey J. Schott
July 1994   ISBN 0-88132-159-1
Currencies and Politics in the United States, Germany, and Japan
C. Randall Henning
September 1994   ISBN 0-88132-127-3
Estimating Equilibrium Exchange Rates
John Williamson, editor
September 1994   ISBN 0-88132-076-5

Managing the World Economy: Fifty Years Afte Bretton Woods   Peter B. Kenen, editor
September 1994   ISBN 0-88132-212-
Reciprocity and Retaliation in U.S. Trade Polic
Thomas O. Bayard and Kimberly Ann Elliott
September 1994   ISBN 0-88132-084-
The Uruguay Round: An Assessment*
Jeffrey J. Schott, assisted by Johanna W. Buurma
November 1994   ISBN 0-88132-206-
Measuring the Costs of Protection in Japan*
Yoko Sazanami, Shujiro Urata, and Hiroki Kawa
January 1995   ISBN 0-88132-211-3
Foreign Direct Investment in the United States,
3rd Ed. Edward M. Graham and Paul R. Krugma
January 1995   ISBN 0-88132-204-0
The Political Economy of Korea-United States Cooperation*
C. Fred Bergsten and Il SaKong, editors
February 1995   ISBN 0-88132-213-X
International Debt Reexamined* William R. Cli
February 1995   ISBN 0-88132-083-
American Trade Politics, 3rd Ed. I.M. Destler
April 1995   ISBN 0-88132-215-6
Managing Official Export Credits: The Quest fc a Global Regime*   John E. Ray
July 1995   ISBN 0-88132207-5
Asia Pacific Fusion: Japan's Role in APEC*
Yoichi Funabashi
October 1995   ISBN 0-88132-224-5
Korea-United States Cooperation in the New World Order*
C. Fred Bergsten and Il SaKong, editors
February 1996   ISBN 0-88132-226-
Why Exports Really Matter!*   ISBN 0-88132-221-
Why Exports Matter More!*   ISBN 0-88132-229-
J. David Richardson and Karin Rindal
July 1995; February 1996
Global Corporations and National Government
Edward M. Graham
May 1996   ISBN 0-88132-111-7
Global Economic Leadership and the Group of Seven   C. Fred Bergsten and C. Randall Henni
May 1996   ISBN 0-88132-218-0
The Trading System After the Uruguay Round*
John Whalley and Colleen Hamilton
July 1996   ISBN 0-88132-131-1
Private Capital Flows to Emerging Markets Afte the Mexican Crisis*   Guillermo A. Calvc
Morris Goldstein, and Eduard Hochreiter
September 1996   ISBN 0-88132-232-6
The Crawling Band as an Exchange Rate Regim Lessons from Chile, Colombia, and Israel
John Williamson
September 1996   ISBN 0-88132-231-8
Flying High: Liberalizing Civil Aviation in the Asia Pacific*
Gary Clyde Hufbauer and Christopher Findlay
November 1996   ISBN 0-88132-227-X

leasuring the Costs of Visible Protection
. Korea*   Namdoo Kim
ovember 1996   ISBN 0-88132-236-9
ne World Trading System: Challenges Ahead
ffrey J. Schott
ecember 1996   ISBN 0-88132-235-0
as Globalization Gone Too Far?   Dani Rodrik
arch 1997   ISBN cloth 0-88132-243-1
orea-United States Economic Relationship*
 Fred Bergsten and Il SaKong, editors
arch 1997   ISBN 0-88132-240-7
ummitry in the Americas: A Progress Report
chard E. Feinberg
pril 1997   ISBN 0-88132-242-3
orruption and the Global Economy
mberly Ann Elliott
ne 1997   ISBN 0-88132-233-4
egional Trading Blocs in the World Economic
stem   Jeffrey A. Frankel
ctober 1997   ISBN 0-88132-202-4
ustaining the Asia Pacific Miracle:
nvironmental Protection and Economic
tegration   Andre Dua and Daniel C. Esty
tober 1997   ISBN 0-88132-250-4
ade and Income Distribution   William R. Cline
ovember 1997   ISBN 0-88132-216-4
obal Competition Policy
ward M. Graham and J. David Richardson
cember 1997   ISBN 0-88132-166-4
nfinished Business: Telecommunications after
e Uruguay Round
ry Clyde Hufbauer and Erika Wada
cember 1997   ISBN 0-88132-257-1
nancial Services Liberalization in the WTO
endy Dobson and Pierre Jacquet
ne 1998   ISBN 0-88132-254-7
storing Japan's Economic Growth
lam S. Posen
ptember 1998   ISBN 0-88132-262-8
easuring the Costs of Protection in China
ang Shuguang, Zhang Yansheng, and Wan
ongxin
vember 1998   ISBN 0-88132-247-4
reign Direct Investment and Development:
e New Policy Agenda for Developing
untries and Economies in Transition
eodore H. Moran
cember 1998   ISBN 0-88132-258-X
hind the Open Door: Foreign Enterprises in the
inese Marketplace
niel H. Rosen
uary 1999   ISBN 0-88132-263-6
ward A New International Financial
chitecture: A Practical Post-Asia Agenda
rry Eichengreen
ruary 1999   ISBN 0-88132-270-9

Is the U.S. Trade Deficit Sustainable?
Catherine L. Mann
September 1999   ISBN 0-88132-265-2
Safeguarding Prosperity in a Global Financial
System: The Future International Financial
Architecture, Independent Task Force Report
Sponsored by the Council on Foreign Relations
Morris Goldstein, Project Director
October 1999   ISBN 0-88132-287-3
Avoiding the Apocalypse: The Future of the
Two Koreas   Marcus Noland
June 2000   ISBN 0-88132-278-4
Assessing Financial Vulnerability: An Early
Warning System for Emerging Markets
Morris Goldstein, Graciela Kaminsky, and Carmen
Reinhart
June 2000   ISBN 0-88132-237-7
Global Electronic Commerce: A Policy Primer
Catherine L. Mann, Sue E. Eckert, and Sarah
Cleeland Knight
July 2000   ISBN 0-88132-274-1
The WTO after Seattle   Jeffrey J. Schott, editor
July 2000   ISBN 0-88132-290-3
Intellectual Property Rights in the Global
Economy   Keith E. Maskus
August 2000   ISBN 0-88132-282-2
The Political Economy of the Asian Financial
Crisis   Stephan Haggard
August 2000   ISBN 0-88132-283-0
Transforming Foreign Aid: United States
Assistance in the 21st Century   Carol Lancaster
August 2000   ISBN 0-88132-291-1
Fighting the Wrong Enemy: Antiglobal Activists
and Multinational Enterprises   Edward M.Graham
September 2000   ISBN 0-88132-272-5
Globalization and the Perceptions of American
Workers
Kenneth F. Scheve and Matthew J. Slaughter
March 2001   ISBN 0-88132-295-4
World Capital Markets: Challenge to the G-10
Wendy Dobson and Gary C. Hufbauer,
assisted by Hyun Koo Cho
May 2001   ISBN 0-88132-301-2
Prospects for Free Trade in the Americas
Jeffrey J. Schott
August 2001   ISBN 0-88132-275-X
Lessons from the Old World for the New:
Constructing a North American Community
Robert A. Pastor
August 2000   ISBN 0-88132-328-4
Measuring the Costs of Protection in Europe:
European Commercial Policy in the 2000s
Patrick A. Messerlin
September 2001   ISBN 0-88132-273-3
Job Loss from Imports: Measuring the Costs
Lori G. Kletzer
September 2001   ISBN 0-88132-296-2

No More Bashing: Building a New Japan-United States Economic Relationship
C. Fred Bergsten, Takatoshi Ito, and Marc Noland
October 2001   ISBN 0-88132-286-5

Why Global Commitment Really Matters!
Howard Lewis III and J. David Richardson
October 2001   ISBN 0-88132-298-9

Leadership Selection in the Major Multilaterals
Miles Kahler
November 2001   ISBN 0-88132-335-7

The International Financial Architecture: What's New? What's Missing?   Peter Kenen
November 2001   ISBN 0-88132-297-0

Delivering on Debt Relief: From IMF Gold to a New Aid Architecture
John Williamson and Nancy Birdsall, with Brian Deese
April 2002   ISBN 0-88132-331-4

Imagine There's No Country: Poverty, Inequality, and Growth in the Era of Globalization
Surjit S. Bhalla
September 2002   ISBN 0-88132-348-9

Reforming Korea's Industrial Conglomerates
Edward M. Graham
January 2003   ISBN 0-88132-337-3

SPECIAL REPORTS

1   Promoting World Recovery: A Statement on Global Economic Strategy*
    by Twenty-six Economists from Fourteen Countries
    December 1982   ISBN 0-88132-013-7

2   Prospects for Adjustment in Argentina, Brazil, and Mexico: Responding to the Debt Crisis*   John Williamson, editor
    June 1983   ISBN 0-88132-016-1

3   Inflation and Indexation: Argentina, Brazil, and Israel*   John Williamson, editor
    March 1985   ISBN 0-88132-037-4

4   Global Economic Imbalances*
    C. Fred Bergsten, editor
    March 1986   ISBN 0-88132-042-0

5   African Debt and Financing*
    Carol Lancaster and John Williamson, editors
    May 1986   ISBN 0-88132-044-7

6   Resolving the Global Economic Crisis: After Wall Street*
    by Thirty-three Economists from Thirteen Countries
    December 1987   ISBN 0-88132-070-6

7   World Economic Problems*
    Kimberly Ann Elliott and John Williamson, editors
    April 1988   ISBN 0-88132-055-2

Reforming World Agricultural Trade*
by Twenty-nine Professionals from Seventeen Countries
1988   ISBN 0-88132-088-9

8   Economic Relations Between the United States and Korea: Conflict or Cooperation?*
    Thomas O. Bayard and Soogil Young, editors
    January 1989   ISBN 0-88132-068-4

9   Whither APEC? The Progress to Date and Agenda for the Future*
    C. Fred Bergsten, editor
    October 1997   ISBN 0-88132-248-2

10 Economic Integration of the Korean Peninsula
    Marcus Noland, editor
    January 1998   ISBN 0-88132-255-5

11 Restarting Fast Track*
    Jeffrey J. Schott, editor
    April 1998   ISBN 0-88132-259-8

12 Launching New Global Trade Talks: An Action Agenda   Jeffrey J. Schott, editor
    September 1998   ISBN 0-88132-266-0

13 Japan's Financial Crisis and Its Parallels to U.S. Experience
    Ryoichi Mikitani and Adam S. Posen, eds.
    September 2000   ISBN 0-88132-289-X

14 The Ex-Im Bank in the 21st Century: A New Approach?   Gary Clyde Hufbauer and Rita M. Rodriguez, eds.
    January 2001   ISBN 0-88132-300-4

15 The Korean Diaspora in the World Economy
    C. Fred Bergsten and Inbom Choi, eds.
    January 2003   ISBN 0-88132-358-6

WORKS IN PROGRESS

Deunionization in the United States: The Role of International Trade
Robert E. Baldwin

Changing Direction: The New Economy in the United States, Europe, and Japan
Martin Baily

New Regional Arrangements and the World Economy
C. Fred Bergsten

The Globalization Backlash in Europe and the United States
C. Fred Bergsten, Pierre Jacquet, and Karl Kaiser

China's Entry to the World Economy
Richard N. Cooper

The ILO in the World Economy
Kimberly Ann Elliott

Can Labor Standards Improve under Globalization?
Kimberly Ann Elliott and Richard B. Freeman

Reforming Economic Sanctions
Kimberly Ann Elliott, Gary C. Hufbauer, and
Jeffrey J. Schott
Free Trade in Labor Agency Services
Kimberly Ann Elliott and J. David
Richardson
IMF and the World Bank
Michael Fabricius
Food Regulation and Trade: Toward a Safe
and Open Global Food System
Timothy Josling, David Orden, and Donna
Roberts
Imports, Exports, and American Industrial
Workers since 1979
Lori G. Kletzer and Robert Lawrence
Crimes and Punishments? An Analysis of
Retaliation under the WTO
Robert Lawrence
Paying the Price: The Costs of Fragmented
International Markets
Robert Lawrence and Scott Bradford
Globalization and Creative Destruction in
the US Textile and Apparel Industry
James Levinsohn
Reforming OPIC for the Twenty-first
Century
Theodore Moran

Foreign Direct Investment, Taxes,
and Tax Competition
John Mutti
Industrial Policy in an Era of
Globalization: Lessons from Asia
Marcus Noland and Howard Pack
Dollarization, Currency Blocs, and
US Policy
Adam S. Posen
Germany in the World Economy
after the EMU
Adam S. Posen
Sizing Up Globalization: The
Globalization Balance Sheet
Capstone Volume
J. David Richardson
Reintegrating India with the World
Economy
T. N. Srinivasan and Suresh D.
Tendulkar
Inflation Targeting
Edwin Truman
Curbing the Boom-Bust Cycle
John Williamson
Policy Reform in Latin America:
After the Washington Consensus
John Williamson, editor

DISTRIBUTORS OUTSIDE THE UNITED STATES

Australia, New Zealand,
and Papua New Guinea
D.A. Information Services
648 Whitehorse Road
Mitcham, Victoria 3132, Australia
tel: 61-3-9210-7777
fax: 61-3-9210-7788
email: service@adadirect.com.au
http://www.dadirect.com.au

United Kingdom and Europe
(including Russia and Turkey)
The Eurospan Group
3 Henrietta Street, Covent Garden
London WC2E 8LU England
tel: 44-20-7240-0856
fax: 44-20-7379-0609
http://www.eurospan.co.uk

Japan and the Republic of Korea
United Publishers Services, Ltd.
KenkyuSha Bldg.
9, Kanda Surugadai 2-Chome
Chiyoda-Ku, Tokyo 101 Japan
tel: 81-3-3291-4541
fax: 81-3-3292-8610
email: saito@ups.co.jp
For trade accounts only.
Individuals will find IIE books in
leading Tokyo bookstores.

Thailand
Asia Books
5 Sukhumvit Rd. Soi 61
Bangkok 10110 Thailand
tel: 662-714-07402 Ext: 221, 222, 223
fax: 662-391-2277
email: purchase@asiabooks.co.th
http://www.asiabooksonline.com

Canada
Renouf Bookstore
5369 Canotek Road, Unit 1
Ottawa, Ontario KIJ 9J3, Canada
tel: 613-745-2665
fax: 613-745-7660
http://www.renoufbooks.com

India, Bangladesh, Nepal, and Sri Lanka
Viva Books Pvt.
Mr. Vinod Vasishtha
4325/3, Ansari Rd.
Daryaganj, New Delhi-110002
India
tel: 91-11-327-9280
fax: 91-11-326-7224
email: vinod.viva@gndel.globalnet.
ems.vsnl.net.in

Southeast Asia (Brunei, Cambodia,
China, Malaysia, Hong Kong, Indonesia,
Laos, Myanmar, the Philippines, Singapore,
Taiwan, and Vietnam)
Hemisphere Publication Services
1 Kallang Pudding Rd. #0403
Golden Wheel Building
Singapore 349316
tel: 65-741-5166
fax: 65-742-9356

Visit our Web site at:
http://www.iie.com
E-mail orders to:
orders@iie.com